Diana R. Harrington
University of Virginia

MODERN PORTFOLIO THEORY, THE CAPITAL ASSET PRICING MODEL, AND ARBITRAGE PRICING THEORY
A User's Guide

second edition

Prentice-Hall, Inc., *Englewood Cliffs, New Jersey 07632*

Library of Congress Cataloging-in-Publication Data

HARRINGTON, DIANA R. (date)
Modern portfolio theory, the capital asset
pricing model, and arbitrage pricing theory.

Previous ed. published as: Modern portfolio
theory and the capital asset pricing model. 1983.
Includes bibliographies and index.
1. Capital assets pricing model. 2. Portfolio
management. 3. Arbitrage. I. Harrington,
Diana R. Modern portfolio theory
and the capital asset pricing model. II. Title.
HG4637.H37 1987   332.6   86-22693
ISBN   0-13-597261-2

To Will

Editorial/production supervision
  and interior design: **Joan E. Foley**
Cover design: **Lundgren Graphics, Ltd.**
Manufacturing buyer: **Ed O'Dougherty**

Printed in the United States of America

10 9 8 7 6 5 4 3 2 1

ISBN 0-13-597261-2   01

Prentice-Hall International (UK) Limited, *London*
Prentice-Hall of Australia Pty. Limited, *Sydney*
Prentice-Hall Canada Inc., *Toronto*
Prentice-Hall Hispanoamericana, S.A., *Mexico*
Prentice-Hall of India Private Limited, *New Delhi*
Prentice-Hall of Japan, Inc., *Tokyo*
Prentice-Hall of Southeast Asia Pte. Ltd., *Singapore*
Editora Prentice-Hall do Brasil, Ltda., *Rio de Janeiro*

Contents

2

THE ASSUMPTIONS
BEHIND MPT AND THE CAPM,   24

3

TESTS OF THE CAPM,   51

4

ESTIMATING BETA,   99

Preface
to the First Edition

This is a book about one of the most intriguing developments in modern finance theory, the capital asset pricing model (CAPM). Derived from modern portfolio theory, this equity valuation model has intellectually challenged academics and practitioners for years.

One of the first practical uses of the capital asset pricing model was in determining the cost of equity for public utilities. Public utility commissions use the estimated cost of equity to set allowable rates that utilities can charge consumers. Ironically, rate-setting hearings have focused experts' disagreements about the CAPM. Detractors examine the evidence and voice these criticisms:

1. Assumptions are too unrealistic; thus, the simple CAPM is probably seriously flawed.
2. Tests of the CAPM prove that it does not describe what has occurred; thus, it is probably wrong.
3. It is virtually impossible to get reasonable people to agree on the best estimate for the inputs to the model; thus, the CAPM is practically useless.

Proponents of the CAPM, examining the same evidence, come to opposite conclusions.

My interest in the practical problems encountered in the use of the CAPM in public utility cases led to this book. Much of what has been written was dispersed in academic journals. Other information was conveyed solely by word of mouth. The difficulty in assembling information about the model has caused serious misunderstandings. For instance, while researching the book I talked with many students and practitioners who believed that the implementation of the model was theoretically prescribed. Many assumed that rate on 90-day Treasury bills was the theoretically correct risk-free rate to use in the CAPM and that it took five years of historical returns data to calculate a beta. Too often theory has been treated as immutable fact.

In this book I point out what we do and do not know about the model from the viewpoint of 1982. I have endeavored to present as well as to interpret the evidence, to separate fact from fiction. Whether readers decide to use the model or not is up to them. Throughout the book I have attempted to make the theory clear, the empirical evidence understandable, and the descriptions of practical applications numerous.

Over the course of the years that it took to research and write this book I have had help from a number of colleagues and friends: Bob Vandell, who encouraged the project and read and re-read the manuscript as it evolved; Jim Haltiner, who provided structure and critical judgment and who, along with the investment professionals in successive Investment Risk Analysis seminars held at the Darden School, University of Virginia, forced me to make the material more clear and complete. Peter Williamson, Gene Brigham, and a number of generous professionals in money management organizations and public utilities contributed to my understanding of the world in which they operate and the potential for the CAPM.

Beverly Seng edited the manuscript with expertise and more good cheer than I could muster at that late stage. Bette Collins provided early editorial assistance. Cindy Frazier, Cathy Stanley, and Nina Hutchinson typed and retyped successive versions of each chapter, having no stake in the book other than doing their jobs with competence and speed. The Sponsors of the Darden School provided welcome support during the writing of this book.

My husband provided patience, support, the layman's viewpoint—as well as a wealth of titles for the book, which you will never see but which gave me a laugh when I needed it.

The mistakes are mine, as they always are.

Diana R. Harrington
Bent Mountain, Virginia

Preface
to the Second Edition

Since the first edition of this book was published, much has happened. While the concepts behind modern portfolio theory and the capital asset pricing model are still being tested and used by academics and practitioners, academics have become entranced with a new theoretical model—arbitrage pricing theory (APT). As a theory, it has some attractive features: it does not rest on some of the assumptions that made the CAPM seem so restrictive; it appears logical and in concert with activities in the capital markets; and it is fresh and novel. As a consequence of having a new theory of asset pricing, many academics and some practitioners have turned their attention to understanding, testing, and attempting to use this new model. Because of emerging interest, this edition contains a description of arbitrage pricing theory, a summary of the results of research that has been done in testing and defining this model, and a discussion of the practical applications of the model.

In addition to the emergence of arbitrage pricing theory over the past five years, we have had increasingly sophisticated researchers pursuing their concerns about the capital asset pricing model. A summary of the results of their research is also included in this edition of the book.

Special help for the second edition came from both academics and practitioners. Notably, Sharon Graham and Jeff Madura at the University of Central Florida provided assistance in gathering the voluminous information about the research that has been done on asset pricing for the last five years. Jeff Born at the University of Kentucky and Tony Estep at Salomon Brothers reviewed the revised manuscript and provided unexpectedly useful suggestions for changes and additions. To all who helped with the revision, my thanks. The mistakes are mine.

Diana Harrington
Crozet, Virginia

Introduction

One of the most interesting and challenging jobs facing a novice or an experienced student of finance is measuring value. Whether we are evaluating the price per share of a firm's stock or the total value of a potential acquisition or other asset, the process of valuation is vexingly difficult.

By *value* I mean the fair price that an investor would be willing to pay for a firm, a portion of a firm, or any other asset. Value is determined by a combination of three factors:

1. The size of the anticipated returns
2. The date that these returns will be received
3. The risk that the investor takes to obtain the returns

A number of valuation methods have been developed. Most require forecasts for some or all of these determinants of value. Of the three factors, risk has been the most difficult to measure and to incorporate into a valuation. Whether valuation is of practical or theoretical interest, not only is risk difficult to measure but its very definition is controversial.

Over the past 20 years a new group of valuation methods has been developed, tested, and used. The primary difference between these and older valuation techniques is the newer methods' perspective. Instead of evaluating each stock, bond, or company singly, these models evaluate assets or companies in terms of their effects on the investor's portfolio. Thus, these models or theories take an investor's point of view and suggest that the investor is (or should be) concerned with the contribution that a given investment will make to his or her existing portfolio of investments.

This portfolio valuation concept, first called *modern portfolio theory* (MPT), evolved gradually. Over time, modifications and additions were made to the basic theory. The most widely known metamorphosis is called the *capital asset pricing model* (CAPM). You may also know this version for its firm- or asset-specific measure of risk called *beta*.

Recently a new model for asset pricing has been introduced—the *arbitrage pricing theory* (APT). This model suggests that there are many sources of risk that contribute to the returns of an asset. This relatively new theory about asset pricing is now going through the same rigorous examination that has characterized the CAPM over the past 20 years.

The CAPM is widely discussed and is being increasingly used. It and the APT are just versions of a much older valuation technique—the *risk-premium model*. The risk-premium model assigns increasingly high returns for increasing risks. An investment with the lowest possible return would be an investment with no risk. The return on this risk-free investment compensates the investor for his or her illiquidity (having the invested funds tied up) over the life of the investment.

The capital asset pricing model is different from the typical risk-premium method because the CAPM measures risk in a particular way and must, in doing so, rest on some very explicit assumptions. These assumptions, and indeed the CAPM's very definition of risk, have prompted abundant controversy. This book will discuss portfolio theory, with special emphasis on the CAPM. In Chapter 1 we will focus on portfolio valuation theories ranging from Markowitz's modern portfolio theory to the CAPM and beyond. Because this book is designed for readers who have a wide variety of backgrounds, it will describe these sometimes complex subjects in terms accessible to those readers who have had no training in theoretical finance.

In Chapter 2 we will discuss the assumptions that are elemental to the development of MPT and the CAPM. To know the requisite assumptions is to know at once the strengths and the frailties of these models. We will attempt to answer two questions. First, why are the assumptions necessary in the development of the theories? Second, how do unrealistic assumptions affect the theories' validity?

Even more controversial than the model's basic assumptions are the results of sophisticated studies that have been developed to test the logic and realism of the CAPM. In Chapter 3 we will thread our way through these various studies to determine which arguments and findings most appropriately support or call into question the CAPM. This chapter will also discuss some of the problems that practitioners meet as they try to use the capital asset pricing model to select assets or construct portfolios.

Although academics have tested, revised, and adapted basic portfolio theory since the early 1950s, practitioners have encountered problems that theorists could safely ignore. For example, practitioners need to know how to measure variables and how to distinguish good input data from useless garbage. Chapters 4–6, then, will assess many of the current methods of implementing the capital asset pricing model.

In Chapter 4 we will discuss the estimation of beta, the firm-specific or portfolio-specific measure of risk used in the CAPM. Beta has been a widely discussed subject, and this chapter will review a variety of methods used to estimate beta and will report the results of a number of empirical studies designed to test these betas. In Chapters 5 and 6 we will discuss the other two estimates necessary for the practical use of the CAPM—the risk-free rate of return and the market premium. Although problems in estimating beta have received the most attention, the CAPM cannot be used unless reliable estimates can be obtained for these other two key factors.

The arbitrage pricing theory is beginning to receive the same scrutiny the CAPM has undergone. Researchers are evaluating the model's assumptions, testing to see how logical and realistic are its implications, and determining whether ready estimates can be made for the factors necessary for its practical use. Since the APT's history is short, we will be able to discuss it and the results of the research to date in one chapter, Chapter 7.

Because a number of components must be estimated for the CAPM and the APT, the use of these models is a creative and thoughtful venture. Much of what we will cover in Chapters 1–7 has led others to creative adaptations. In Chapter 8 we will discuss some of these current and creative uses of the CAPM and CAPM-derived approaches, as well as emerging uses for the APT. Applications from bank trust departments, investment advisory services, and public utility regulation will be included.

Now that we have surveyed the scope of this book, let us deal with the question of its underlying purpose. Why should anyone but the investment historian find MPT, the CAPM, and the APT of more than passing interest?

In the past decade we have seen managers attempt to use modern portfolio theory, particularly the CAPM, to achieve a strange purpose: to identify market inefficiencies. The purpose is strange because MPT is premised on market efficiency. Simply put, market efficiency suggests that all that is known and knowable by investors is incorporated into the price of the stock (or bond or other asset). The CAPM is derived from a set of assumptions that are even more stringent than those of MPT. Both the CAPM and the APT presume "perfect efficiency." Even so, the various models have been used to identify undervalued stocks, to market-time (that is, to change the debt-equity asset mix in anticipation of strong or weak equity market conditions), to rotate groups (that is, to overrepresent or underrepresent certain industries in the portfolio), and to achieve other active management ends. These models have also been used in other ways that are compatible with the intent of theory—for such purposes as determining asset-mix strategies, diversifying, and evaluating the performance of assets or portfolios. In other words, efficient-market models are being used to identify investment opportunities on which the investment manager can capitalize.

Despite their newness and their questionable theoretical justification, these practical adaptations of the theory often seem to work. Modern portfolio theory and its descendants, it would seem, can be used for aggressive management. Because many of the practical adaptations had their seeds in specific disagreements with one or more of the assumptions or implications of the theories, understanding the theories can help us in evaluating the evolution of the pragmatic adaptations and in participating in what is yet to happen.

The purpose of this book, then, is to review what we are beginning to learn about the CAPM and the APT from the point of view of the practitioner who is striving to adapt theory to useful purposes, and from that of the student who is learning that abstract theory can be useful. In addition to reports of theoretical adaptations and findings, reports of practical and creative uses will be included throughout the book.

What is now clear is that we know a great many things we did not know before, and we have found new ways of looking at old and perplexing problems. There is challenge in this knowledge. To use any model unthinkingly is to court disaster. To use it creatively appears to yield tangible rewards. To gain more than a superficial understanding of the CAPM and the APT, we must rely on almost two decades of articles written in academic journals. Our understanding has evolved over that time. Researchers disagree with one another, and there exists some real confusion about the significance of some research. My objective is to clear away some of the obfuscation and to lay the essential problems and opportunities before you so that you can form your own judgment about the models. Let us begin by reviewing the basics in lay-persons' terms.

chapter

1

Modern Portfolio Theory and the CAPM – Briefly

For as long as anyone can remember, people have been trying to estimate the future. Science fiction writers have plied their trade by responding to their readers' desire to understand the world in which they or their children may live. Often writers of this genre describe methods such as time travel or tomorrow's newspaper found today that grant their characters insight into the future. Such artifices are usually categorized as delightful diversion. But the occasional Jules Verne of stock selection has indeed been viewed as having a special method that could be passed along—a serious business this, not mere diversion. Modern portfolio theory is one imaginative construct. Like all such constructs, it is not the scientific verity that it is sometimes touted to be. Rather, the theory merely offers insights that can help thoughtful, creative analysts and managers do their jobs better. Tracing the evolution of *modern portfolio theory* (MPT) and its widely used adaptation, the *capital asset pricing model* (CAPM), can give us a better feel for their value as methods for divining the future.

Both MPT and the CAPM have great appeal. One of the reasons for their popularity is that these theoretical models evaluate assets on the twin aspects of risk and return. Previous models have considered returns to be paramount. Risk, if considered at all, was evaluated subjectively or intuitively. Another reason for the popularity of MPT and the CAPM is that they evaluate assets in terms of their effect on the risk and return of an investor's entire portfolio of assets.

I. MODERN PORTFOLIO THEORY

Modern portfolio theory is no mystical concept. It relies on simple and basic ideas. Returns are measured in an intuitively logical way. They are simply the returns expected from an investment or portfolio. For instance, the expected return from a bond held for a single period (t) is measured as follows:

Expected total return =
$$\frac{\text{interest income}_t + (\text{sales price}_t - \text{purchase price}_{t-1})}{\text{purchase price}_{t-1}}$$

For a stock, the following formula would be used to calculate the returns over a single period (t):

Expected total return =
$$\frac{\text{dividends}_t + (\text{market price}_t - \text{market price}_{t-1})}{\text{market price}_{t-1}}$$

These forecasts of returns are rarely perfectly accurate. Consequently, we need a means to measure "upside" potential and "downside" danger—that is, the potential that returns may exceed our estimate and the danger that returns may be less than we anticipate. In other words, we need a measure of how wrong our forecast may be.

One measure of forecast uncertainty is called *variance*. Variance measures the breadth of the distribution of expected returns from an investment. It is calculated on the basis of the squared deviations from the *mean* forecast. Basic textbooks in finance and statistics offer simple introductions to the concepts of mean and variance. Appendix A to this chapter also provides a simple example of how to calculate variance. A second and more widely used measure of forecast uncertainty is the square root of variance, called the *standard deviation*. Variance and standard deviation are widely used measures of risk, and they are the measures used in MPT for estimating the potential risk of making an investment. *Risk* is defined as forecast uncertainty or the potential for forecast error.

Exhibit 1-1 shows the distribution of returns that might be expected for two investments, A and B. The mean or average expected

Exhibit 1–1

Possible Outcomes
of Two Independent Investments

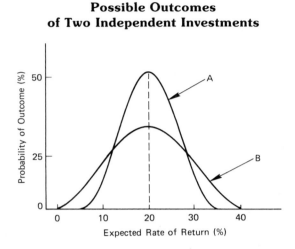

Expected Rate of Return (%)

return, at the vertical dotted line, is the same for both investments. However, investment B is more risky; the upside potential and downside danger are greater. With investment A we are more certain that our forecast will be close to the actual return. Thus, the variance of investment A is smaller than that of investment B.

Exhibit 1–1 shows two investments whose returns are normally distributed. This means that the forecasted upside potential of each is the same size as its forecasted downside danger. We describe such distributions as being *normal.* Any normal distribution can be represented by the familiar bell-shaped curve, which is symmetrical and neither flat nor peaked. A normal distribution has an advantage because we need only two summary measures, mean and variance, to describe the entire distribution. Although distributions of forecasted returns from investments are not always normal, analysts often assume that they are in order to simplify their analysis of the investor's decision. Thus, the analyst only has to give the investor the mean forecasted return and the variance (or the standard deviation), and the investor can then describe the entire forecasted distribution. We need not depict all the potential outcomes graphically because all the forecasted dangers and oportunities can be assessed from those two measures.

When we move from evaluating a single asset in isolation to evaluating a portfolio, some factors change. Return is still the expected return, but for a portfolio the return expected will be the average return from all the assets held in the portfolio. Appendix B includes an example of how the portfolio return is calculated. Risk is still the variance of the expected return from the portfolio: the investor is still concerned with upside potential and downside danger. However, the risk of the portfolio's components—the risk of the individual investments—is viewed quite differently from the risk of the entire portfolio.

To demonstrate the difference, let us look at the expected returns from a portfolio composed of only two investments—the stocks of two firms. The first firm is a major automobile manufacturer; the second firm is in the automotive after-care industry—perhaps a company providing replacements for shock absorbers, tires, or batteries.

Over time, the returns from shares of an automobile manufacturer can be expected to follow a pattern like the line *AC* in Exhibit 1–2. As you can see, the returns are cyclical and are expected to vary over time. Line *AD*, however, represents the returns expected from the second firm's stock. While the general economy remains strong, auto manufacturers prosper and so do their stockholders. But as the economy contracts, new-car purchases are postponed and automotive replacement-part manufacturers prosper. The sales of both companies are cyclical, as are the returns from their stocks. As a result, both stocks hold considerable risk for the investor. You will note, however, that we have been optimistic about the prospects for both stocks since the cyclical returns are increasing over time.

For a portfolio containing shares of both firms, the returns would be the sum of those from the two stocks. However, the risk (variance) of the portfolio would be much smaller than that from either stock. In Ex-

Exhibit 1–2

Variability of Returns Over Time

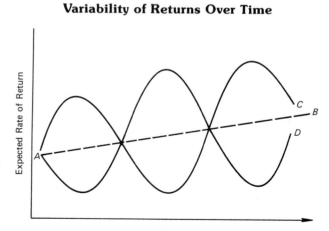

Time

hibit 1-2, dashed line *AB* represents the expected variability of the returns from a portfolio containing equal amounts of these two stocks. The two stocks' returns show a negative correlation—they move opposite each other. Because each stock's returns are counterbalanced by the other stock's returns, the portfolio's overall variance is lower than the variance of either stock's returns. Appendix B shows how portfolio risk is calculated. The relationship between the two stocks' returns can be measured by their correlation, or *covariance.* Covariance is simply the correlation coefficient multiplied by the product of the standard deviations of the expected returns of the two investments.

Although negative correlation (or covariance) reduces the risk of the portfolio, positive correlation does not. For instance, if an investor held stock in two automobile manufacturers, the risk of the portfolio would not be reduced. Instead it would more closely resemble the risk from each of the two stocks.

The interesting lesson from this simple demonstration is that risk can be reduced by judicious diversification—by increasing the number of assets with uncorrelated (or not highly correlated) returns. It is important to remember that to reduce a portfolio's risk, the investor must put together assets whose returns do not follow similar patterns—assets whose returns are not highly correlated.

Exhibit 1-3 illustrates just how risk can be reduced by composing portfolios with several common stocks. The first column indicates the number of stocks in the portfolio; the second column shows the level of variability (variance) above the basic market variability for a stock portfolio of that size. Basic market variability—the effect of changes in general economic activity on the returns of all stocks—cannot be eliminated. Judicious portfolio construction can, however, reduce almost completely the remaining variability—the non-market-related risk. The most dramatic reduction in non-market-related risk is achieved with about 14 stocks. The same diversification effect can be seen with assets other than stocks. Diversification reduces risk. Modern portfolio theory's concept of risk as variability of portfolio returns rather than that of returns of individual assets does, in fact, work.

The Markowitz Model

The first model to deal explicitly with risk in a portfolio sense was devised by practitioner Harry Markowitz (1952).[1] The model is quite simple. First, the investor chooses among all possible investments on the

---

[1] Years in parentheses following an author's name relate to a specific reference at the end of the chapter.

Exhibit 1–3

Risks of Portfolios with Different Numbers of Securities Whose Returns Are Uncorrelated

NUMBER OF SECURITIES	STANDARD DEVIATION OF RETURN IN EXCESS OF THE STANDARD DEVIATION OF THE MARKET
1	10.00%
2	7.07
3	5.77
4	5.00
5	4.47
10	3.16
20	2.24
50	1.41
100	1.00
1,000	.32
5,000	.14
10,000	.10
100,000	.03

Source: William F. Sharpe, *Investments,* 2nd ed., © 1981, p. 130. Reprinted by permission of Prentice-Hall, Inc., Englewood Cliffs, N.J.

Exhibit 1–4

The Efficient Frontier

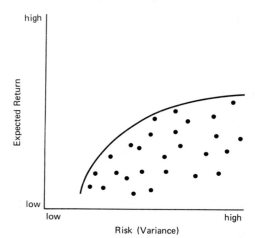

basis of their risk (portfolio variance) and return (portfolio return). These two characteristics can be plotted graphically for a group of investments. Exhibit 1-4 shows one such graph. (If you read the older MPT or CAPM literature, you may find that the axes are reversed in the graphic representations. This book shows the currently accepted method.) Each dot represents a possible investment. Some of the dots represent a single stock, bond, or other asset, whereas other dots represent various combinations of investments. The portfolios are made up of all possible combinations of the individual investments' alternatives. Thus, all possible choices are represented on the graph.

The next question must be, How does an individual choose among all possible portfolios? If the investor is rational, he or she will choose investments that provide the highest return for a given level of risk or those that offer the least risk for a given return. These best-return portfolios are called *efficient.* The curved line in Exhibit 1-4 links all these efficient portfolios together and is called the *efficient frontier.*

Although we have now identified all possible efficient portfolios, we have not given the investor directions as to how to choose his or her particular portfolio. This choice depends on the investor's appetite for risk. A risk-averse investor, such as a person nearing retirement, may prefer a portfolio with low risk (variance), whereas a risk taker may prefer a portfolio with greater variance and commensurately higher returns.

We can graphically represent any investor's preference for risk by plotting his or her trade-offs between risk and return. The lines connecting these points are called *utility curves.* Exhibit 1-5 shows the efficient frontier (note, that for convenience we have removed the dots representing inefficient portfolios or assets) and a set of utility curves that may reflect our older investor's preference for risk and return. As risk increases along each curve, the return required to induce this risk-averse investor to take the risk must also increase. Each curve shown in Exhibit 1-5 represents a single combination of risk and return equally satisfactory for this particular investor. The higher the utility curve, the greater the investor's satisfaction. Obviously, the investor's goal would be to find an investment, or portfolio, that would bring the greatest satisfaction—an investment that lies on the curve that is highest and farthest to the left. In this example, however, there are no investments on the highest curve. The best that the investor can achieve is an investment that lies at the point at which the dashed utility curve touches (is tangent to) the efficient frontier (*AO* line). A number of investments lie on lower utility curves, but these would not give this investor as much utility (satisfaction) as an investment on the frontier.

Other investors with different attitudes toward risk would have dif-

Exhibit 1–5

Efficient Frontier and Investor's Preference

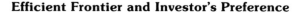

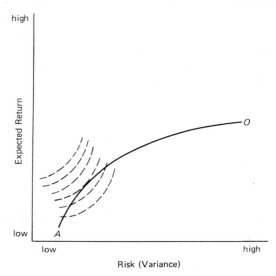

ferent utility functions (sets of utility curves). These curves define which investments, of all those on the efficient frontier, would be attractive to any given investor.

Using the Markowitz Model

In order to plot each investment and portfolio of investments on the graph shown in Exhibit 1–4, we must estimate future returns and variances of returns for each possible investment. For portfolios containing two investments, we would need to forecast returns and, to estimate the portfolio variance, the variances for each of the investments, and the correlation between the two investments' returns. As the size of the portfolio expands, the number of forecasts increases dramatically. For a portfolio with N assets, the number of correlations that must be calculated is $N(N-1)/2$. Thus, for a 14-asset portfolio, 91 correlations are needed to estimate the portfolio's variance. Appendix B to this chapter demonstrates the process we must go through to evaluate the risk and return for just three assets. Recall that this theory was first described in 1952— long before reasonably priced computer time became available. Even in the 1980s, the task of processing the data is quite costly for all but the smallest groups of assets.

Computing or estimating correlations is not the only problem involved in using the Markowitz model. Before we can determine correlations, we must first forecast future returns as well as estimate the uncertainty of those forecasts. Estimating the future return for one asset is hard enough, but we must estimate them for all assets, and under a variety of possible circumstances. If we could make all these forecasts, correlation coefficients would be quite easy to compute. If, however, we are willing or able to make only a few of the necessary forecasts, we increase the possibility that our correlation coefficients may be wrong. If we try to avoid the task of forecasting by using historical returns as proxies for forecasts, we run into complex statistical problems, problems we will discuss in Chapters 3 and 4. If we use forecasts, we find that forecasts of correlations are new and thus difficult for most analysts to make.

II. THE CAPITAL ASSET PRICING MODEL

The mechanical complexity of the Markowitz portfolio model kept both practitioners and academics from adopting the concept for practical uses. Its intuitive logic, however, spurred the creativity of a number of people. Several simplified versions were developed.[2] The most practical version is the capital asset pricing model. The CAPM is a logical extension of MPT, both intuitively and mathematically. In addition, the CAPM is a testable theory, MPT is not.

To understand the relationship between MPT and the CAPM, let us again consider the process we must go through to use MPT techniques to calculate the risk of a portfolio. To do so, we must have the standard deviation of every asset's expected returns, the correlation between the expected returns for every pair of assets, and the amount of each asset being held. For relatively small numbers of assets, the process is lengthy. For larger universes, the process is nearly impossible.

One way to simplify the process is to correlate each asset's expected return with the expected returns of a weighted average or index of all the assets under consideration. If, for example, our universe of assets

---

[2]The Sharpe diagonal model is perhaps the best known of these adaptations of the Markowitz model. See, for example, W. F. Sharpe, "A Simplified Model of Portfolio Analysis," *Management Science,* 9 (January 1963), 227–93. Others who developed the same or similar models virtually simultaneously were J. Lintner, "The Valuation of Risky Assets: The Selection of Risky Investments in Stock Portfolios and Capital Budgets," *Review of Economics and Statistics,* 47 (February 1965), 13–37; J. Treynor, "Toward a Theory of the Market Value of Risky Assets" (unpublished manuscript, 1961); and J. Mossin, "Equilibrium in a Capital Asset Market," *Econometrica,* 34 (October 1966), 768–83.

were only 20 stocks, to calculate the portfolio risk we would need to estimate 20 standard deviations and 20 correlations of the expected returns from each asset with the expected returns from this new (20-stock) index—40 calculations in all. The Markowitz model would have required 20 standard deviations and 190 correlations, a total of 210 estimates.

The beauty of this simplified process is that it gives us the same risk rankings as the Markowitz method. The absolute risk, the portfolio variance, would, of course, depend upon the universe chosen. Note that both methods are concerned only with risk and return. Other characteristics of the assets, such as the assets' quality ratings (e.g., bond rating) or industry affiliation, are assumed to be summarized in these measures of risk and return.

The capital asset pricing model actually takes this simplification of the Markowitz method even further. The CAPM uses a weighted average as the benchmark for calculating correlation, defining this benchmark as an index of the market-value-weighted portfolio of *all* possible risky investments.[3] This market-value-weighted portfolio or index is called the *market portfolio*. In addition to defining the index as the market portfolio, the CAPM's second adaptation of the Markowitz model is the addition of another asset to the universe of assets under consideration. This additional asset is known as the *risk-free asset*. You may have noted in Exhibit 1–1 that all the plotted investments had some risk; none lay on the *Y*-axis of the graph. This risk-free asset, added in the CAPM, has zero variance and zero covariance with any other asset—no risk. The risk-free asset provides a small but positive return—the return that investors require for their temporary illiquidity.

While in Chapters 4, 5, and 6 we will discuss how the risk-free asset and the market-value-weighted portfolio are identified, notice that the addition of the risk-free asset changes the investor's opportunities considerably. Exhibit 1–6 shows these changes. The MPT efficient frontier is the curved line *AO*. However, the risk-free asset allows us to create a new and more efficient frontier, R_fZ. The portfolios (except for the market portfolio) or assets lying on this new straight line provide more return for the same risk, or they offer less risk for the same level of return as those on the old efficient frontier. The straight line R_fZ, the new efficient frontier, is called the *capital market line* because it represents all possible capital market investments proportionately. The capital market line changes the risk-return trade-offs that are available to investors from those available from the MPT efficient frontier.

---

[3]Market-value-weighted, since this weighing captures the amount of any given asset that is available, as well as the price that results from the balance of the supply and demand for each asset in the marketplace.

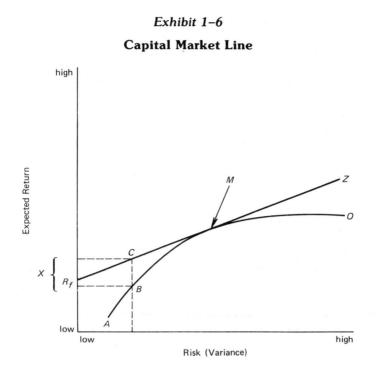

Exhibit 1–6

Capital Market Line

Our risk-averse investor, first shown in Exhibit 1–5, chose a portfolio shown at point *B* in Exhibit 1–6. By holding the portfolio shown at point *C* in Exhibit 1–6, this investor could improve his or her return by *X* with no change in risk. To obtain this improved return, the risk-averse investor would have to purchase portions of the market portfolio (*M*) and of the risk-free security (*R_f*) in a combination that suited his or her tolerance for risk. The more aggressive risk taker would borrow money to buy as much of *M* as possible. This debt-supported or leveraged portfolio would lie on the portion of the line labeled *MZ*. The average investor would hold the market portfolio *M*.

The CAPM's Definition of Risk

The CAPM defines *risk* as the covariability of the security's returns with the market's returns. We can also say that *risk* is the volatility of the security's returns relative to the volatility of the market portfolio's returns. All other variability can be diversified away by proper portfolio formation, as was demonstrated in Exhibit 1–3. Normally, investors require increased returns from an asset to compensate them for tolerating the risk that the forecasted returns may not be realized. But investors will not require any extra return to compensate them for risk or variability that can be eliminated—diversified away—from the portfolio. Since assets are priced to reflect the impact of their risk (variability of returns) on the portfolio, investors who choose to be less than fully diversified will not be compensated for the full risk of each asset: only systematic risk is priced and rewarded. Thus, there is a real incentive for being fully diversified in a world where prices are fair.

The risk that can be eliminated is called *unsystematic, non-market-related,* or *extramarket risk* because it is caused by changes that are specific to the firm issuing the security. For example, changes in a firm's management may affect its stock's returns. Unsystematic risk is unexpected, unpredictable, and, *in prospect,* unrewarded. Looking back, we can, of course, see unsystematic sources of superior returns or losses. But because these uncertainties can be diversified away, they are not relevant to the investors' forecasts of the future returns.

Investors, however, require compensation for risks that cannot be diversified away. These risks are called *systematic,* or *market-related, risks.* Systematic risks are caused by socioeconomic and political events that affect the returns of all assets, For example, an outburst of inflation may affect different companies in different ways, but all companies are affected to some extent. Stocks with greater-than-average systematic, or market-related, risk will be priced so that they are expected to have commensurately greater-than-average returns.

Systematic risk, then, is an estimate of how the expected returns from an asset or portfolio will move relative to the returns from the market portfolio. A firm relying on coal-fired generators, for example, may be relatively immune to rising oil prices; consequently, its systematic risk may be lower than that of the market as a whole. This firm, however, may be adversely affected by increased inflation. The systematic risk of a stock issued by this firm is a composite figure describing the asset's sensitivity to these factors and a host of others.

The CAPM designates systematic risk as *beta* (β). The beta of the market is 1.0.[4] Assets with less systematic risk (less volatility) than that

---

[4]The beta of the market is 1.0 because

$$\beta_m = \frac{\text{covariance } (R_m, R_m)}{\text{variance } (R_m)}$$

$$= \frac{\text{variance } (R_m)}{\text{variance } (R_m)}$$

$$= 1.0$$

of the market would have betas of less than 1.0; more risky assets would have betas in excess of 1.0. For any asset, beta is calculated as follows:

$$\tilde{\beta} = \frac{\text{covariance } (\tilde{R}_m, \tilde{R}_j)}{\text{variance}(\tilde{R}_m)}$$

where

R_m = expected returns from the market portfolio

R_j = expected returns from a given investment

covariance R_m, R_j = [correlation j, m] [(standard deviation of R_m) (standard deviation of R_j)]

$\sim$ = a forecast

In the CAPM, the beta for a portfolio is the weighted average of the betas for each asset contained in the portfolio. The returns are also the weighted average of the expected returns from the assets in the portfolio. R_f is the minimum return any investor would expect to receive from any asset. For assets with risk, the investor would expect the risk-free rate of return plus extra compensation for the systematic risk of the asset. This extra compensation is known as the *market price of risk*. For the average asset the market price of risk would be the difference between the risk-free rate of return and the return from the market (R_m $-R_f$). For an asset with more risk or less, the return would be proportionally higher or lower.

The formula for determining the expected returns from a given asset or portfolio is as follows:

$$\tilde{R}_j = \tilde{R}_f + \tilde{\beta}_j \, (\tilde{R}_m - \tilde{R}_f)$$

where

R_j = return from the asset or portfolio

R_f = return from the risk-free security

R_m = return from the market

β_j = volatility of asset or portfolio relative to that of the market m

$\sim$ = a forecast

Exhibit 1–7 plots the forecasts of risk and return for individual assets that make up the market portfolio. The solid line is called the *security market line*. Because the forecasted return for every asset depends

Exhibit 1–7

Security Market Line

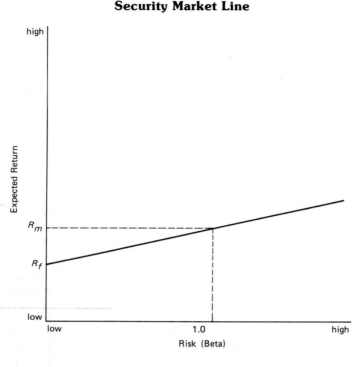

upon its systematic risk, the line represents the trade-off between systematic risk and return for every asset. Risk is labeled *beta*. Beta can replace variance as the measure of portfolio risk because we are assuming that investors will hold only fully diversified portfolios. Thus, the risk any asset contributes to the portfolio is the only risk that is important to the investor in pricing assets. Systematic risk is nondiversifiable and directly, and linearly, related to return. In a fully diversified portfolio only systematic risk remains, and therefore beta is a measure of an asset's risk, and is all the investor needs to know about the risk of an asset or a portfolio.

Evaluating the CAPM

Earlier we noted that the CAPM is just one version of a group of capital market models, called *risk-premium models,* which have been used for years by investment bankers, corporate financial officers, and investment analysts. These models start with the assumption that every holder of a risky investment requires a return that is greater than the return he or she would get from a risk-free security. In other words, the investor receives a premium as compensation for his or her risk. Most risk-premium models calculate the required rate of return by adding to the risk-free rate of return certain premiums for industry risk, operating risk, or financial risk. These calculations remain subjective because the analysts' estimates of business risks are likewise subjective.

The CAPM, by contrast, defines *risk* explicitly as the volatility of an asset's returns relative to the volatility of the market portfolio's returns. The advantage of this precise definition of risk is that risk is the only asset-specific forecast that must be made in the CAPM. Both R_f and R_m are forecasts that are the same from stock to stock or from asset to asset. Once calculated, R_f and R_m can be used to forecast returns for every asset.

The definition of risk as relative volatility of returns has some disadvantages, however. First, forecasts of future volatility are difficult to make and to verify. Second, it is possible that systematic risk or beta is too limited a definition of a security's risk. These two problems will be discussed in Chapter 4.

It is also possible that the capital asset pricing model as a whole may be flawed. Its very simplicity rests on some rigorous assumptions that underlie and build on MPT—assumptions about market efficiency, interest rates, and taxes on income from investments. These assumptions have repeatedly been challenged. To use the model wisely, we must understand the relevance of these charges. Chapter 2 will describe these assumptions in greater detail, explain why they are necessary, and determine whether they are so restrictive that they invalidate the model.

The model is also based on the fundamental premise that return and risk are interdependent. This hypothesis has been tested with historical data. The evidence that these tests offer to support the hypothesis will be represented in Chapter 3.

Finally, some problems with the CAPM become manifest when practitioners try to use it. Because the theory provides no definitions of the risk-free rate of return (R_f) or of the returns from the market portfolio (R_m), these forecasts must be made by the practitioner. Methods of determining R_f and R_m will be discussed in Chapters 5 and 6.

In Chapter 7 a recent addition to the equilibrium pricing models, arbitrage pricing theory, is discussed. In some ways this model is richer, and deals with some of the theoretical and empirical difficulties researchers and practitioners have had with both the CAPM and MPT.

Our challenge is to understand the advantages and limitations of these models so that we can capitalize on their insights while remaining aware of their flaws.

APPENDIX A
MEAN AND STANDARD DEVIATION
OF INDIVIDUAL ASSETS

The following forecasts were made for investments A and B. These investments were graphed in Exhibit 1-1. To calculate the variance and standard deviation for each investment the following steps would be used:

INVESTMENT A		INVESTMENT B	
Probability of Return (P_A)	Forecasted Return (X)	Probability of Return (P_B)	Forecasted Return (X)
05%	10%	05%	2%
20	15	25	12
50	20	40	20
20	25	25	28
05	30	05	38

The expected mean return would be calculated as follows:

$$\text{Expected mean return} = E(\tilde{X}_i) = \sum_{i=1}^{\eta} P_i X_i$$

For investments A and B:

$$E(X_A) = .05(.10) + .20(.15) + .50(.20) + .20(.25) + .05(.30)$$
$$= .20 \text{ or } 20\%$$

$$E(X_B) = .05(.02) + .25(.12) + .40(.20) + .25(.28) + .05(.38)$$
$$= .20 \text{ or } 20\%$$

The variance (and standard deviation) would be calculated as follows:

$$\sigma_j^2 = \sum_{i=1}^{n} P_i(E(X_j) - X_i)^2$$

For investments A and B:

$$\sigma_A^2 = .05(.20 - .10)^2 + .20(.20 - .15)^2 + .50(.20 - .20)^2 + .20(.20 - .25)^2 + .05(.20 - .30)^2$$

$$\sigma_A^2 = .20$$

$$\sigma_A = .0447 \text{ or } 4.47\%$$

$$\sigma_B^2 = .05(.20 - .02)^2 + .25(.20 - .12)^2 + .40(.20 - .20)^2 + .25(.20 - .28)^2 + .05(.20 - .38)^2$$

$\sigma_B{}^2 = .644$

$\sigma_B = .0802$ or 8.02%

    The advantage of this approach is that a standard deviation describes all the possible outcomes. For instance, within one standard deviation of the mean lie 68 percent of all forecasted returns. Within two standard deviations lie 95 percent, and within three standard deviations, 99.7 percent. So for investment A, 99.7 percent of all the expected outcomes will be within 33.4 and 6.59. For investment B, 99.7 percent of the time the outcomes will be between 44.06 and -4.06. Thus, investment B, with its larger standard deviation and identical mean is more risky than investment A.

APPENDIX B
USING THE MARKOWITZ PORTFOLIO MODEL:
THREE ASSETS

    The expected return $E(X)$ for a portfolio $(_p)$ is simply the weighted average (w) of the expected returns $(E(X))$ for each of the portfolio's assets (i):

$$E(X_p) = \sum_{i=1}^{n} w_i E(X_i)$$

    For a portfolio with three assets that have the following characteristics

ASSET	MEAN EXPECTED RETURN $E\ (X\ )$	PROPORTION IN THE PORTFOLIO (w)
A	20%	50%
B	20	20
C	20	30

the expected return for the portfolio would be

    Portfolio mean return $= .50\ (.20) + .20\ (.20) + .20\ (.30)$

                                 $= .20$ or 20%

The portfolio variance is not the simple average of the variances of each of the assets.

The general formula for variance to be used with a portfolio containing any number of assets is

$$\sigma^2(\bar{X}_p) = \sum_{i=1}^{n} \sum_{j=1}^{n} w_i w_j \rho_{ij} \sigma_i \sigma_j$$

where

$w =$ proportion in portfolio

$\sigma =$ standard deviation

$_{ij} =$ correlation of i and j

$_p =$ the portfolio

$n =$ the number of assets

$i,j =$ specific assets, here numbered 1, etc.

$\rho_{ij}\sigma_i\sigma_j =$ covariance, also written as cov_{ij}

Thus, the variance of a portfolio containing *three* assets must be calculated using this expanded version of the formula:

$$\sigma^2(\bar{X}p) = w_1^2 \sigma_1^2 + w_2^2 \sigma_2^2 + w_3^2 \sigma_3^2 +$$

$$2w_1 w_2 \, \text{cov}_{1,2} + 2w_1 \, w_3 \, \text{cov}_{1,3} + 2w_2 w_3 \, \text{cov}_{2,3}$$

Calculation of the Expected Risk and Return
for a Three-Asset Portfolio

SECURITY	MEAN EXPECTED RETURN ($\bar{X}$)	VARIANCE (σ^2)	STANDARD DEVIATION (σ)	PROPOR-TION IN PORTFOLIO (w)
A	20%	20.0	4.5%	50%
B	20	64.4	8.0	20
C	20	225.0	15.0	30

PAIRED ASSETS	CORRELATION COEFFICIENT (ρ_{ij})	COVARIANCE ($\text{cov}_{i,j}$)
A,B	.48	21.6
A,C	.30	22.5
B,C	.60	81.0

Portfolio variance $= (.5)^2(20) + (.2)^2(64.4) + (.3)^2(225) + 2(.5)(.2)(21.6) +$
$$2(.5)(.3)(22.5) + 2(.3)(.2)(81)$$

$$\sigma_p^2 = 48.6$$

$$\sigma_p = 6.97\%$$

REFERENCES

Lintner, J., "The Valuation of Risky Assets: The Selection of Risky Investments in Stock Portfolios and Capital Budgets," *Review of Economics and Statistics*, 47 (February 1965), 13-37.

Markowitz, Harry M.,"Portfolio Selection," *Journal of Finance*, March 1952, pp. 77-91.

Mossin, Jan, "Equilibrium in a Capital Asset Market," *Econometrica*, 34 (October 1966), 768-83.

Sharpe, W. F., "A Simplified Model of Portfolio Analysis," *Management Science*, 9 (January 1963), 277-93.

——, *Investments*. 2nd ed. Englewood Cliffs, N.J.: Prentice-Hall, 1981.

Treynor, Jack, "Toward a Theory of the Market Value of Risky Assets." Unpublished manuscript, 1961.

chapter

2

The Assumptions
Behind MPT and the CAPM

Wall Street is a tough testing ground for new ideas. New theories are a
dime a dozen, and many are not worth half the price. Investors' best
attitudes are skepticism toward the unproven and reluctance to accept
the unlikely.

When modern portfolio theory and the capital asset pricing model
were first described, investors and investment managers greeted them
with less than the usual enthusiasm. There were several reasons for this
reception. First, the models are normative, not descriptive; they describe
what should be, not necessarily what is. On the basis of certain logical
economic objectives, the theories describe how investors' behavior should
affect security prices. Neither MPT not the CAPM attempted to describe
what had been observed in the marketplace.

Ordinarily, the normative quality of a model would not daunt an
investment practitioner. It was a second problem that caused more dis-
may. Both MPT and the CAPM are based on certain assumptions—assumptions that some practitioners considered to be "ivory tower" dis-
tortions of reality. Although all theories abstract fundamental
relationships from complex environments, what made practitioners suspect these assumptions was that overzealous proponents of theory tended
to emphasize the models' most basic assumption, that of the market's
efficiency. The efficient-market dogma is particularly unpalatable to

practitioners, as it seems to say that research and active management have not added value to portfolios and will not do so in the future. Furthermore, index funds based on the concept of market efficiency, portfolios constructed to imitate the market, added an observable threat to the implicit message that security analysis was worthless. Under the circumstances, we could hardly expect investment professionals to greet this theory with open arms.

The academic community found the CAPM much more intriguing than did investment professionals. Although academics had long accepted the axiom that risky securities should promise more return than those with less risk, no widely accepted theory existed to explain how this risk premium could be calculated. MPT did not provide an answer since the risk of an asset was relative and depended upon the other assets being considered. The CAPM did provide one answer—risk was the relative volatility of returns. Academics hoped that this definition would be usable—that a security's relative volatility, its beta, could be measured.

The concept of risk as relative volatility also had intuitive appeal. Just as academics looked to the free market as the arbitrator of true security value, so did they look to market action as the arbitrator of relative riskiness. The model seemed sensible.

Academics are much more accustomed than practitioners to working with simplifying assumptions. They tend to be more concerned with the acceptability of a theory's implications, pending its empirical verification, than with its perfect veracity. That empirical testing would follow was taken for granted. In fact, the CAPM, at first blush, appeared to lend itself to empirical testing better than had any previous expression of the mechanism by which risky assets are priced—certainly much better than MPT. The CAPM was a beginning, not a fully tested answer.

The academic world is also accustomed to working with "foundation" models—models that oversimplify reality. Academics know that, in time, these models are usually revised and elaborated to incorporate more realistic assumptions. A foundation model serves as a point of departure. If later testing proves that the assumptions are too strict and too abstract, the assumptions can be modified.

In this light, we can see why academics were enthusiastic about the CAPM and why they pursued the testing and adapting of it. We can also see why practitioners were reluctant at first to adopt the CAPM.

The model is simple, is controversial, and holds promise. We should not be dismayed by the unrealistic claims of the overzealous. The advantage of a simpler model is that it is easier to understand, test, and use. Although we do not want a model that is so simplistic that it ignores important factors, a model's purpose is to abstract from the noisy complexity of reality. To be useful, a model must either describe what is occurring or forecast the future. A good model will both describe and forecast as simply as possible. A complex model would be of marginal value if a simple asset pricing model could explain most of the variability of past returns and could predict the future with reasonable accuracy. Even if the simpler model failed to explain how prices changed or failed to predict future prices, it might still serve as a building block for constructing a more useful model.

The simple CAPM and its assumptions have been the subject of considerable discussion. In this chapter we will look at the model's simplifying assumptions. We will begin with MPT's assumptions since it is on these CAPM is first based. Without academic jargon, we will describe what role the assumptions played in the theory's evolution and why the assumptions are needed. We will also describe how MPT and the CAPM would change if each assumption were removed. After looking at the assumptions in detail, we will be able to understand the tests of the CAPM's accuracy and its predictive ability, which will be described in Chapter 3. To know how the model may be oversimplified is to begin its adaptation to reality. We should not cringe from what is new but endeavor to know it with greater intimacy.

The CAPM rests on eight assumptions.[1] The first five assumptions are those that underlie the efficient-market hypothesis and thus underlie both MPT and the CAPM. The last three assumptions are necessary to create the CAPM from MPT. The eight assumptions are the following:

1. The investor's objective is to maximize the utility of terminal wealth.
2. Investors make choices on the basis of risk and return. Return is measured by the mean returns expected from a portfolio of assets; risk is measured by the variance of these portfolio returns.
3. Investors have homogeneous expectations of risk and return.
4. Investors have identical time horizons.
5. Information is freely and simultaneously available to investors.
6. There is a risk-free asset, and investors can borrow and lend unlimited amounts at the risk-free rate.
7. There are no taxes, transaction costs, restrictions on selling short, or other market imperfections.
8. Total asset quantity is fixed, and all assets are marketable and divisible.

---

[1]In this chapter we will discuss the eight assumptions needed for the CAPM. Additional assumptions are needed when the model is adapted. These additional assumptions are often complex.

One final reminder before we begin: the CAPM is an *expectational* model. We are not trying to describe what has happened, but what investors believe will occur, because investors' beliefs determine security prices. When, as sometimes happens, the distinction between an expectational model and a descriptive model is forgotten, the significance of the assumptions and the importance of test results can be misinterpreted.

To provide the needed familiarity with each assumption we will take them one at a time, discussing why each is needed theoretically and what the result of relaxing each would be. We will begin with the first five—those needed for market efficiency.

I.   THE EFFICIENT-MARKET ASSUMPTIONS

1.   THE INVESTOR'S OBJECTIVE IS TO MAXIMIZE THE UTILITY OF TERMINAL WEALTH.

MPT and the CAPM are just models that describe how consumers (investors) make choices. Thus, we must begin a theory of investor choice with a description of the objective the investor has in mind. We assume that the investor's objective is to maximize the utility of wealth at the end of a given holding period. For MPT and the CAPM, the investor is maximizing the *utility* of wealth, not maximizing wealth (or return) itself.

Utility is a way of describing the differences in individual preferences. For instance, if you are a dessert lover and you prefer ice cream to pie, to you the utility of ice cream exceeds the utility of pie. In addition to a preference for ice cream, the typical dessert lover has what is called "a diminishing positive marginal utility"—in other words, more ice cream is preferred to less, but each dish of ice cream is enjoyed less than the last. A risk-averse investor can also be described in the same way except that it is wealth, not ice cream, that is of interest. Each increment of wealth is enjoyed less than the last because each increment is less important in satisfying the basic needs and desires of the individual. A diminishing marginal utility for wealth is the most frequently described utility function. There are other forms of utility functions. For instance, an investor with a preference for risk would have an increasingly positive marginal utility for wealth: for the risk taker, more is preferred to less, but each increase in wealth makes the individual more acquisitive. A risk-neutral investor would find each increment of wealth equally attractive—that is, each increment would have the same utility. Given the investor's wealth, the total utility (or satisfaction) he or she obtains will depend upon the combinations of risk and return that are available.

Although this assumption about the investor's objective is quite straightforward and logical, it has some hidden problems. For instance, one problem is that the concept of maximizing terminal wealth makes no distinction among the forms that wealth can take. The assumption implies, for instance, that capital gains and dividends are equivalent and that the investor has no preference for one over the other. If investors do prefer one to the other, returns would have to be reclassified as dividends and capital gains, and the simple single risk measure used in MPT and the CAPM (the covariance of returns) would no longer be adequate. The obvious drawback to separating dividends and capital gains is that the model becomes more complex.

This assumption about the investor's objective is only the first step in the process of defining how investors behave. To make this description useful, we must describe the criteria that investors use in choosing among investments. We assume that investors take risk and return alone into consideration when maximizing their utility of terminal wealth.

2. INVESTORS MAKE CHOICES ON THE BASIS OF RISK
   AND RETURN. RISK AND RETURN ARE MEASURED
   BY THE VARIANCE AND THE MEAN OF THE
   PORTFOLIO'S RETURNS.

In Chapter 1 we discussed the difference in the way risk is measured when assets are evaluated as part of a portfolio rather than singly. Portfolio risk is total risk, is measured by variance, but since rational investors diversify away diversifiable risk, it can also be described by beta. Portfolio variance (or beta) is the sole factor determining investors' perceptions of risk. Return, the only other influence on investors' choices, is the expected mean rate of return. These descriptions of risk and return are critical to both MPT and the CAPM. Although there is little disagreement over using the mean[2] (or average) expected rate of return as the measure of return, using variance as the measure of total risk has provoked controversy.

The obvious advantage of using variance as the measure of risk is that it allows us to describe (graphically if desired) any distribution of returns by using only two numbers, the mean and the variance. The key problem in using variance is that it is an accurate description only for normal distributions. Not all distributions are normal, as many research-

[2]The mean is the most frequently used measure of location. In a normal distribution it coincides with the median (the outcome in the middle of the distribution) and the mode (the most frequent outcome). In non-normal distributions it does not.

Exhibit 2–1

Normal and Skewed Distributions of Returns

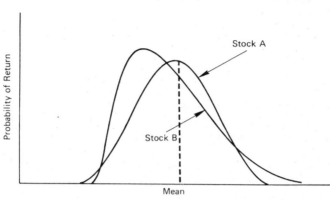

ers have shown.[3] Distributions may have identical means and variances, yet they may still be quite different. In fact, it is intuitively obvious that distributions of returns in the capital markets are not normal. After all, although the investor can lose 100 percent of most investments (excepting some leveraged futures and options investments), the upside potential is theoretically unlimited.

Exhibit 2–1 shows the forecasted returns for two stocks. The two returns' distributions have exactly the same mean and variance. However, the two stocks would not be equally attractive to an investor. Stock B has more upside potential and less downside risk than stock A, even though the means and variances for both are the same. Many investors would prefer stock B to stock A because the long shot is quite attractive when the two stocks' mean expected returns are the same. A distribution like that of stock B is called *skewed* because it deviates from the normal distribution.

Skewing of returns' distributions is ignored by the model's use of variance as the sole measure of risk. Yet we can see that skewing may be an important factor in investment decisions. Curiously enough, skewing can be a problem for the model even if returns are not actually skewed. Because MPT and CAPM are anticipatory, skewing need only be important in the *minds* of investors for it to invalidate these simple models'

[3]See, for example, M. A. Simkowitz and W. L. Beedles, "Diversification in a Three-Moment World," *Journal of Finance and Quantitative Analysis*, 13 (December 1978), 924–41.

predictions. If skewing is important, these simple models could provide a poor description of the data investors use and thus of investor behavior. As a result, the CAPM and MPT, which make their forecasts on the basis of normal distributions, could make poor predictions.[4]

One solution to this problem is to substitute for variance some other measure of risk. Semivariance is one alternative.[5] Semivariance measures only the downside risk (or upside potential) from the investor's chosen target, instead of measuring both up and downside from the mean. Variance and semivariance will yield the same results only when the distribution is normal and the investor's return target is the mean. Even using the means as the targets, the two investments shown in Exhibit 2-1 would not have identical measures of semivariance.

We can easily imagine an example in which the MPT mean-variance efficient frontier (like that shown in Exhibit 1-4) would differ from that calculated on the basis of mean and semivariance. Any group of stocks with skewed returns distributions would produce these contrasting results. Portfolios that would appear efficient on the basis of mean-variance criteria would appear inefficient on the basis of mean-semivariance criteria, and vice versa. Because the investor's decision would depend on the risk measure chosen, it is important to use an appropriate measure of risk.

In using MPT and the CAPM we assume that portfolio variance is an appropriate measure of risk because it allows us to use two factors, mean and variance, to describe each asset's relative attractiveness. In moving from MPT to the CAPM we presume that since rational investors diversify away diversifiable risk (unsystematic risk), beta is a measure of the remaining risk (the variance) of the portfolio. Thus, we presume that beta and return are directly and linearly related. Some researchers[6] have contended that when investors' diversification efforts are constrained, for instance by transaction costs, the model would have to include both beta and variance as reward-providing factors. As a result the total return the investor would expect, and get, would come from two kinds of risk, not just one.

When the first two assumptions are joined—that the investor's goal is to maximize the utility of terminal wealth and that the investor's de-

[4]Many suggest that because returns over time are skewed, a lognormal distribution better reflects reality. They replace the simple, linear, CAPM with a log, log construct.

[5]For a description of semivariance, see James C. T. Mao and J. F. Brewster, "An E-Sh Model of Capital Budgeting," *Engineering Economist,* 15 (January–February 1970), 103–21.

[6]See, for instance, Haim Levy, "Equilibrium in an Imperfect Market: A Constraint on the Number of Securities in the Portfolio," *American Economic Review,* 73 (September 1978), 643–58; and Joram Mayshar, "Transaction Costs in a Model of Capital Market Equilibrium," *Journal of Political Economy,* 86 (August 1979), 673–700.

cisions are based on expected risk and rates of return—we can conclude that investors choose only those portfolios with the highest rate of return for their preferred level of risk (variance), or those with the lowest risk for their preferred rate of return. This definition of preferred investments is the same as that given in Chapter 1 for portfolios on the efficient frontier.

Still, with only these two assumptions every investor could have his or her own estimates of mean and variance for each asset, and thus each would have a unique efficient frontier. To move from an investor-specific efficient frontier to the single efficient frontier of modern portfolio theory, we need one further assumption about investors' expectations.

3.   INVESTORS HAVE HOMOGENEOUS EXPECTATIONS
     OF RISK AND RETURN.

This assumption simply states that all investors' estimates of risk and return are the same. To have the single efficient frontier of modern portfolio theory, we must have consensus estimates of the mean and variance and thus of the relative value of each investment. Without a consensus, each investor or group of investors could have very different forecasts for variance and for mean return. Consequently, the efficient portfolio for one investor could be quite different from that for another.

For an example of the problems this assumption removes, let us return to the issue of dividends versus capital gains. If some investors prefer dividends (a bird in the hand) to capital gains, high-yield stocks would be valued differently from those with high, but longer-term, potential. Varying preferences could produce a number of investor-specific efficient frontiers instead of the single frontier of modern portfolio theory. This complex, investor-specific model would have multiple efficient frontiers, each dependent on a different set of preferences for capital gains versus dividends. Furthermore, investors could define the market portfolio (and/or its risk and return) differently. That, too, would endanger the single efficient frontier of MPT and the CAPM, making the models useless.

Thus, MPT, and CAPM, and the efficiency of the market portfolio are inseparable. All rest on the assumption of homogeneous expectations. We could not state an equilibrium relationship without this assumption.[7] Now we know why homogeneity is a necessary assumption. But is homogeneity realistic?

---

[7]In equilibrium, buying equals selling, and all investors agree on the market price of risk, regardless of their personal attitude toward risk.

There is good reason to suspect that homogeneity is not a marketplace phenomenon. We know that investors rarely agree on the future; we need only look at the forecasted returns published by various research groups. Yet the question is not whether people have diverse expectations but whether such diversity affects prices. The efficient-market hypothesis suggests that the price of an asset (specifically a stock) is the best estimate of the present value of future returns from that asset.[8] How would the efficient-market hypothesis be affected if the world were populated by nonhomogeneous investors? How would prices be determined?

Several alternative theories could be used to explain investor behavior. One alternative is a group of models called *state-preference models*.[9] Each model is investor-specific, depending on that investor's expectations of the world and or his or her other preferences, given that world. However, because these are investor-specific models, they are difficult to generalize.

A state-preference model is not the only alternative explanation of investors' pricing behavior. Miller (1977) suggested that consensus pricing does not exist. Rather, he suggested it is the optimistic investor who keeps security prices up. Buying may occur at a variety of levels of optimism and thus at different prices. The quantity of buying, Miller said, continues from the most optimistic investor down, until there is a supply-demand equivalence. Although no particular model has been derived to deal with Miller's theory of investor optimism, this theory and other alternatives to homogeneous pricing are intriguing. In the CAPM and MPT we use homogeneity because it yields a simple, more easily generalized, model. Other choices might lead to a richer framework, one that would describe capital market activity more accurately, but these models would be much more complex.

Thus far these three assumptions lead us to a consensus model of investor behavior. However, the concept of a consensus rests upon yet another assumption. Recall that our first assumption was that investors

---

[8]There are three forms or levels of market efficiency; each implies a more vigorous translation of information into price. The first, called the weak form, states that information conveyed by historical prices and returns is reflected in the current price. The second version, the semistrong form, states that other publicly available information (e.g., the information contained in annual reports) is also fully reflected in the price. The strong form of the efficient-market hypothesis states that neither special-interest groups (e.g., corporate management) nor those with information not generally available can outguess the current asset price. There is, to be sure, evidence that contradicts the strong form, at least in the short run. There is also some evidence that casts doubt on the other forms of the efficient-market hypothesis. However, the market is clearly more efficient than we would have believed years ago—but not perfectly efficient.

[9]For a simple description of state-preference models, see Thomas E. Copeland and J. F. Weston, *Financial Theory and Corporate Policy*, 2nd ed., (Reading, Mass.: Addison-Wesley, 1985).

maximize terminal wealth. Terminal wealth implies that there is a specific time period over which the investor makes his or her forecasts.

4. INVESTORS HAVE IDENTICAL TIME HORIZONS.

This assumption suggests that investors form portfolios to achieve wealth at a single, common terminal date. That single, common horizon allows us to construct a single-period model. The model implies that investors buy all the assets in their portfolios at one point in time and sell them at some undefined but common point in the future.

Although necessary, this assumption is also obviously unrealistic. The world of investors is composed of short-term speculators, buy-and-holders, and everyone in between. Furthermore, the chosen horizon may depend upon the characteristics of the asset and could even change for any group of investors over time. This single-period assumption implies that investors operate on a single horizon. Yet investors act as if they make a series of reinvestments rather than a single-period buy-and-hold decision. Thus, a continuous model may be more appropriate.

In addition to being an inaccurate description of investors' behavior, the assumption is not realistic regarding risk. We know that risk for a short-term speculator is not the same as that for investors with longer horizons; in other words, risk changes over time.[10] As the horizon is extended, short-term fluctuations cancel out and longer-term cycles gain importance. Risk for day-traders is quite different from risk for those seeking long-term capital gains. The use of a single-period model to depict what is clearly a sequential decision-making process has hidden difficulties. If the nature of risk varies over time, then investors with quite different horizons may act (and in fact should act) quite differently. Because their assessments of beta, the risk-free rate, and the market premium depend upon their horizons, the simple, single-period model would be wrong.

Continuous-time models have been developed,[11] but they are more complex than the single-period models. Some include another asset in addition to the two used in the CAPM (the risk-free asset and the market portfolio)—an asset to hedge against unforeseen changes in the risk-free

---

[10]See Robert F. Vandell, D. Harrington, and S. Levkoff, "Cyclical Timing: More Return for Less Risk," Darden School Working Paper No. 78–12 (Charlottesville, Va.: Darden Graduate School of Business Administration, 1978).

[11]See Robert C. Merton, "An Intertemporal Capital Asset Pricing Model," *Econometrica,* 41 (September 1973), 867–87; Eugene F. Fama, "Multiperiod Consumption Investment Decisions," *American Economic Review,* 55 (March 1970), 163–74; and Douglas T. Breeden, "An Intertemporal Asset Pricing Model with Stochastic Consumption and Investment Opportunities," *Journal of Financial Economics,* (September 1979), 265–96.

rate. Others presume the investor's consumption-investment choices are independent over time, and create multiperiod betas.[12] However, these models continue to see risk and return as the only important characteristics of an asset. Other characteristics are believed to be completely summed up in the measures of risk and return.

We can use the single-period model to approximate multiperiod investor behavior, but only if the following conditions are true:

1. Returns are independent over time. For the stock market, this is equivalent to saying that the weak form of the efficient-market hypothesis holds.[13]

2. Expectations are independent of past or current information. For instance, we must be able to say that the returns from a retail food chain are independent of such things as past and current inflation and past food prices.[14]

To the investment practitioner, these two conditions are clearly not realistic. Thus, continuous-time adaptations are intriguing, but complex.[15]

Just what would be the impact if we misestimate the horizon length investors are using in pricing assets? As the horizon lengthens the capital market line could intersect the efficient frontier at different points. If this were so, investors with different horizons would hold different, but still efficient, portfolios. The result would be no single efficient frontier, and no single market price of risk. However, while the horizon length affects the absolute value of the slope and intercept in the CAPM, it may not affect the linearity of the capital market line,[16] or the rankings of securities. Thus, if the horizon is overestimated, the intercept would be lower than it actually is, and low-risk portfolios would appear to underperform high-risk portfolios. Still, the CAPM assumes that there is a common horizon being used by investors.

One last assumption is needed to complete the underpinning of efficient-market theory and thus of these models.

[12]Most models, except that by Douglas T. Breeden, ibid., presume that the investors' preference for consumption versus investment is independent from time period to time period. Yaacov Z. Bergman, "Time Preference and Capital Asset Pricing Models," *Journal of Financial Economics* 14 (1985), 145–59, shows that if preferences are intertemporally dependent, Breeden's more simple, single-consumption beta, model does not hold.
[13]For a description of the weak form of the efficient-market hypothesis, see footnote 8 in this chapter.
[14]For more detail regarding these propositions, see Eugene F. Fama and J. MacBeth, "Tests of the Multiperiod Two Parameter Model," *Journal of Financial Economics*, 1 (May 1974), 43–66.
[15]See N. Gressis, G. Philippatos, and J. Hayya, "Multiperiod Portfolio Analysis and the Inefficiency of the Market Portfolio," *Journal of Finance*, 31 (September 1976), 1115–26.
[16]See J. E. Gilster, Jr., "Capital Market Equilibrium with Divergent Investment Horizon Length Assumptions," *Journal of Finance and Quantitative Analysis*, 18 (June 1983), 257–65.

5. INFORMATION IS FREELY AND SIMULTANEOUSLY AVAILABLE TO INVESTORS.

Market efficiency also rests on this assumption. If groups of investors were privy to special, not widely available, information on which they could make superior decisions, markets would not be efficient and MPT and the CAPM would be affected. Without a set of common forecasts, a single efficient frontier could not exist.

Is this assumption realistic? Intelligent people can of course disagree. Still, most of the market value of the stock market consists of stocks of the most carefully analyzed firms. And the information about these companies is broadly available to managers of large portfolios. For other assets, such as the stocks and bonds of smaller firms, information is not as widely available.

What can we conclude about the reality of the efficient-market assumptions? The validity of the first four assumptions will depend on whether they are important to the way that investors' expectations are formed. If investors price assets as if they are true, then they are true. If, however, any of the assumptions is sufficiently unrealistic, there may be no unique parameters to the model. In other words, the model's results could be different for each investor or group of investors. There may be multiple efficient frontiers, depending on the investors' time horizons. The optimal portfolio for each investor would depend on that investor's estimates of risk and return over his or her holding period. A model reflecting these diverse factors would be much more complex and virtually impossible to test.[17]

Do not despair. Although these assumptions and those that we are about to discuss are clearly not realistic, we must remember our criterion for a good model: does it explain or forecast or both? If it does either or both, we can use it to make better decisions. In the ensuing chapters we will see that, despite its flaws, the CAPM has positive and exciting uses. But first we need to make several additional assumptions to create the CAPM.

II. THE CAPM ASSUMPTIONS

1. THERE IS A RISK-FREE ASSET, AND INVESTORS CAN BORROW AND LEND UNLIMITED AMOUNTS AT THE RISK-FREE RATE.

This may be the most crucial assumption for the CAPM. The risk-free asset is needed to simplify the complex pairwise covariances of Markow-

---

[17]See Fama and MacBeth, "Tests of the Multiperiod Two-Parameter Model."

itz's theory. The risk-free asset simplifies the curved efficient frontier of MPT to the linear efficient frontier of the CAPM, and the investor has ceased to be concerned with the characteristics of individual assets. Instead, the investor can create a portfolio from his or her own risk-preferred combination of R_f and R_m.[18] Risk is decreased or increased by adding a portion of the risk-free asset or by borrowing at the risk-free rate to invest additional funds in the market portfolio.

This assumption raises two questions. First, is there such a thing as a risk-free asset? And second, can all investors both borrow and lend at the risk-free rate?

In the next chapter we will look at some CAPM tests that use the rate of return on a 90-day Treasury bill as the proxy for the risk-free rate, and in Chapter 6 we will discuss alternative proxies. Note that the R_f of the CAPM is not the Treasury bill rate but the rate of return on a theoretical zero-risk asset or portfolio. This theoretical asset has no risk—that is, it has no covariance with the market.

Does the risk-free security exist?

Several researchers have questioned the very existence of a truly risk-free asset, and they have developed models that do not depend on the existence of a risk-free security. Black (1972) suggested that the *minimum*-risk asset is not in fact risk free because it is subject to the buffeting of inflation. Black created an alternative CAPM using short-selling as a proxy for the risk-free asset. If the investor can short-sell assets, then any portfolio of risky assets can be balanced by short-sold assets, creating a riskless portfolio in any economic environment. To short-sell, the investor borrows securities and sells those securities in anticipation of replacing them later at a lower price. Black assumed that short-selling was the means that allowed market prices to be in equilibrium—that is, to be balanced between market pessimists and market optimists, buyers and sellers. For Black short-selling would be similar to issuing securities at an uncertain rate. Because short-selling could occur at any time, it could be used as a proxy for the risk-free asset. Black assumed that all investors could participate in the short-selling of risky securities, which is not actually true. Many large portfolios are restricted from short-selling. However, Black's model retained the CAPM's linear relationship between risk and return. The method of combining two portfolios, the risk-free asset and the market portfolio, still worked.

---

[18]The investor is concerned with risk and return, not with the individual characteristics of each asset. The investor's particular attitude toward risk will determine how much of the risk-free asset and the market portfolio will be held. This principle is more formally known as the separation theorem.

Black's replacement for the risk-free asset was a portfolio that had no covariability with the market portfolio. Because the relevant risk in the CAPM is systematic risk, a risk-free asset would be one with no volatility relative to the market—that is, a portfolio with a beta of zero. All investor-preferred levels of risk could be obtained from various linear combinations of Black's zero-beta portfolio and the market portfolio. Exhibit 2–2 graphs the traditional CAPM and Black's version of it. Since R_z (the rate of return on the zero-beta asset) and R_m are uncorrelated (as R_f and R_m were assumed to be in the simple CAPM), the investor can choose from various combinations of R_z and R_m. On segment R_z, R_m, Y is sold short and the proceeds are invested in R_m. On segment $R_z R_m$, portions of the zero-beta portfolio and R_m are purchased. At R_m the investor is fully invested in the market portfolio.

The equilibrium CAPM was rewritten by Black as follows:

$$E(R_i) = (1 - \beta_i)E(R_z) + \beta_i E(R_m)$$

where E indicates "expected," $E(R_z)$ is less than $E(R_m)$, and R_z holdings over the whole market must be in equilibrium. That is, the number of short sellers and lenders of securities must be equal.

Black's adaptation is intriguing. If, as many think, R_z is larger than R_f, the capital market line would have a less steep slope and a higher

Exhibit 2–2

Zero-Beta CAPM and R_f CAPM

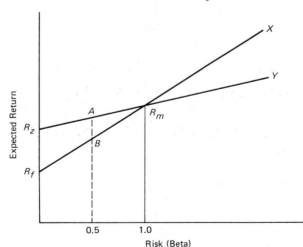

intercept than those of the simple CAPM. If Black's model is more correct in its description of investor behavior in the marketplace, then the use of the simple model would produce equity return predictions that would be too low for stocks with betas greater than one and too high for stocks with betas of less than one. Exhibit 2-2 shows the difference between the two models' predictions for a stock with a beta of less than one. The difference between the prediction from the simple model and that from Black's is the difference between B and A.

Unfortunately, we do not have, and neither did Black, an explanation of just what the zero-beta portfolio or asset might be. Nor do we know how restrictions on short-selling would affect the Black adaptation. Certainly there are substantial real-world restrictions against short-selling, as well as significant investor aversion to short-selling.

Do R_f or R_z even exist? We don't know. We do know that to use either model, R_f or R_z must be available to investors and its returns must be independent of the rate of return from the market (have zero covariance). Is it likely that R_f and Black's R_z are independent of the market's returns—that they have betas of zero? If these returns are not independent, special statistical problems occur.[19] R_f and R_m must be independent. If they are not, investors cannot separate their risk preferences from specific asset choices. The ability to make choices on the basis of risk and return alone, without other information about the individual asset, is essential to the CAPM. If this separation were not possible, then we could not use the CAPM.

Because inflation affects both risky and riskless assets, inflation alone could cause the interdependence of R_m and R_f (or R_m and R_z). Because there was considerable inflation in the 1970s, many researchers examined its effect on the CAPM. Unfortunately the interdependence of R_f and R_m is not the only impact inflation has on the CAPM.

Frankly, our understanding of the relationship between market returns and investors' expectations of inflation is limited. For some time it was believed that stocks acted as an inflation hedge; market returns were positively correlated with inflation. Lintner (1975) pointed out how little we understand about the impact of inflation. He suggested a negative relationship between returns and inflation. During outbursts of inflation, the firm's rate of return and equity value are reduced because of the firm's increased dependence on outside financing. The need for additional financing, Lintner suggested, is caused by accounting practices that are insensitive to inflation. His is one explanation of the effects of

---

[19]For a discussion of this problem, see, for example, R. L. Hagerman and E. H. Kim, "Capital Asset Pricing with Price Level Changes," *Journal of Finance and Quantitative Analysis*, 11 (September 1976), 381–92.

inflation on returns. Our question is, How would inflation affect the basic CAPM?

The CAPM has been adapted to deal with inflation. Biger (1975) came to the conclusion that uncertain inflation would change the composition of the optimal portfolio. He suggested that a more accurate model might be

$$R_j = \text{real } R_f + \text{inflation} + \beta_j(R_m - R_f)$$

Yet this model may be far too simplistic.

Hagerman and Kim (1976) suggested a more complex adaptation to account for inflation:

$$E(\tilde{R}_j) = E(\tilde{R}_f) + \frac{\overbrace{\text{covariance } (R_j, R_m - R_f)}}{\text{covariance } (R_m, R_m - R_f)} [E(\tilde{R}_m) - E(\tilde{R}_f)]$$

Their change is in the second term, the beta term outlined by a bracket. In the simple model, this term is

$$\frac{\overbrace{\text{covariance } R_i, R_m}}{\text{variance } R_m}$$

indicating that Hagerman and Kim expected an interrelationship among the returns of the market, the returns of the stock, and inflation.

Theirs is not the only version of inflation-adjusted CAPM. Friend, Landskroner, and Losq (1976) provided another CAPM adapted for inflation. All of their factors are expressed in nominal terms:

$$E(R_j) = R_f + \text{cov}(R_j, R_p)$$
$$+ \frac{E(R_m - R_f) - \text{cov}(R_m, R_p)}{\alpha\sigma_m^2 - \text{cov }(R_m, R_p)} \ \text{cov}(R_j, R_m) - \text{cov}(R_m, R_p)$$

where

    R_p = expected inflation rate
    α = percentage of total investors' capital in risky investments

When the correlation between an asset's return and the rate of inflation is positive, their model yields a lower cost of equity (expected return) than would the simple CAPM. If inflation rises, so do returns. This finding is important. In times of uncertain inflation, the size of errors from the simple, but erroneous, CAPM would be magnified. The real cost of equity could well be misestimated—and we have no way of knowing by how much.

It is important to note that an inflation rate is really a weighted average of the effects of inflation of the prices of various goods and services. Because companies use different goods and services in producing their products, the net cash flows of some firms will increase as a result of inflation, while others will not. Thus, even if the rate of return investors require to compensate them for expected inflation increases, some of the cash-flow winners will increase in value.

Lewellen and Ang (1982) looked at the effect of inflation on expected stock and bond returns. They examined the "Fisher effect"—the expected nominal rate of return is the product of the real rate of return (R_R) and expected inflation (R_I):

$$R_i = (1 + R_R)(1 + R_I)$$

and concluded that when inflation is uncertain, the Fisher relationship works for equities, but not for debt. While they admit such a finding seems odd, they ascribe it to the fact that in an inflationary environment, ex ante, the fixed-dollar payoff of debt will decline in comparison to such things as equities, which "are insulated from inflation because they are claims against real-goods outputs . . . the inflation down-side income protection provided is worth more on balance than the inflation-upside income constraint is dangerous."[20]

The impact on the CAPM of Lewellen and Ang's findings is that while expected, or certain, inflation would shift the capital market line parallel and upward, like line AB to CD in Exhibit 2-3, uncertain inflation of the same magnitude would result in a nonparallel shift, like line $A'B'$.

Exhibit 2-3 is plotted for a certain, and uncertain inflation rate of 20 percent. While this is an extreme example, at least in the United States, if the world is as Lewellen and Ang suggest, the beta of any asset will misestimate the expected rate of return when inflation is uncertain. The "Fisher effect" would not hold, and only for a portfolio whose beta is 1.0 would the forecast be accurate.

The presentation of these adaptations is not meant to demonstrate practical and usable inflation-adapted CAPMs. Rather, it is to demonstrate the diversity of the adaptations and to show the increased complexity that results. Unfortunately, we do not know which, if any, of these models is most accurate. Our understanding of inflation and our ability to adapt the model for the complex impacts of inflation are primitive.

---

[20]Lewellen, Wilber G., J. S. Ang, "Inflation, Security Values, and Risk Premia," *The Journal of Financial Research*, 5 (Summer 1982), 110.

Exhibit 2–3

Security Market Lines with Varying Forecasts for Inflation

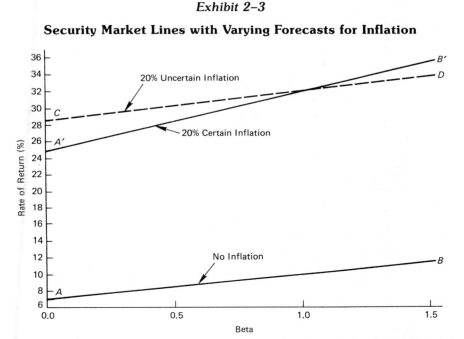

Source: Data from Wilber G. Lewellen and J. S. Ang, "Inflation, Security Values, and Risk Premia," *Journal of Financial Research*, 5 (Summer 1982), 109–10.

Still, we are sure that the simple model does not properly represent even our limited understanding of inflation. The simple CAPM relies on the existence of a risk-free asset that does not covary with the market. Inflation alone makes the existence of a truly risk-free asset unlikely and makes the covariance of the least-risk asset with other assets very likely. The result of these inaccuracies would be a model that incorrectly describes the world, and thus we must be suspicious of the simple CAPM.

Can all investors borrow and lend at the risk-free rate?

The second problem in using the risk-free security as one of the two factors in the CAPM is that we assume that this security is available to all investors. The theory suggests that investors must be able to lend and borrow at the risk-free rate. A risk taker creates a portfolio that is riskier than the market portfolio by borrowing at the risk-free rate to invest in the market portfolio. This borrowing and lending at the risk-free rate results in the single straight line $R_f R_m X$ shown in Exhibit 2-2.

Obviously, few investors can borrow at the risk-free rate. They can lend (for instance, buy U.S. Treasury securities), but not borrow.

Several researchers have attempted to make the model more realistic with regard to the borrowing and lending assumption. For example, assume that all investors can lend at a nominally risk-free rate but few investors, if any, can borrow at that rate. If we set the borrowing rate higher, at, say, R_z, the relationship would change from the traditional straight line of the CAPM. That is, the capital market line, line $R_f R_m X$ shown in Exhibit 2–2, would become line $R_f R_m Y$. Line $R_f R_m Y$ is a broken line, which would seem to reflect reality better. In fact, the $R_m Y$ section of the line could really be a number of lines, each dependent on the borrowing rate available to a different group of investors.

The assumption regarding the equality of borrowing and lending rates and the free access to the risk-free security is clearly an inaccurate description of the world. Relaxing the assumption leads at best to a broken capital market line, and at worst to an investor-specific fan of lines. In short, relaxing this assumption changes the model in ways that affect the slope, intercept, and linearity of the capital market line. The borrowing-lending assumption is critical to the model's integrity, and its relaxation causes changes that we are not yet able to describe well.

2.   THERE ARE NO TAXES, TRANSACTION COSTS,
     RESTRICTIONS ON SHORT SALES, OR OTHER
     MARKET IMPERFECTIONS.

This assumption has several implications for the CAPM. First, the assumption about short sales complements the assumption about a risk-free asset. Roll (1977) showed that there must be either a risk-free asset or a portfolio of short-sold securities for the capital market line to be straight: if there were no risk-free asset, the investor could create one by short-selling securities. If there were no risk-free asset, and the investor could not create a proxy risk-free security by short-selling, the capital market line would not be linear and the direct linear relationship between risk (beta) and return would not exist. In reality, there are considerable restrictions on short sales in most portfolios.

Second, of the three assumptions specific to the CAPM, this one removes the real-world problem of transaction costs and taxes. The CAPM treats dividends and capital gains as equivalent and transaction costs as irrelevant. Assuming that all returns are equally desirable allows us to use the simple CAPM.

We know that different investors have different transaction costs and different taxes. Still, the differences are important only if investors consider these potential costs and taxes in discriminating among different assets or portfolios. For example, some securities or assets are available to small investors but are not available to large institutions, or quality restrictions may remove a group of assets from a given investor's consideration. If situations like these create diverse expectations, we are back to a market portfolio that is investor-specific. And we would be left, once again, with multiple efficient frontiers.

Are transaction costs and taxes important to the pricing of assets? In the late 1970s and early 1980s, transaction costs were probably less important than taxes. In May 1975 the Securities and Exchange Commission deregulated transaction costs, allowing them to seek competitive levels. The deregulated costs were on average lower than pre-1975 transaction costs and thus less important.

The assumption that taxes are irrelevant has several implications. First, the assumption implies that capital gains and dividend income are equally attractive to investors and that higher dividend-paying stocks have a greater market value, all other things being equal. Miller and Modigliani (1961) and Modigliani and Miller (1963) showed that where dividends are taxed at higher rates than capital gains, capital gains should have greater after-tax value. Otherwise, given an investment policy, dividends and capital gains would be equally attractive. However, other researchers suggested that dividends are irrelevant;[21] that is, that given a range of investors, a company would simply adjust its dividend policy until a change in its dividend policy would not affect the price of another's shares. Brennan (1970, 1971) suggested that different securities are attractive to investors in different tax brackets. The price of a security at any time would be the result of a tug of war among investors with different expected taxes. The effect of this would be multiple capital market lines if taxes were important enough to affect security pricing.

The CAPM has been adapted to include taxes. Among others, Brennan (1971) has demonstrated that the risk-return relationship would be linear despite different tax rates on dividends and capital gains—if dividends were certain. The Brennan model shown below is considerably more complex than the original CAPM.

$$E(\tilde{R}_i) - R_f = b\beta_i + \tilde{i}\,(d_i - R_f)$$

[21]For evidence that dividends are not relevant, see Fisher Black and M. Scholes, "The Effects of Dividend Yield and Dividend Policy on Common Stock Prices and Returns," *Journal of Financial Economics,* 20 (May 1974), 1–22; and M. Miller and M. Scholes, "Dividends and Taxes: Some Empirical Evidence," *Journal of Political Economy,* 90 (June 1982), 1118–41. For contrary findings, see S. Bar Yosef and R. Kolodny, "Dividend Policy and Capital Market Theory," *Review of Economics and Statistics,* May 1976, 181–90; and Robert Litzenberger and K. Ramaswamy, "The Effect of Personal Taxes and Dividends on Capital Asset Prices," *Journal of Financial Economics,* 7 (June 1979), 163–96.

where

$$R = \text{before-tax total return from a security}$$

$\beta =$ beta, the security's systematic risk

$b =$ after-tax excess return on the market:
$$E(R_m) - R_f = d_m - R_f$$

$R_f =$ return on the riskless asset

$d_i =$ dividend yield

$\tilde{i} =$ a positive coefficient accounting for the taxation of dividends as ordinary income and capital gains at a preferential rate

$i =$ a subscript to designate a particular security or portfolio

In addition, the slope and intercept that result from his model would not be the same as that produced by the simple CAPM. Using his model, the higher the security's before-tax dividend yield, the higher the security's before-tax expected returns. Brennan's adaptation could be especially important for firms or industries with particularly high dividend payouts. In 1980 the average payout for Standard and Poor's utilities was 66 percent, and the payout for industrials was 41 percent. In 1983 these payouts were 63 and 50 percent, respectively. Thus, you can see that for utility stocks (or others with high dividend payout ratios), where the CAPM is used in rate setting with frequency, the potential for error is sizable.[22]

Although we have a vague idea of the effective difference between high-yield and growth stocks, it is not clear whether the investor fully perceives the difference and whether this difference is reflected in the pricing of securities. Theoretically, investors should prefer capital gains to dividends. Then why do so many firms continue to pay dividends? This question has not been fully answered, although most researchers agree that investors value dividends for more than their dollar value. Investors seem to feel that dividends are a sign of management's confidence in future earnings.

The issue of the importance of taxes in security pricing is still not resolved. Even so, some investment management organizations have adapted the CAPM to include effect of taxes. These models describe not a security market line but a security market plane. In addition to risk

[22]For a report on regulatory use of the CAPM, see Diana R. Harrington, "The Changing Use of the Capital Asset Pricing Model in Utility Regulation," *Public Utilities Fortnightly,* August 13, 1980; and "Trends in Capital Asset Pricing Model Use," *Public Utilities Fortnightly,* August 13, 1981.

and return, the tax rate is added as the third dimension. The relative attractiveness of securities changes, depending upon the individual's tax rate. A security that would look fairly valued using the simple CAPM could be very attractive to a low-tax-bracket investor but uninteresting to a high-tax-bracket investor.

Nonetheless, the simple CAPM treats taxes as being irrelevant. Finding this assumption unrealistic, some investment management organizations are using an adapted form of the CAPM. In later chapters we will discuss these adaptations in greater detail.

3. TOTAL ASSET QUANTITY IS FIXED, AND ALL ASSETS
   ARE MARKETABLE AND DIVISIBLE.

This assumption suggests that we can ignore liquidity and new issues of securities. If such things cannot be ignored, then the simple CAPM cannot capture all that is important in pricing securities.

Liquidity—the ease of buying and selling large dollar amounts of a given security—is a serious concern for investors with large portfolios. Small investors are free to enter and leave all sectors of the market virtually at will. But managers of large portfolios feel that they are restricted to the most actively traded securities. For these managers, investing in the securities of small firms has some dangers. The manager must invest in a large number of small firms, which would require considerable research; or the manager must take a large position in the small firm's securities, which would make any rapid changes in portfolio composition virtually impossible. Consequently, some investment research groups have begun to add liquidity as a factor in making their market estimates. The adaptation produces multiple capital market lines—one line for each particular group of investors (or each desired level of liquidity). Other firms have used the market value (the size) of the company as another factor in determining return, presuming that small firms yield greater ex post returns.

In addition to ignoring investors' objectives concerning liquidity, this assumption also ignores the existence of nonmarketable assets—such as human capital or individuals' employability. The fact is that a large portion of most portfolios is made up of either very illiquid assets or unmarketable assets. To exclude these assets could mean that we are ignoring important parts of "the market." Mayers (1972) proposed an adaptation of the CAPM that includes unmarketable assets. In his model, systematic risk is the covariation of returns from the stock with those from the market *plus* the covariation of returns from the stock with those from nonmarketable assets. His model is obviously more complex than our basic CAPM, and the returns from nonmarketable assets and covariance of those returns with the market returns would indeed be difficult to estimate. Still, Mayers's notion of a CAPM that includes non-marketable assets provides perspective on the complexity that can be reduced by an assumption—and on the practical difficulties that we encounter with the richer versions of the CAPM.

These eight assumptions are basic to the CAPM. Interestingly enough, the CAPM may be usable even if several of the assumptions are invalid. Even if markets are not perfect,[23] Mao (1971) and Levy (1978) show that the model can be used.[24]

III. CONCLUSION

In this chapter we have looked at the assumptions needed to create the simple CAPM. Because these assumptions are critical to understanding the CAPM, let us review their implications. The following list describes the logical consequences of these assumptions:

1. Risk is the variance of expected portfolio returns.
2. Risk can be broken into two components: diversifiable (nonsystematic) risk and nondiversifiable (systematic) risk.
3. Proper diversification can reduce unsystematic risk.
4. Beta is the relevant measure of risk for investors with diversified portfolios.
5. Risk and return are linearly related by beta—that is, risk and return are in equilibrium.
6. Return is total return.
7. An investor holds portions of two portfolios: the risk-free asset and the market portfolio.
8. The return that an investor actually receives is derived from only two sources: risk-proportional market return plus nonsystematic random return. No other factor is consistent in its effect on security returns.

These are *not* the assumptions in their strict sense. Instead, they are statements that describe the model and its meaning. To the practitioner, the assumptions seem patently untrue. Academics have found the as-

---

[23] Perfect markets are frictionless—that is, without such things as taxes and transaction costs—perfectly competitive, informationally efficient, and they maximize the investor's expected utility of terminal wealth.

[24] Lawrence Kryzanowski and T. M. Chau, "Asset Pricing Models When the Number of Securities Held Is Constrained: A Comparison and Reconciliation of the Mao and Levy Models," *Journal of Financial and Quantitative Analysis,* 17 (March 1982), 63–73, compare the Mao and Levy adaptations and describe how they might be used to test the veracity of the CAPM.

sumptions restrictive, at the least, and have created alternative models designed to reflect reality more accurately. We have seen that some of these adaptations are more complex than the simple CAPM.

To various degrees, all the CAPM assumptions are violated in the real world. But that fact alone is insufficient to damn the model. Models are meant to abstract from reality and to ignore irrelevant or trivial factors. *Irrelevant* is the key word. Because all the assumptions are unrealistic, the real questions are, Does the factor's exclusion from the model destroy the model's ability to describe or predict? Will adding any factor enhance the model's value enough to compensate for the increased complexity?

We have made conjectures; we have looked at the assumptions and played a "what if" game. If we added this or that factor, what would be its effect on the model's predictions? Each of the model's adaptations tends to move us in one of two directions. Either we have a market line that is higher in intercept and lower in slope than the CAPM's market line, or we find multiple market lines rather than the simple homogeneous efficient frontier.

To understand the assumptions is to know both the strengths and the weaknesses of the model. Too many analysts have thrown the model out on the basis of their shallow understanding of the assumptions when adaptation rather than rejection was the logical and fruitful action. Some of the adaptations that we have described come from practitioners who sought a better answer, and some of them come from academic researchers who tested the theoretical strength of this simple concept.

Still, we need to know much more. Early in this chapter we said that one of the things that intrigued researchers was that this model presented a testable hypothesis. We do not have to accept the CAPM on gut feel, but we can examine the evidence. In the next chapter we will look at that evidence, evaluating it against what we have learned about the model and its assumptions. Only then can we judge whether the model is worth our pursuit or whether it must be cast aside while we wait for a more realistic concept.

REFERENCES

Bar Yosef, S., and R. Kolodny, "Dividend Policy and Capital Market Theory," *Review of Economics and Statistics* (May 1976), 181-90.

Bergman, Yaacov Z., "Time Preference and Capital Asset Pricing Models," *Journal of Financial Economics*, 14 (1985), 145-59.

Biger, Nahum, "The Assessment of Inflation and Portfolio Selection," *Journal of Finance,* 45 (July 1975), 451-67.

Black, Fisher, "Capital Market Equilibrium with Restricted Borrowing," *Journal of Business,* 45 (July 1972), 444-55.

Black, Fisher, and M. Scholes, "The Effects of Dividend Yield and Dividend Policy on Common Stock Prices and Returns," *Journal of Financial Economics,* 20 (May 1974), 1-22.

Breeden, Douglas T., "An Intertemporal Asset Pricing Model with Stochastic Consumption and Investment Opportunities," *Journal of Financial Economics,* 7 (September 1979), 265-96.

Brennan, Michael J., "Taxes, Market Valuation and Corporate Financial Policy," *National Tax Policy,* 23 (December 1970), 417-27.

———, "Capital Market Equilibrium with Divergent Borrowing and Lending Rates," *Journal of Financial and Quantitative Analysis,* 6 (December 1971), 1197-1205.

Copeland, Thomas E., and J. F. Weston, *Financial Theory and Corporate Policy,* 2nd ed., Reading, Mass.: Addison-Wesley, 1985.

Fama, Eugene F., "Multiperiod Consumption Investment Decisions," *American Economic Review,* 55 (May 1970), 163-74.

Fama, Eugene F., and J. MacBeth, "Tests of the Multiperiod Two Parameter Model," *Journal of Financial Economics,* 1 (May-June 1973), 43-66.

Friend, Irwin, Y. Landskroner, and E. Losq, "The Demand for Risky Assets under Uncertain Inflation," *Journal of Finance,* 31 (December 1976), 1287-98.

Gilster, J. E., Jr., "Capital Market Equilibrium with Divergent Investment Horizon Length Assumptions," *Journal of Finance and Quantitative Analysis,* 18 (June 1983), 257-65.

Gressis, N., G. Philippatos, and J. Hayya, "Multiperiod Portfolio Analysis and the Inefficiency of the Market Portfolio," *Journal of Finance,* 31 (September 1976), 1115-26.

Hagerman, R. L., and E. H. Kim, "Capital Asset Pricing with Price Level Changes," *Journal of Finance and Quantitative Analysis,* 11 (September 1976), 381-92.

Harrington, Diana R., "The Changing Use of the Capital Asset Pricing Model in Utility Regulation," *Public Utilities Fortnightly,* August 13, 1980.

———, "Trends in Capital Asset Pricing Model Use," *Public Utilities Fortnightly,* August 13, 1981.

Kryzanowski, Lawrence, and T. M. Chau, "Asset Pricing Models When the Number of Securities Held Is Constrained: A Comparison and Reconciliation of the Mao and Levy Models," *Journal of Financial and Quantitative Analysis*, 17 (March 1982), 63-73.

Levy, Haim, "Equilibrium in an Imperfect Market: A Constraint on the Number of Securities in the Portfolio," *American Economic Review*, 73 (September 1978), 643-58.

Lewellen, Wilber G., and J. S. Ang, "Inflation, Security Values, and Risk Premia," *Journal of Financial Research*, 5 (Summer 1982), 105-123.

Lintner, John, "Inflation and Security Returns," *Journal of Finance*, 30 (May 1975), 259-80.

Litzenberger, Robert, and K. Ramaswamy, "The Effect of Personal Taxes and Dividends on Capital Asset Prices," *Journal of Financial Economics*, 7 (June 1979), 163-96.

Losq, Etienne, and J. P. D. Chateau, "A Generalization of the CAPM Based on a Property of the Covariance Operator," *Journal of Financial and Quantitative Analysis*, 17 (December 1982), 783-97.

Mao, James C. T., "Security Pricing in an Imperfect Capital Market," *Journal of Financial and Quantitative Analysis*, 6 (September 1971), 1105-16.

Mao, James C. T., and J. F. Brewster, "An E-Sh Model of Capital Budgeting," *Engineering Economist*, 15 (January-February 1970), 103-21.

Mayers, David D., "Non-Marketable Assets and Capital Market Equilibrium under Uncertainty," in *Studies in the Theory of Capital Markets*, ed. M. Jensen, pp. 223-48. New York: Praeger, 1972.

Mayshar, Joram, "Transaction Costs in a Model of Capital Market Equilibrium," *Journal of Political Economy*, 86 (August 1979), 673-700.

Merton, Robert C., "An Intertemporal Capital Asset Pricing Model," *Econometrica*, 41 (September 1973), 867-87.

Miller, Edward, "Risk, Uncertainty and Divergences of Opinion," *Journal of Finance*, 32 (September 1977), 1151-68.

Miller, Merton, and F. Modigliani, "Dividend Policy, Growth and the Valuation of Shares," *Journal of Business*, 34 (October 1961), 411-33.

Miller, Merton, and M. Scholes, "Dividends and Taxes," *Journal of Financial Economics*, 7 (December 1978), 333-64.

——, "Dividends and Taxes: Some Empirical Evidence," *Journal of Political Economy*, 90 (June 1982), 1118-41.

Modigliani, Franco, and M. Miller, "Corporate Income Taxes and the Cost of Capital: A Correction," *American Economic Review*, 52 (June 1963), 433-42.

Roll, Richard, "A Critique of the Asset Pricing Theory's Tests, Part I: On Past and Potential Testability of the Theory," *Journal of Financial Economics*, 4 (March 1977), 129-76.

Simkowitz, M. A., and W. L. Beedles, "Diversification in a Three-Moment World," *Journal of Finance and Quantitative Analysis,* 13 (December 1978), 924-41.

Vandell, Robert F., D. Harrington, and S. Levkoff, "Cyclical Timing: More Return for Less Risk." Darden School Working Paper No. 78-12. Charlottesville, Va.: Darden Graduate School of Business Administration, 1978.

chapter

3

___

Tests of the CAPM

___

The assumptions underlying the capital asset pricing model are restrictive, as we know. They abstract from reality in ways that we realize are untrue. We do pay taxes and at different rates; there are transaction costs; there is inflation; and borrowing and lending at the risk-free rate are unlikely. We can easily cite evidence that the world is quite different from that postulated by the CAPM.

The CAPM has been adapted to make it more realistic. In Chapter 2 we discussed several of these adaptations (as well as adaptations to the assumptions behind MPT). Most of these adaptations either predict multiple market lines or present a theoretical market line with a higher intercept and lower slope than that predicted by the simple CAPM.

Although many of these models are useful, all of them leave something to be desired. We do not know which adaptation or adaptations are theoretically correct or appropriate. Separately, each adaptation seems to change theory in one of two directions; taken together, the adaptations have an uncertain effect.

So far we have only looked at theory. In this chapter we will examine empirical tests of the CAPM. Researchers have asked, Is the model realistic? Does it provide a good description of investor behavior? The tests that will be reported in this chapter are, for the most part, tests of how well the model fits history. In reviewing each test, our purpose is to determine whether the CAPM fits the real world and, if it does not, to determine the source and size of the discrepancies between the model and the world. We will not examine empirical tests of MPT for MPT does not provide a testable hypothesis like the CAPM.

The CAPM's form is simple. Thus, it is vulnerable to two potential sources of error. The first potential problem is that the form of the model may simply be wrong. Instead of being linear, the actual risk-return relationship could be nonlinear (for example, the "true" market line could be J-shaped). A model that is wrong is termed *misspecified*. The second potential problem is austerity; the model may not include all the relevant factors. If a certain factor (or factors) does influence the way the investors determine the price of an asset, and if this factor (or factors) is not included in the simple CAPM, the model would be termed *inadequate* to describe the real behavior of investors.

If the model is either misspecified or inadequate, it would be difficult to use. An example of the real and practical result of misspecification is shown in Exhibit 3–1. The line $R_f X$ is the theoretical capital market line. The intercept is at R_f, just as the theory says it should be, and the slope indicates the incremental return for each additional unit of risk.

Exhibit 3–1

Theoretical Market Line

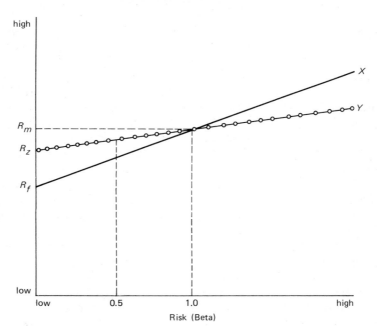

Risk (Beta)

The line $R_z Y$ indicates the sort of market line postulated by some of the adaptations we discussed in Chapter 2: the intercept is above R_f and the slope is less steep.

Now, looking at the two lines in Exhibit 3-1, let us put ourselves in the position of setting rates for a public utility. In determining the allowed rate of return, the public utility commission attempts to set the rates charged customers at a level that will cover all the costs of providing the electricity, gas, or telephone service—including the costs of capital. Thus, the commission needs an estimate of the firm's cost of equity. Because utilities typically have betas of less than 1.0, the effect of a misspecified market line is to underestimate the cost of equity. (Of course, for stocks with betas exceeding the market's, the effect is the opposite—an overestimation.) For the utility in question, the allowed rate of return would be lower than the true cost of equity for the firm, that is, the rates the company would be allowed to charge would be lower than those needed to cover its costs.

The same sort of problem can have other impacts. For instance, if you are the manager of a company estimating the cost of capital (the hurdle rate) for an investment (even an acquisition), if the investment has a beta less than 1.0, a misspecified market line would cause you to underestimate the return it should provide to be acceptable. For an investment with a beta greater than 1.0, the rate chosen would exceed that which should have been used. The effect of these errors is to penalize riskier projects unnecessarily, and to make low-risk projects seem overly attractive.

Let us look at the effect of misspecification from another viewpoint. If you are a portfolio manager in an investment management organization and are attempting to keep or lure clients over the long term, where should you position your portfolio regarding risk? What if you know that theory incorrectly draws the capital market line, as shown in Exhibit 3-1? If your clients will eventually be evaluating your performance against this incorrect, theoretical capital market line, would you choose to position your portfolio with a low beta or a high beta? If your portfolio were low risk, the simple CAPM would forecast a return lower than that forecast by the respecified model. If your return were exactly like the return forecast by the respecified model, on the line $R_z Y$, you would appear to have outperformed the average. This superior performance is not a sleight of hand but simply the result of comparing actual results with a forecast made from the wrong model. Conversely, the risk-taking portfolio manager would consistently look bad when evaluated against the respecified CAPM's capital market line.

There are other possible market lines, curves, slopes, and intercepts. Exhibit 3-1 merely demonstrates the practical problems that can result from a model that is wrong. An erroneous model can lead investors, and those evaluating performance, to wrong conclusions and wrong decisions.

Is the capital asset pricing model misspecified or inadequate? And if it is, what is the real relationship among the factors affecting stock prices? Recall that to be useful, a model does not have to be an exactly accurate representation of the system it seeks to describe. We would like it to be, because a model that adequately describes a system as complex as investors' behavior would be most useful. We would, however, be satisfied if the model could be used to make predictions. We are all familiar with correlated factors that do not describe an underlying relationship but are useful in making predictions—high hemlines and high stock prices, large hips and high IQ. Such correlations often work, although we are not sure why.

The problem with a predictive but nondescriptive model is that if any of the underlying causal factors changes in importance, we cannot examine the change nor can we predict its resulting effect on the underlying relationship. For instance, what would happen to the hemline–stock price model if the real determinants of stock prices changed?

Our question is, What is the CAPM? Is it a useful predictor, a good descriptor, both, or neither? Let us look at what researchers have found. We will discuss only a small sample of the flood of work that has been done and published. Other writers might choose to report different research. What we will report here are the results of major works that provide new insights. There are two reasons for reporting these works. First, we want to clarify what is already known. Second, we want to describe research that has real and practical implications. All too often these practical implications are described in academic jargon and published in infrequently read journals. Both advocates and detractors of the CAPM can find support in the literature. Much of the evidence presented in this chapter will appear to refute the CAPM. Certainly, many researchers have had difficulty finding evidence of the simple relationship expressed by the CAPM. There are several reasons why this is true, prime among them the fact that our research techniques may not be up to the task (there may be so much extraneous information that the basics are obfuscated), and that we may have used the wrong data in our research. Keep these concerns in mind while you read this chapter, since, as you will discover, we have learned much, but perhaps not whether the simple CAPM is flawed beyond usefulness.

Behavior is always hard to describe and difficult to study. Requiring too much out of a theory of human behavior virtually ensures that it will be rejected. On the other hand, if the CAPM is obviously and seriously flawed, and research confirms these flaws, we must move on to other theories. After we look at a summary of more than 20 years of inquiry, we can decide for ourselves.

I. MISSPECIFICATION

There are two basic tests of the reliability of the model. To determine whether the model explains past behavior, researchers have studied past market activity (ex post data) to find out whether the relationships were the same as those predicted by the model. To determine whether the model predicts future behavior, past data has been used to form forecasts for R_m, R_f, and beta, and these forecasts have then been tested against more recent history.

Using history for either purpose creates some problems. First, investors' expectations or beliefs are not really being tested; rather, it is what actually occurred that is under study. The problem is that there is no reason to believe that realized, or ex post, results will be anything like the predictions that investors made at the beginning of the period. In fact the historical, or ex post, model, the model used to analyze historical data, can have a negative intercept or slope. This negative slope and intercept is not in concert with CAPM theory. Or is it?

If at the beginning of 1986 and 1987 we were forecasting the relationship shown in Exhibit 3–2, and at the beginning of 1986 we invested

Exhibit 3–2

Forecasted and Realized Returns

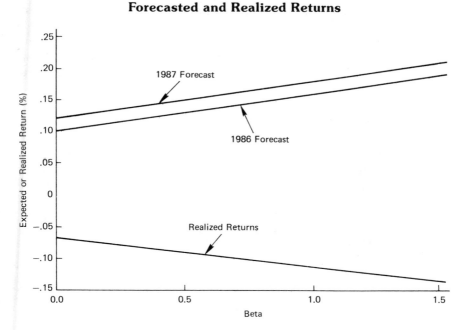

$1000 in the risk-free asset and $1000 in the market portfolio (perhaps U.S. Treasury securities and an index fund), by January 1, 1987, we would have lost money.

Investors' Expectations: 1986 and 1987

	EXPECTED RETURN		REALIZED RETURN
	1/1/1986	1/1/1987	1/1/1986 to 1/1/1987
R_f	10%	12%	− 6.7%
R_m	16	18	−11.2

The reason is that investors' expectations for returns rose over the period, and to satisfy their increased expectations the prices of the Treasury security and the index fund dropped.[1] The ex ante market lines are both positive; however, as is clearly shown in Exhibit 3–2, the ex post, realized, market line has a negative slope and intercept. Here we have a situation where both forecasts were positive (as the CAPM would suggest), but the investor lost. This does not suggest that the CAPM is wrong, only that what you think you will get is not always what you get.

By using history, we are mixing two sets of data: We are mixing expectations and realizations. This data mixing is an inherent difficulty in testing an expectational model. Only recently have we begun to see work that looks specifically at expectations, the ex ante data.[2] The results are still entirely too tentative to rely on, however. Until more is done in creating and testing ex ante data, it is important to keep in mind that we do have data problems. As we recount the history of CAPM testing, we will try to interpret the results as well as their implications, given the data problem.

1. SLOPE AND INTERCEPT: DOES THE MODEL DESCRIBE THE REAL WORLD?

So far we have learned some very interesting things about the CAPM and reality. Some of the earliest work tested realized data (history) against data generated from simulated portfolios. Early studies by

---

[1]In calculating the realized return we are presuming the U.S. Treasury security has a simple yield of 10 percent ($100 per year) and the index fund's dividend yield is zero. While other assumptions would change the realized return, the result would still be a negative intercept and slope.

[2]See, for example, W. Lewellen, R. Lease, and G. Schlarbaum, "Patterns of Investment Strategy and Behavior among Individual Investors," *Journal of Business,* July 1977, pp. 296–333; or R. F. Vandell and J. Stevens, "Personal Taxes and Equity Security Pricing," *Financial Management,* 11 (Spring 1982), 31–40.

Douglas (1969) and Lintner (Douglas [1969]) showed discrepancies between what was expected on the basis of the CAPM and the actual relationships that were apparent in the capital markets. Theoretically, they
expected the minimal rate of return from the portfolios (the intercept)
and the actual risk-free rate for the period would be equal. They were
not.

These early results caused some concern. Many analysts suggested
that the tests were faulty and were thus not giving accurate results.[3]
However, the Douglas and Lintner results could have been caused by
either of two things: the CAPM could have been wrong or the test procedure could have been faulty. Other researchers reformulated the test
procedures, and these new procedures were used on different data in the
hope that more accurate results would follow. One retest hypothesized
that the proxies used for R_m and R_f (the CAPM gives us no direction as
to which real-world figures to use) are correlated. Thus, these proxies
would produce a higher intercept and lower slope than would be realistic—the precise results that Douglas and Lintner had obtained. These
retests did not find that this problem caused the results. The conclusion
was that the Douglas and Lintner findings could be caused by a faulty
model. The simple CAPM might be wrong.

Miller and Scholes (1972) reformulated the test procedures to deal
with other problems. They asked, Was the form of the model[4] accurate
(that is, were risk and return linearly related)? Was beta the best risk
measure? Could the choice of the index change the results? Was beta
correlated with unsystematic risk? Could the returns be nonnormal? Any
of these problems might have caused Lintner's results. In typically academic jargon, Miller and Scholes reported that they did not find good

---

[3]See Merton Miller and M. Scholes, "Rate of Return in Relation to Risk: A Reexamination of Some Recent Findings," in *Studies in the Theory of Capital Markets*, ed. M.
Jensen (New York: Praeger, 1972), pp. 47–78.

[4]In testing the CAPM, the model is usually written

$$R_{jt} = \gamma_0 + \gamma_1 (\beta_j) + \epsilon_{jt}$$

where

$$\gamma_1 = R_{mt}$$
$$R_{jt} = \text{the return on the portfolio } (j)$$

In testing the results should be as follows:

1. γ_0 should be zero. If it is not zero, some factor could be missing from the model.
2. Increases in beta should result in linear increases in return.
3. γ_1 is R_{mt}. It may also be written in risk-premium form by subtracting R_{ft} from
R_{mt}. γ_0 would be expected to be zero.

reason to reject Lintner's results. Lintner's results could have been accurate reflections of the world—in other words, the model could be wrong. Although not able to discredit Lintner's results, the Miller-Scholes study did provide solid footing on which to begin the design of future studies.

Another study, now more famous than Lintner's, was done by Black, Jensen, and Scholes (1972). Lintner had used what is called a cross-sectional method (looking at a number of stock returns during one time period), whereas Black, Jensen, and Scholes used a time-series method (using returns for a number of stocks over several time periods). To make their test, Black, Jensen, and Scholes assumed that what had happened in the past was a good proxy for investor expectations (a frequent assumption in CAPM tests). Using historical data, they generated estimates using what we call the market model:

$$R_{jt} = \alpha_{jt} + \beta_j \, (R_{mt} - R_{ft}) + \epsilon_{jt}$$

where

R = total returns

β = the slope of the line (the incremental return for risk)

α = the intercept or a constant (expected to be R_f)

ϵ = an error term (expected to be random, without information)

m = the market

f = the risk-free asset

j = the asset or portfolio

t = the time period

Instead of testing the CAPM with individual stocks, they used portfolios of stocks. The use of portfolios can be justified for two reasons. First, the CAPM suggests that investors will invest in more than one asset— they hold portfolios. Thus, studying portfolios is realistic. Second, by studying portfolios, errors in measuring individual assets' systematic risk can be reduced. Since an asset's risk typically is estimated using historical data, albeit recent history, it contains some sampling or measurement error. This measurement error can have the effect of making systematic risk appear unstable for individual assets. Measurement error can reduce the probability of finding what is expected—a positive linear relationship between systematic risk and return. If the errors are random for individual assets, they would cancel out in portfolios in much the same way that a portion of an asset's returns are offset by the returns of other assets in a portfolio. Thus, the individual asset measurement errors that might confuse the results when studying the returns of different assets can be reduced if portfolio returns are studied.

Based on the relationships developed in the CAPM, Black, Jensen, and Scholes expected to find

1. That the intercept was equal to the risk-free rate (their proxy was the Treasury bill rate)
2. That the capital market line had a positive slope and that riskier (higher-beta) securities provided higher return

Instead, they found

1. That the intercept was different from the risk-free rate
2. That high-risk securities earned less and low-risk securities earned more than predicted by the model
3. That the intercept seemed to depend on the beta of any asset: high-beta stocks had a different intercept than low-beta stocks

Their results are shown in Exhibit 3–3. The dashed lines represent the capital or theoretical market line. The Black, Jensen, and Scholes results, the solid line, are not what the simple CAPM would predict, but the results are just what some of the theoretical adaptations suggested we might find: the intercept is different from the Treasury bill rate for the period and the line's slope does not coincide with the capital market line that links the return on Treasury bills and the return on the stock market index. These results are similar to the controversial Lintner results. Because they are important, many researchers felt they should be verified.

Fama and MacBeth (1974) criticized the Black, Jensen, and Scholes (BJS) study. In a reformulation of the study, they supported the first of the BJS findings. They found that the intercept exceeded the risk-free proxy, but they did not find evidence to support the other BJS conclusions.

Controversial or contrary findings are not uncommon in the testing of this model. With each new piece of research, we gain insight into the approaches we must take to test the model. However, by 1974 most researchers agreed that the intercept often exceeded the CAPM-predicted R_f, proxied by Treasury bill rates of return.

One other study sheds further light on these findings. Fama and MacBeth (1973) calculated the actual risk premium and the predicted intercept from 1935 to 1968 and over a variety of subperiods. They too used a technique that settled down the beta instability from individual

Exhibit 3-3

Theoretical and Empirical Market Lines

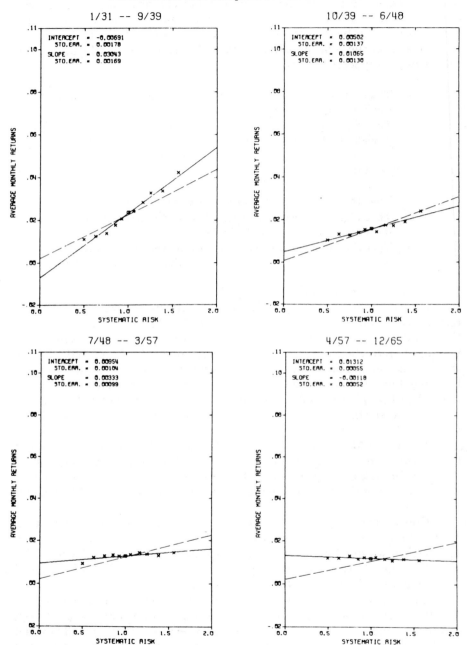

Source: Michael C. Jensen, *Tests of Capital Market Theory and Implications of the Evidence* (Charlottesville, Va.: Financial Analysts Research Foundation, 1975), p. 26.

security errors. They formed portfolios and reformed them (grouping by betas) at the beginning of each year. The returns of these groups were related to the market returns in each period. If the model was accurate, Fama and MacBeth believed they would find an intercept equal to the risk-free rate for the period. Exhibit 3–4, an adaptation of their results, shows that in no period did the intercept from this study match the Treasury bill rate. In fact, Fama himself concluded that in only one period (1961–June 1968) did the model describe the market well. He said that this finding led him to "a negative conclusion with respect to the Sharpe-Lintner hypothesis" (the CAPM).[5]

Something was not quite right. The results were not what theory had led us to expect. However, these tests alone do not allow us to determine whether the model is wrong, whether there is something missing, or just what is creating the problem.

In addition to testing the CAPM, Black, Jensen, and Scholes (1972) tried to provide a better explanation of the underlying security-pricing system. They suggested the adaptation of simple CAPM as follows:

$$R_{jt} = (1 - \beta_j)R_{zt} + \beta_j R_{mt} + \epsilon_{jt}$$

where

$$R_z = \text{some factor usually exceeding } R_f$$

The authors provided no explanation for the added factor, often called the zero-beta portfolio.

Exhibit 3–4

Tests of the Two-Factor Model (in Yearly Rates of Return)

DATES	INTERCEPT	R_f*	INTERCEPT $- R_f$
1935–6/1968	7.5 (3.8)†	1.7	5.8
1935–1945	4.7 (5.2)	0.2	4.5
1946–1955	10.9 (2.6)	1.2	9.7
1956–6/1968	7.4 (3.0)	3.3	4.1
1935–1940	2.9 (6.4)	0.2	2.7
1941–1945	6.9 (3.4)	0.3	6.6
1946–1950	6.1 (3.1)	0.7	5.4
1951–1955	15.8 (1.9)	1.7	14.1
1956–1960	19.2 (2.0)	2.0	16.4
1961–6/1968	1.2 (3.4)	4.6	−3.4

*Actual return on Treasury bills for the period.
†Standard error of the estimate.

Source: Adapted from E. F. Fama and J. D. MacBeth, "Risk, Return and Equilibrium: Empirical Tests," *Journal of Political Economy,* 71 (May–June 1973), 622–23.

[5]Eugene F. Fama, *Foundations of Finance* (New York: Basic Books, 1976).

Using a method like that of Black, Jensen, and Scholes, Reinganum (1981c) again examined the relationship of beta and return. He initially studied a period of time different from that studied by Black, Jensen, and Scholes—one in which the available data included stocks from both the American and New York Stock Exchanges. Using daily data he estimated betas using at least 100 days of data, and reformed beta-ranked portfolios yearly. In addition, Reinganum used three beta measures, a simple beta and two betas adapted to take infrequent stock trading effects into account. The results of his study did not depend upon the beta used: the average returns from low-beta stocks were not statistically different from the average returns from high-beta stocks. Exhibit 3-5 shows his findings for the simple beta for the period 1962-79.

Reinganum tested his data for a variety of potential causes for the unexpected results. Only when the data from 1926-79 were used and the portfolios were formed from betas that were calculated from five years of monthly data, do the portfolio returns look as the CAPM would suggest they should: the higher the beta the higher the returns. Unfortunately, these results, as alluring as they may seem, are not statistically significant.

Once again we are left with the conclusion that using ex post, historical, data results in risk-return relationships that are not as CAPM theory would predict.

2. IS THE CAPITAL MARKET LINE STRAIGHT OR CURVED?

Is the risk-return relationship linear? Here we have conflicting evidence. Many intuitive arguments suggest that the risk-return relationship should be curved rather than straight: the securities markets are filled with such things as options and convertible securities that have some downside protection, but no upside barriers.

Fama and MacBeth (1973), in addition to testing the intercept and slope, added factors to verify linearity. Their results suggested nonlinearity. Although other researchers have had similar results, the evidence is still somewhat mixed and the argument about linearity continues.

McDonald (1983) further tested the CAPM's linearity. In particular he was concerned with whether nonlinearities that had been found were related to the horizon problem. Using a sophisticated approach for determining whether more complex models would improve the results, McDonald concluded that they did not. The simple model did about as well. In addition, he said that while the nonlinear model is often more appropriate, the nonlinearities do not seem to be due to misspecifying the horizon. In fact, McDonald suggested that the superior results from the

Exhibit 3-5

Daily Return Statistics for the Ten Beta Portfolios with Betas Estimated Using Daily Returns, a Value-Weighted Index, and the "Market Model" Estimator

PORT-FOLIO	MEAN RETURN*	ESTI-MATED PORT-FOLIO BETA†	SKEW-NESS	KURTOSIS	AUTO-CORRELATIONS 1	2	3
Low Beta	.893 (.079)	.05	-.101	5.601	.48	.28	.25
2	.695 (.081)	.33	.131	6.601	.52	.24	.21
3	.689 (.094)	.50	-.074	6.125	.47	.19	.18
4	.673 (.107)	.64	-.098	5.864	.47	.15	.16
5	.738 (.116)	.79	-.105	4.810	.45	.14	.14
6	.736 (.130)	.95	.056	6.025	.42	.11	.13
7	.716 (.143)	1.13	.012	5.569	.40	.09	.10
8	.660 (.158)	1.34	.177	5.730	.38	.07	.09
9	.668 (.181)	1.64	.166	5.764	.33	.06	.08
High Beta	.584 (.221)	2.25	.314	5.788	.26	.02	.06

*A mean return is calculated using 4009 trading day returns from 1964 through 1979. Mean daily returns are multiplied by 1000 for reporting purposes. Standard errors are in parentheses. Skewness and kurtosis measures are based on moments of the normal distribution.

†The estimated portfolio beta is just the linear combination (equal weights) of security betas. These betas are estimated in the year prior to the portfolio holding period.

Source: Marc R. Reinganum, "A New Empirical Perspective on the CAPM," *Journal of Financial and Quantitative Analysis*, 16 (November 1981), 443.

nonlinear model may come from the use of ex post data in testing an ex ante model, or choosing an incorrect measure of market return. Furthermore, he suggested that nonlinearity probably comes from a variety of sources, the least likely of which is a theoretical misspecification, like the horizon problem.

One effect of real nonlinearities in the data is that betas based on history could be misestimated. McDonald looked at that question, too. He calculated betas for each of four models: a simple linear model, a logarithmic model, and the two models that allowed for horizon and market-level changes. He found that, regardless of the model, the betas were close to each other, although the linear model had slightly higher betas. Thus, "when betas are used to rank securities, the linear or logarithmic estimates are excellent approximations."[6]

3. DOES BETA MEASURE RISK?

One cause of misspecification could be that beta is an incorrect or insufficient measure of risk. Other, traditional measures such as standard deviation certainly appeal to investors. These measures are familiar and thus comfortable. Variance and standard deviation could be used to describe single-asset risk. However, early portfolio theory and the CAPM adaptation describe risk in the context of a portfolio. When assets are placed in a portfolio, variance is not a relevant risk measure for individual assets. Understanding this difference in risk measurement allows us to define *investors* as those who would seek to reduce the reducible risk by holding diversified portfolios. The only risk that remains in a diversified portfolio is systematic risk. However, few of the studies have investigated whether investors see risk in the portfolio sense. Studies that have explicitly investigated investors' portfolios have found that investor holdings are markedly undiversified.

Blume and Friend (1975) analyzed the major classes of liabilities and assets (including stock portfolios) held by individuals. They studied the Federal Reserve Board's 1962 *Survey of the Financial Characteristics of Consumers* and a sample of 1971 individual federal income taxes. What they found was that individuals had remarkably undiversified holdings. Blume and Friend studied not only share holdings but home ownership and human capital (in the form of employment) as well. (Although it would be interesting to include in individuals' holdings those assets held by their pension funds, this Blume and Friend did not do.) There seemed to be greater diversification by older individuals and by those who owned

[6]Bill McDonald, "Functional Forms and the Capital Asset Pricing Model," *Journal of Financial and Quantitative Analysis,* 18 (September 1983), 326.

their own businesses. The results differed among income groups. Generally, only persons whose net worth exceeded $1 million owned more than ten stocks. Even considering the individual's other assets, Blume and Friend found that diversification was still not greatly increased. Individuals were not particularly diversified.

Why not? Friend and Blume suggest a number of possible reasons. The investors' heterogeneous expectations, plus their improper assessment of portfolio risk, could cause the CAPM to describe investors' behavior badly. This is speculation, to be sure, but interesting food for other researchers. One final point about this study: Blume and Friend noted that certain groups of investors appear to have more diversified portfolios. For these groups, they say that "the underlying model is most likely to hold."[7] For other investors, a different model could be more appropriate.

Does this evidence prove that the model is in error? Blume and Friend did demonstrate that investors are quite undiversified. However, they did not demonstrate how investors evaluate securities; they merely described the cumulative results of their decisions. If investors price assets *as if* they hold a diversified portfolio, that is enough to ratify the model. The Blume and Friend work does not study or answer that question.

One source of the inconsistencies between reality and what the model seems to suggest could lie with the model's basic assumptions—that investors have homogeneous forecasts of the future. While some testing as been done,[8] it is really too tentative, and has encountered substantial problems in obtaining usable expectational data.

The Blume and Friend study is rich in information. For instance, when 1000 stockholders were asked to describe the measure of risk that they used in evaluating stocks, 82 percent said that they evaluated risk, but of that group only 17 percent used betas, whereas the remainder used earnings volatility (45 percent) or price volatility (30 percent). Although earnings or price volatility could be proxies for beta, Blume and Friend further found that the wealthy segment of their sample had little intuitive understanding of covariance or of what effect this sort of risk would have on the risk of a portfolio.

Beta is not the only measure of risk that we could use in evaluating the future. Beta may not be the best or even a complete measure of risk.

---

[7]Marshall Blume and I. Friend, "The Asset Structure of Individual Portfolios," *Journal of Finance*, 30 (May 1975), 601.

[8]See, for instance, Pamela P. Peterson and D. R. Peterson, "Divergence of Opinion and Return," *Journal of Financial Research*, 5 (Summer 1982), 125–34, with a critique by Steve Swindler and P. Vanderheiden, *Journal of Financial Research*, 6 (Summer 1983), 47–50.

In an attempt to evaluate beta, Friend and Blume (1970) tested 200 random portfolios to determine whether the risk-return relationship was linear. They were particularly interested in the risk-adjusted portfolio performance measures that had been proposed earlier by Jensen, Treynor, and Sharpe.[9] Friend and Blume regressed measures of risk-adjusted performance against two measures of risk—beta and standard deviation. Risk-adjusted performance measures should be independent of standard deviation—if there are no systematic differences in risk-adjusted performance among portfolios with different degrees of risk, if the CAPM assumptions are real-world approximations, if it is realistic to test expectations with history, and if statistical problems (such as measurement errors) do not invalidate the results.

What Friend and Blume found was that risk-adjusted performance was still dependent on risk; systematic risk did not seem to provide a complete explanation of actual performance. What is even more interesting is that in some periods the relationship was the opposite of what one would expect. Exhibit 3-6 shows this perverse result from January 1960 to March 1964. This 1960–64 period had an actual market return (S&P 500) of 9.3 percent and a return from Treasury bills of 2.8 percent. The results shown in Exhibit 3-6 are, at the least, curious. In other periods, the line was upward sloping to the right. From their study, Friend and Blume concluded that using the CAPM with its rigid risk-return relationship was not justified. A less explicit relationship of risk and return, they said, was preferable.

Blume and Friend are not the only researchers who have looked at the question of whether beta is a complete risk measure. Lakonishok and Shapiro (1984) added variance to the simple CAPM. They were attempting to determine whether, when an asset is held in an undiversified portfolio, both beta and variance determine return. Using total return data for the New York Stock Exchange from 1958 to 1980 they grouped securities into portfolios by beta then variance (A), by variance then beta (B), by beta alone (C), and by variance alone (D). As shown in Exhibit 3-7, they found that the market rate of return was 7.7 percent greater than that from holding U.S. Treasury bills—taking risk was rewarded. However, you can see that it was variance (γ_2) that was rewarded, not beta (γ_1).

In addition, Lakonishok and Shapiro looked at the performance of their model in up (down) markets, that is, in months in which the market return exceeded (was less than) the Treasury bill return. As shown in Exhibit 3-8, they found both beta and variance significant, and that

[9]For an explanation of these performance measures, see, for example, Jack C. Francis and S. H. Archer, *Portfolio Analysis,* 2nd ed. (Englewood Cliffs, N.J.: Prentice-Hall, 1979).

Exhibit 3–6

Scatter Diagram of Jensen's Performance Measure* on Risk, January 1960–March 1964

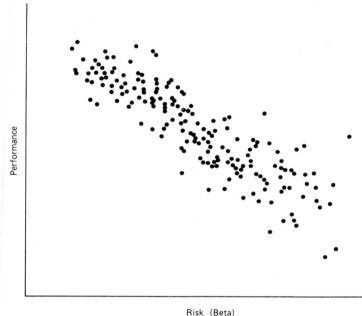

Risk (Beta)

*Using *log relatives.*
Source: Irwin Friend and Marshall Blume, "Measurement of Portfolio Performance under Uncertainty," *American Economic Review,* 60 (September 1970), 573.

Exhibit 3–7

Summary of Results over the 1962–80 Period (228 observations)

	γ_0	γ_1	γ_2	$\overline{R}^2$
A	0.0042*	0.0033	−0.0736	0.2995
B	0.0058*	−0.0016	0.3497*	0.3034
C	0.0045*	0.0014		0.2120
D	0.0055*		0.1661*	0.2110

*Statistically significant at the 5 percent level.
Source: Josef Lakonishok and A. C. Shapiro, "Stock Returns, Beta, Variance and Size: An Empirical Analysis," *Financial Analysts Journal,* 40 (July–August 1984), 38.

Exhibit 3-8

Summary of Results over Up and Down Markets

OVER UP MARKETS (122 OBSERVATIONS)

	γ_0	γ_1	γ_2	$\overline{R}^2$
A	0.0150*	0.0233*	0.9219*	0.2031
B	0.0105*	0.0206*	1.3197*	0.3045
C	0.0122*	0.0333*		0.2039
D	0.0247*		2.5400*	0.2041

OVER DOWN MARKETS (106 OBSERVATIONS):

	γ_0	γ_1	γ_2	$\overline{R}^2$
A	−0.0083*	−0.0197*	−1.2194*	0.3067
B	−0.0052*	−0.0272*	−0.9266*	0.3028
C	−0.0044*	−0.0354*		0.2212
D	−0.0166*		−2.5661*	0.2189

*Statistically significant at the 5 percent level.

Source: Josef Lakonishok and A. C. Shapiro, "Stock Returns, Beta, Variance and Size: An Empirical Analysis," *Financial Analysts Journal,* 40 (July–August 1984), 38.

"individual stocks . . . are behaving as expected: High-beta stocks do better in up markets and worse in down markets than low-beta stocks; the same is true for high-variance stocks."[10] Both beta and variance seem to contain information important to determining returns.

Arnott (1983) looked at the relationship of returns to the following measures of risk he says are used by investors:

1. True beta. A 52- or 156-week regression beta calculated from the stock's returns and the returns of the S&P 500.

2. Expected beta. A regression of exponentially weighted data for the stock's returns and those of the S&P 500, with the results adjusted toward 1.0.

3. Expected risk. An exponentially weighted standard deviation of stock price changes.

4. Earnings per share uncertainty. The standard deviation of seven years of a stock's returns divided by the stock's price. This measure, Arnott says, is a measure of risk, since unexpected earnings changes result in stock price changes.

5. Capitalization. The log of the market value of the company's common stock. This is used by Arnott as a measure of size, presuming

[10]Josef Lakonishok and A. C. Shapiro, "Stock Returns, Beta, Variance and Size: An Empirical Analysis," *Financial Analysts Journal,* 40 (July–August 1984), 39.

companies of larger market value have a risk different from that of small capitalization firms.

6. Total sales. The log of the total sales from the previous year. Another measure of company size.

7. Book value/market value. This, and earnings yield, are used by Arnott as a measure of the investment community's assessment of the company's fundamental risk.

8. Return (earnings yield). The earnings yield divided by the dividend yield.

Arnott correlated each of these risk measures with the returns from the company's stock in the next year. The results are presented in Exhibit 3–9. What you see are information coefficients (ICs)—the correlation between the risk measure and the subsequent returns. Arnott uses ICs instead of another measure, like the R^2, the coefficient of determination, because he says that "it is widely used in the investment community"[11] and it is simple. The correlations between the risk measures for one-year returns are shown in Exhibit 3–10.

Arnott finds little relationship between beta as he measures it and other measures of risk. In addition, for the period he studied, his true

Exhibit 3–9

Information Coefficient Summary: One- and Three-Year Returns

	ONE-YEAR DATA		THREE-YEAR DATA	
	Mean IC	Standard Deviation	Mean IC	Standard Deviation
True beta	+.07	.26	+.03	.17
Expected beta	+.04	.19	+.06	.12*
True risk	+.04	.30	+.08	.24
Expected risk	+.06	.23†	+.13	.19*
EPS uncertainty	+.11	.19†	+.18	.15†
Capitalization	+.20	.18†	+.28	.13†
Total sales	+.16	.12	+.23	.10†
Book/market price	+.04	.19	+.07	.17*
Earnings yield	+.07	.16*	+.07	.14*
Return EPS yield	+.10	.12†	+.11	.11†

*Significant at the 90.0% level.
†Significant at the 99.9% level.

Source: Robert D. Arnott, "What Hath MPT Wrought: Which Risks Reap Rewards," *Journal of Portfolio Management,* Fall 1983, pp. 6–7.

[11]Robert D. Arnott, "What Hath MPT Wrought: Which Risks Reap Rewards," *Journal of Portfolio Management,* Fall 1983, p. 6.

Exhibit 3-10

Risk Measure Correlations

	TRUE BETA	EXP. BETA	TRUE RISK	EXP. RISK	EPS UNCER.	CAP.	TOTAL SALES	BOOK/ PRICE	EPS YIELD
Expected beta	0.53								
True risk	0.61	0.54							
Expected risk	0.50	0.67	0.73						
EPS uncertainty	-0.01	0.00	0.19	0.18					
Capitalization	-0.02	0.00	0.35	0.37	0.36				
Total sales	0.00	0.01	0.31	0.31	-0.03	0.70			
Book/market price	0.01	-0.03	0.07	0.06	0.58	0.29	-0.14		
Earnings yield	0.02	-0.06	-0.09	-0.11	0.44	0.11	-0.17	0.32	
Return (EPS yield)	0.01	-0.01	0.03	0.03	0.52	0.19	-0.06	0.27	0.77

Source: Robert D. Arnott, "What Hath MPT Wrought: Which Risks Reap Rewards," Journal of Portfolio Management, Fall 1983, p. 6.

beta did not yield the highest IC; rather, it yields the lowest. Unfortunately, the Arnott study leaves much to be desired, but it does provide a glimpse at some of the measures of risk that investment practitioners use, and their relationship to a historically calculated beta.[12]

Cooley, Roenfeldt, and Modani (1977) also studied the question of the completeness of beta as a measure of risk by looking at a number of more traditional risk measures to see whether they served the same purpose or whether these other measures added more richness to the explanation of returns' behavior. Using a technique that clustered risk measures into affinity groups, they looked at a number of risk measures over two time periods. Some of these measures are familiar; some are more obscure:

1. Range
2. Semi-interquartile range
3. Mean absolute deviation
4. Standard deviation
5. Variance
6. Semivariance
7. Lower confidence limit
8. Beta
9. Coefficient of quartile variation
10. Skewness
11. Peakedness (kurtosis)
12. Coefficient of variation

If beta was an inadequate risk measure, then distinct and uncorrelated groupings of other risk measures would occur. The 12 measures fell into three distinct groups. The first 7 measures, from *range* to *lower confidence limit*, were almost interchangeable; they seemed to be measuring the same thing. *Beta* provided some additional information but overlapped with the first group. What was most interesting was that *skewness* and *kurtosis* provided distinct (non-beta-related) and useful information. These findings suggest that if we have two stocks, one with normally distributed returns and the other with returns skewed to the right, an investor will not find them equally attractive. Although the mean and standard deviations would be the same, skewing would make one more attractive: a stock skewed to the right would have less down-

---

[12]In Chapter 5 we will explore beta and how to calculate it. Some of the concerns readers have about the Arnott study—for instance, how a historical beta should be calculated—are discussed in that chapter.

side risk and more upside potential—which means, for an investor, less risk.

4. WHAT ABOUT SKEWING?

In Chapter 2 we hypothesized that the assumption of normal distributions (the assumption of the irrelevance of skewing) might be dangerous. Empirical studies have shown that as a measure of risk, skewness does seem to provide additional useful information. In an early study, Arditti (1967) evaluated the importance of a number of factors, skewness among them. He found that the rate of return on stocks was directly related to variance but inversely related to skewness. The magnitude of each asset's return was correlated with its variability, but the increase in return was less than proportionate for each increase in risk. Arditti concluded that skewness was important in explaining return behavior.

On the issue of skewness, Kraus and Litzenberger (1976) went one step further. They suggested that it is not skewness but systematic and nondiversifiable skewness that is important, and that investors prefer increases in beta as surrogates for proportionally greater increases in systematic or co-skewness. Risk would appear to be preferred because it acts as a proxy for skewness. Thus, when returns are skewed, beta would be the result of two opposing forces, and naive beta estimates could be in error.

Not only does logic suggest that skewness is important in asset pricing but evidence also indicates that realized returns are skewed. Some studies purporting to show skewing have been criticized because the result could have been caused by outliers (data points that lie at the extreme). By laying out the data as in Exhibit 3–11, we can see that the skewing is not the result of a couple of unusual observations: more errors are positive than negative even at ten standard deviations from the mean. Furthermore, practical experience tells us that returns should be skewed. An investor's unlevered downside risk is a 100 percent loss, but upside potential is unrestricted.

The Reinganum results that we examined in Exhibit 3–5 also show that beta-ranked portfolios have skewed results. Even when he excluded very unusual data (years in which the returns were abnormal), the returns were still significantly skewed.

Simkowitz and Beedles (1978) also looked at the effect of diversification on portfolio skewness. They found that as diversification increased, skewness decreased. By the time the portfolio reached five stocks, 92 percent of the skewing had been eliminated. Exhibit 3–12 gives their results. The variance (systematic plus unsystematic risk) drops as the portfolio size increases (column 3), and the skewness (column 4) drops

Exhibit 3–11

Error Distribution Summary

STANDARD DEVIATION BOUNDS	FREQUENCY OF NEGATIVE ERRORS	FREQUENCY OF POSITIVE ERRORS
Between 0 and 1 SDs	57974	47255
Between 1 and 2 SDs	14279	12395
Between 2 and 3 SDs	1744	2955
Between 3 and 4 SDs	247	852
Between 4 and 5 SDs	51	307
Between 5 and 6 SDs	4	128
Between 6 and 7 SDs	1	68
Between 7 and 8 SDs	4	39
Between 8 and 9 SDs	1	9
Between 9 and 10 SDs	2	14
Greater than 10 SDs	1	18

Source: M. A. Simkowitz and W. L. Beedles, "Diversification in a Three-Moment World," *Journal of Finance and Quantitative Analysis,* 13 (December 1978), 934.

dramatically. Column 6 indicates the relationship of skewness to total risk (here measured as standard deviation). Positive skewness disappears completely after six assets are held in a portfolio. Note, these are not just any six assets, but those with relatively uncorrelated returns.

These results pose something of a dilemma. If investors prefer skewing but abhor variance, should they compose diversified portfolios? Simkowitz and Beedles suggest that investors who prefer skewing will not diversify, but those who are concerned with the range of possible returns will diversify. Perhaps a measure that relates skewness to variance may be useful in developing a portfolio strategy.

What we have learned so far is that returns are not normally distributed. Thus, the assumption of normal distributions may be an inaccurate approximation. Beta may be too simplistic a measure of risk and, therefore, a source of considerable error.

The real question is, Is skewing sufficiently important to destroy the basic linear relationship of the CAPM? Fama (1976) believed that the distribution of returns was close enough to normal that the assumption of normalcy was appropriate. This is an accommodation—one that was made, no doubt, because our ability to deal with nonnormal distributions is still quite primitive. It is quite difficult to include skewing into the model. It is much easier to deal with a model premised on normalcy.

The question of skewing remains troublesome. Moreover, remember that returns do not even need to be skewed to invalidate the model; investors must simply *believe* that returns are skewed. The result of real or imagined skewing can be either a nonlinear risk-return relationship or an

Exhibit 3-12

Distributional Measures Averaged Over Portfolios of Varying Sizes

PORTFOLIO SIZE	NUMBER OF PORTFOLIOS [1]	HOLDING PERIOD RETURN [2]	VARIANCE (× 100) [3]	RAW SKEWNESS (× 100) [4]	PERCENTAGE RETURN TO STANDARD DEVIATION [5]	CUBE ROOT OF RAW SKEW TO STANDARD DEVIATION [6]
1	549	1.012858	.582320	.046209	.184332	.743956
2	274	1.012864	.373904	.013092	.220674	.608219
3	183	1.012858	.301102	.005399	.241560	.463321
4	137	1.012854	.265995	.002614	.255659	.323158
5	109	1.012888	.247009	.001339	.265002	.165966
6	91	1.012851	.230559	.000571	.272274	.033614
7	78	1.012863	.220846	.000159	.278376	−.036336

Source: M. A. Simkowitz and W. L. Beedles, "Diversification in a Three-Moment World," *Journal of Finance and Quantitative Analysis,* 13 (December 1978), 936.

inaccurate prediction of the regression coefficients.[13] Neither result is desirable because, in either case, considerable error in estimating potential equity returns would result.

Substantial evidence exists that something is basically wrong with the simple form of the CAPM. No one piece of research is sufficiently strong to allow us to reject the model outright, but we should at least be skeptical of the model at this point. Roll (1977) has even pointed out that the CAPM is not a good hypothesis to test. The CAPM is an expectational model and requires using the full set of assets available to the investor (in the broadest sense) as an index. Roll says that because we cannot know what that complete index is, and because our proxies cannot be tested for similarity to this *unknown* portfolio, our tests have not been tests of expectations but of what actually occurred. When the model is tested on historical data, if we find returns above or below the security market line, the index chosen is not ex post efficient. Since the true market index contains all assets—stocks, bonds, and even human capital—it is unlikely that we will ever be able to gather the data necessary to use it. Thus, no test of the CAPM using history would be a valid theoretical test. Thus, we cannot draw any satisfactory conclusions from any test of the CAPM. All tests have been joint tests of the model and of the data on which it has been tested.

Roll's article has caused quite a stir among both academics and practitioners.[14] From the beginning, however, there was no doubt that the CAPM was an expectational model. It should have been evident that problems occur any time that expectations are tested on the basis of realizations. What we hope to get is rarely what we get. Thus, the problems of testing an expectational model are clear. Still it is disturbing to find a model is theoretically but not practically testable. The broader question for the practitioner then should be, Does this model in its simple or in its adapted forms provide me with insights that can help me do my job better?

Before completing our discussion of empirical studies, let us look a bit more at the problem of the inadequate index.

5.   DO OTHER INDEXES YIELD DIFFERENT RESULTS?

Some attempts have been made to create broader indexes, in part simply to test the results of using such indexes. Friend, Westerfield, and Granito (1978) formulated a test that attempted to respond to Roll's concerns.

---

[13]See Miller and Scholes, "Rate of Return in Relation to Risk: A Reexamination of Some Recent Findings," *Studies in the Theory of Capital Markets,* ed. M. Jensen, (New York: Praeger, 1972), pp. 47–78.
   [14]See, for example, Anise Wallace, "Is Beta Dead?" *Institutional Investor,* July 1980, pp. 23–30.

They first used a stock index alone, then added a bond index, and finally a joint stock-bond index. Their results are shown in Exhibit 3–13. Their regression is of this form:

$$R_i = \gamma_0 + \gamma_1\beta_1 + \gamma_2\sigma_{ri}$$

Exhibit 3–13

Return-Risk Regressions for Individual Assets Adjusted for Order Bias and for Asset Groups, 4th Quarter 1968–2nd Quarter 1973

	FOR INDIVIDUAL ASSETS*			
	Estimates of Regression Coefficients			
TYPE OF ASSET	γ_0	γ_1	γ_2	$\overline{R^2}$
Common stocks	1.025	−.018		0.087
	(.0032)	(.0020)		
	1.030	−.015	−.078	0.097
	(.0035)	(.0022)	(.0245)	
Corporate bonds	1.016	.001		−0.001
	(.0009)	(.0022)		
	1.017	.001	−.037	0.013
	(.0009)	(.0022)	(.0102)	
Common stocks	1.022	−.016		0.209
and	(.0009)	(.0008)		
Corporate bonds	1.023	−.012	−.060	0.216
	(.0009)	(.0011)	(.0141)	
	FOR ASSET GROUPS†			
Common stocks	1.032	−.022		.556
	(.0046)	(.0027)		
	1.037	−.004	−.284	.643
	(.0044)	(.0054)	(.0784)	
Corporate bonds	1.016	.001		−.020
	(.0018)	(.0048)		
	1.016	−.001	.011	−.039
	(.0018)	(.0058)	(.0331)	
Common stocks	1.022	−0.16		.693
and	(.0013)	(.0011)		
Corporate bonds	1.024	−.010	−.099	.706
	(.001)	(.0029)	(.0428)	

*The regressions are of the general form $\overline{R}_i = \gamma_0 + \gamma_1\beta_1 + \gamma_2\sigma_{rr}$. The number of observations is 867 for stocks, 891 for corporate bonds, and 1758 for stocks and corporate bonds combined.

†Observations are based upon the means for groups of individual assets (50 groups for each of stocks and corporate bonds and 100 groups for stocks and corporate bonds combined).

Source: I. Friend, R. Westerfield, and M. Granito, "New Evidence on the Capital Asset Pricing Model," *Journal of Finance*, 33 (June 1978), 910.

where

γ_0 = alpha or the intercept

γ_1 = the coefficient of the market volatility factor

γ_2 = the coefficient for the residual standard deviation, with the third factor, $\gamma_2\sigma_{ri}$, entering the second, fourth, and sixth equations

Many believe that the CAPM implies that the regression coefficients will be quite similar regardless of the index used. Friend, Westerfield, and Granito found that they were not. Exhibit 3–13 reports regression coefficients for individual and grouped data (50 groups of stocks, 50 groups of bonds, and 100 mixed stock-bond groups) over the period 1968–73.

The intercepts, γ_0, shown in the first column of Exhibit 3–13 were not the same, and they were not close to any of the normally quoted riskfree rates for the period. To provide some perspective on their intercepts, the average Treasury bill rate for the same period was 5.5 percent.

For two of the regressions, both of which used the corporate bond index alone, the coefficient of determination ($\bar{R}^2$) showed that the index and the asset's returns were virtually unrelated. The joint stock and bond index, however, showed a higher $\bar{R}^2$ than did the stock index alone.

Adding residual errors (the leftover data that should have no pattern or useful information) should not have improved the results. Much to our theoretical chagrin, the results did improve. We would have expected that the error terms would provide irrelevant additional data. In this study, they provided additional information that was sometimes more important than that provided by the market itself.

The choice of index can have very important consequences. International diversification—that is, adding stocks traded on non-U.S. exchanges to a portfolio comprised primarily of securities of U.S.-based corporations—has been touted as a portfolio strategy that can increase returns *and* reduce risk. If the market proxy used to demonstrate this phenomenon is a U.S. proxy like the S&P 500, the results are not clear because our index proxy represents only part of the whole market. To be sure of the effect, we must use a proxy for the world market, not a U.S. market index. Although world stock indexes have recently been developed and tested,[15] what is clear is that an incorrect proxy for the market can provide incorrect information.

Friend, Westerfield, and Granito also gathered and tested expec-

---

[15]See, for instance, Capital International's index, or First Chicago Bank—First Chicago Investment Advisors' Multiple Market Index.

tational data—in particular, they used estimates of future returns that had been made by financial institutions (banks, insurance companies, and investment counseling firms) in 1974, 1976, and 1977. In Exhibit 3-14 we can see their results for all three periods. The analysts' estimates are noted as γ_3, and the coefficients are positive and significant in all three periods and are more significant than the market volatility factor (γ_1). In fact, the market factor in several periods was either negative or almost zero. Analysts' estimates, they concluded, yielded important information.

This study by Friend, Westerfield, and Granito is one of the few early attempts to look at ex ante data to verify the model. It is certainly important. They found again that systematic risk was not the sole de-

Exhibit 3-14

Expected Return-Risk Regressions* for Individual Stocks for Three Periods: August 1974, March 1976, and February 1977

PERIOD	ESTIMATES OF REGRESSION COEFFICIENTS				$\overline{R}^2$
	γ_0	γ_1	γ_2	γ_3	
August '74	1.171	-0.28			.02
	(.018)	(.021)			
	1.121	-0.27	.918		.21
	(.022)	(.018)	(.273)		
	1.103	$-.017$	.919	.491	.25
	(.024)	(.019)	(.265)	(.267)	
March '76	1.132	$-.002$			0
	(.010)	(.014)			
	1.144	.004	$-.282$		.02
	(.012)	(.014)	(.170)		
	1.143	.005	$-.283$	.021	0
	(.014)	(.014)	(.173)	(.252)	
February '77	1.210	$-.071$			.06
	(.031)	(.037)			
	1.179	$-.097$	.875		.08
	(.038)	(.041)	(.604)		
	1.180	$-.080$	.256	.575	.21
	(.035)	(.038)	(.598)	(.196)	

*These are cross-section regressions of the general form $E(R_i) = \gamma_0 + \gamma_1\beta_i + \gamma_2\sigma_{ri} + \gamma_3 h_i$. $\overline{R}^2$ is the coefficient of determination adjusted for degrees of freedom. The standard error of a regression coefficient is indicated by ( ). The number of observations is 46 for 1974, 34 for 1976, and 48 for 1977.

Source: I. Friend, R. Westerfield, and M. Granito, "New Evidence on the Capital Asset Pricing Model," *Journal of Finance*, 33 (June 1978), 907.

terminant of returns. If these findings hold up to further study, they would suggest that forming a portfolio with large residual risk, denoted as γ_2, might be beneficial. Such a portfolio would outperform the market on both risk *and* return dimensions because residual risk has information useful to the forecasting of returns.

What we have found thus far is that the simple capital asset pricing model does not describe history or expectations very well. At the very least, the "true" slope is less steep and the intercept is higher than theory would predict, and, in addition, the efficient frontier may not be linear. We also found that beta does not seem to provide a full description of risk. Other risk measures are important in determining security returns. In particular, the problem of skewed returns cannot be ignored. When returns are tested, they are found to be skewed; when the model is tested, adaptations that include skewness are found to improve results. Thus, the model appears to be misspecified.

II.   INADEQUACY

At the beginning of this chapter, we suggested that errors in the CAPM could be of two types. First, the model could be inaccurate, as we have already seen. Second, the model could omit important factors—that is, the model could be inadequate.

We found that the model does not reflect the world well—at least, that is our conclusion when we test it using ex post data. Some of these inaccuracies may be due to the model's austerity. One way that we can test the adequacy of the model is to add other factors that seem intuitively relevant and then test the result of using this new model. If the added factor is important, we should find better explanatory power (for instance, a higher R^2), more stable parameters, or the ability to form equally diversified portfolios with fewer assets.

1.   WHAT ABOUT DIVIDENDS AND TAXES?

Researchers have added factors to the CAPM and tested them for significance. Dividends, as we pointed out in Chapter 2, have always been considered a factor influencing share price. To provide a richer explanation than that offered by total returns alone, we could segment total returns into dividends and capital gains. The evidence on dividend importance is conflicting, however. The tide has shifted from dividend importance to dividend irrelevance and has recently shifted back again to importance. The facts are not clear.

Vandell and Stevens (1982) looked specifically at the effect of taxes on security pricing. Their study examined the differences between the simple CAPM and one with a personal tax factor included. Using forecasts from analysts at a major institution, they looked at the difference between the ex post capital market line (using 90-day Treasury bills and the market return) and a plane derived from a combination of risk and yield. Their research suggests that beta does not capture the tax effect. Furthermore, their adjusted model produced a security market line much closer to what would have been expected theoretically. They found a strong negative correlation between yield and beta; high-yield stocks tended to have low betas.

Representative of the controversy, Black and Scholes (1974) found no significant relationship between dividends and stock returns, before or after taxes. Academic researchers nonetheless remained perplexed as to why the market did not demand higher returns from high-dividend-paying stocks to compensate for the higher tax rate on dividends. Using new data or techniques, a number of researchers, Litzenberger and Ramaswamy (1979, 1980) and Banz (1981) among others, found conflicting results about the yield-related tax impact.

Correcting for what they believed was a bias-inducing error (previous researchers had used the previous year's dividend to proxy for the expected yield, without taking into account the seasonal nature of dividends), Litzenberger and Ramaswamy (1979) found the existence of a clientèle effect with regard to dividend yield: investors with different characteristics preferred different yields. In particular, they found "that the aversion for dividends is lower for high yield stocks,"[16] and "that the before-tax expected return on a security is linearly related to its systematic risk and dividend yield."[17]

Of findings like Litzenberger and Ramaswamy's, Miller and Scholes (1982) say that they come from "using short-run definitions of dividend yield . . . in tests seeking to deduce the differential tax burden on dividends over long-term capital gains from differences in rates of return on shares that do and shares that do not pay out a cash dividend during the return interval."[18] In effect, what researchers may have found is a dividend announcement effect, not a systematic tax effect resulting from corporate dividend policy.

Using a technique to correct for the information effects of dividend announcements, Miller and Scholes found "no significant remaining re-

[16]Robert H. Litzenberger and K. Ramaswamy, "The Effect of Personal Taxes and Dividends Capital Asset Prices," *Journal of Financial Economics*, 7 (1979), 165.
[17]Ibid., p. 190.
[18]Merton Miller and M. S. Scholes, "Dividends and Taxes: Some Empirical Evidence," *Journal of Political Economy*, 90 (June 1982), 1119.

lation between returns and expected dividend yields."[19] They do not conclude that there is no effect, only that using short-term yield measures provides these negative results.

Do taxes affect the returns of equity securities? The only conclusion that we can draw now is that we do not know.

2. DOES LIQUIDITY AFFECT SECURITY PRICING?

Liquidity is another factor that has been added to the basic CAPM with some success. Fouse (1976) used ex ante (analyst-generated) data to project returns for individual shares. He aggregated the data into projected capital market lines.[20] To this risk-return relationship Fouse added liquidity, segmenting the universe into five liquidity groups. Exhibit 3–15 shows his "liquidity fans" for two different time periods. Fouse's fans are not the only or necessarily the best approach to the liquidity problem, but these fans clearly demonstrate the added dimension that liquidity could bring to analysts' forecasts.

For those engaged in portfolio management, this work has several interesting implications. The first is that analysts' projections of securities' values change and sometimes change quite rapidly. Let us look for a moment at Fouse's lines for December 31, 1974. High-risk stocks were expected to provide high yields. Do these facts suggest an investment strategy? Yes and no. If we can project the next configuration, the line at some future point in time, the answer is yes. In fact, at December 31, 1974, we might have suspected that the high-risk stocks would perform better over the long run: if returns expectations dropped, prices would rise and capital gains would result. That is in fact what happened by June 30, 1975. The reverse occurred from February 1976, to mid-1977. By mid-1977 a low flat line became a line with a higher intercept and slope. If the investor had bought a diversified portfolio of stocks on the basis of the February 1976 forecast, by mid-1977 that portfolio would have shown a capital loss. That is because the required returns had increased and stock prices consequently dropped to reflect those increased expectations.

Beyond the question of investment strategy, what do Fouse's liquidity groupings suggest for those engaged in security selection? Stocks that previously appeared attractive when a single liquidity grouping was used might not appear attractive when sorted into liquidity groupings. Exhibit 3–16 shows the projected risk and return for two stocks, X and

[19]Ibid., p. 1131.

[20]Wells Fargo, Fouse's employer at the time, reports success in using this expectational method for stock selection. The full story is not yet available regarding the longer-term strength of this methodology.

Exhibit 3-15
Dynamic Capital Market Lines and Liquidity Considerations

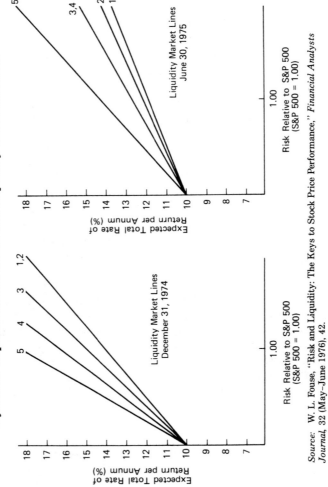

Source: W. L. Fouse, "Risk and Liquidity: The Keys to Stock Price Performance," *Financial Analysts Journal,* 32 (May–June 1976), 42.

Exhibit 3–16

Projected Risk and Return with Liquidity Consideration for Two Securities

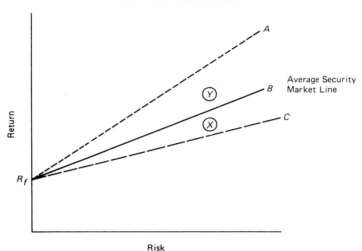

Y. Stock *Y* definitely seems more attractive. However, *Y* is an over-the-counter, lightly traded stock and *X* is a market giant. If we add liquidity sectors (the dotted lines) similar to Fouse's, we can see that our illiquid stock (*Y*) is unattractive vis-à-vis the least liquid sector (line R_fA), whereas our liquidity giant is expected to outperform the most liquid group (line R_fC). Obviously, our selection will be different when we see the stocks in this light.

3. FIRM SIZE AND SECURITY PRICES

Firm size as a determinant of return is another factor that has received considerable attention over the past five years. In fact some researchers have found that holding the stocks of small firms not only increased realized returns, but did so by almost 20 percent per year from 1963 to 1977. These returns have been large and persistent.

Using the CAPM and data from 1962 to 1975, Reinganum (1981b) ranked each company on its stock market value and placed them, revising them annually, in ten groups (deciles). The risk- (beta-) adjusted returns for each market-value-ranked portfolio was calculated, and the results are shown in Exhibit 3–17. The abnormal returns are the portfolio's returns less the return from the equally weighted American–New York

Exhibit 3-17

Mean Abnormal Daily Returns of Ten Market Value Portfolios During the First Year*
(Based on Equal-Weighted NYSE-AMEX Index)

PORTFOLIO NO.	MEAN ABNORMAL RETURNS† (IN 1/10%)	BETA	AVERAGE PERCENT-AGE ON AMEX‡	AVERAGE MEDIAN VALUE§ ($ IN MILLIONS)	DAILY AUTOCORRELATION OF ABNORMAL RETURNS		
					1	2	3
1	0.500 (6.42)	1.00 (101.7)	82.61	8.3	0.06	0.03	0.06
2	0.193 (3.47)	1.02 (144.9)	48.35	20.0	-0.05	0.01	-0.00
3	-0.033 (-0.71)	1.00 (171.3)	23.81	34.1	0.01	-0.00	0.02
4	-0.050 (-1.11)	1.00 (177.1)	11.29	54.5	0.05	-0.02	0.00
5	-0.115 (-2.60)	0.94 (170.3)	8.59	86.1	0.09	0.04	0.01
6	-0.193 (-4.18)	0.88 (160.9)	4.42	138.3	0.20	0.07	0.11
7	-0.189 (-3.99)	0.90 (156.8)	4.35	233.5	0.27	0.17	0.16
8	-0.214 (-4.00)	0.83 (135.9)	2.71	413.0	0.37	0.22	0.17
9	-0.292 (-5.24)	0.83 (126.3)	2.46	705.3	0.38	0.23	0.21
10	-0.343 (-4.79)	0.82 (96.3)	1.60	1,759.9	0.37	0.25	0.21

*Following portfolio recomposition.
†Average abnormal return per trading day. There are approximately 250 trading days per year.
‡Percentage of firms in portfolio listed on the American Stock Exchange.
§The median firm size in each portfolio averaged over the 14 years included in the study.

Source: Marc Reinganum, "Abnormal Returns in Small Firm Portfolios," Financial Analysts Journal, 37 (March–April 1981), 54.

Stock Exchange Index. These abnormal returns should have been zero, since all the betas were about 1.0. They were not. Not only were they different from zero, but "on the basis of firm size data, an investor can form portfolios that systematically earn abnormal returns."[21] Even more interesting is the fact that investors in the largest market-value stocks had negative returns. The small differences in betas did not account for the differences in returns. In addition, these abnormal returns persist. In the second year after portfolio composition, portfolio 1 had a return of 0.496 (about 12 percent per year) while portfolio 10 had a return of −0.408.

Banz (1981) at about the same time reported similar findings. However, he points out that if the investor owns only small stocks, he or she will be less diversified, and thus open to the significantly higher degree of unsystematic risk of small-firm stocks.

To give some idea of the impact of the size effect, when Lakonishok and Shapiro (1984) added size to their regression containing beta and variance, size was the only significant variable, regardless of the time period studied.

There is some speculation about what the source of this small-firm effect might be. One idea is that size is just a proxy for some other, yet unknown factor. Banz (1981) says, "Basu believed to have identified a market inefficiency but his P/E-effect is just a proxy for the size effect. Given its longevity, it is not likely that it is due to a market inefficiency but it is rather evidence of a pricing model misspecification."[22]

4. DO INDUSTRY GROUPINGS AFFECT PRICES?

As analysts, portfolio managers, and investors, we all know of factors beyond the basic changes in the market returns that are important in the way we estimate a security's value. For instance, the CAPM makes no distinction among industry groups. Yet many feel that industry-related factors do affect returns and that adding industry factors could enhance the CAPM's power. We know that industries have different betas. Those differences are pointed out in Exhibit 3–18. However, for an industry index to provide additional information there must be effects that are semisystematic, that affect all companies in an industry to a greater or lesser degree. Different betas for different industries may simply mean that companies in the same industry operate in similar product-

[21]Marc Reinganum, "Abnormal Returns in Small Firm Portfolios," *Financial Analysts Journal,* 37 (March–April 1981), 55.
[22]Rolf W. Banz, "The Relationship Between Return and Market Value of Common Stocks," *Journal of Financial Economics,* 9 (1981), 17.

Exhibit 3–18

Industry Betas

INDUSTRY	BETA	INDUSTRY	BETA
Brokerage	1.69	Tire and rubber	0.99
Computers	1.42	Steel	0.99
Oilfield services	1.33	Multiform	0.99
Electronics	1.22	Trucking and transport	0.99
Air transport	1.18	Toiletries and cosmetics	0.98
Oil producers	1.17	Maritime	0.96
Precision instruments	1.15	Ethical drugs	0.95
Aerospace	1.15	Insurance—property, and casualty	0.94
Health care/hospital suppliers	1.10	Apparel	0.93
Building products	1.08	Home appliance	0.93
Diversified chemicals	1.08	Publishing	0.92
Hotels/gaming	1.07	Machine tools	0.91
Paper and forest products	1.06	Construction equipment	0.91
Travel/recreation	1.06	Metal fabricating	0.89
Retail stores	1.04	Machinery	0.89
Chemicals	1.04	Textile	0.87
Telecommunications	1.04	Tobacco	0.87
Fast food	1.04	Household products	0.86
Integrated steel	1.03	Insurance—life	0.86
Broadcasting	1.03	Food processing	0.80
Auto manufacturing	1.01	Brewing	0.79
Office equipment	1.00	Electric utilities	0.65

Source: Calculated from data available from *Value Screen,* Value Line, Inc.

markets with the same or similar means of production. Such companies would, of course, be affected in similar ways by macroeconomic events.

While the betas you see in Exhibit 3–18 are the average for each industry, the betas of companies within most industries are quite similar. For instance, the electric utility beta is 0.65, and the range for the companies in the industry is 0.83 to 0.43. Other industries have wider ranges. Thus a single index (representing the entire market) could be inadequate if multiple, industry-specific indexes better reflect the true underlying returns-generating process.

King (1966) studied this very problem and concluded that the market index accounted for about 50 percent of the volatility of stock returns over time. An additional 10 percent could be attributed, he believed, to industry classification, specifically to SIC (Standard Industrial Classifications used by the U.S. Department of Commerce) code groups. Over the periods he studied, the importance of the market index in the regression dropped. In 1927–35 the R^2 was .53; in 1952–60 it was .26. King concluded that industry indexes could add value in a regression. Others tended to dismiss King's study with the objections that SIC codes were not a good classification scheme and that, theoretically, the industry factor was a random variable—unsystematic and diversifiable.

Cohen and Pogue (1967) looked at the problem as well. They also used SIC codes and Markowitz portfolio model. They found some evidence to support King's study, but there were severe statistical problems with their work. As a result, little more was done until Farrell (1974, 1975, 1976) expanded on the industry-specific, multi-index concept.

Farrell suggested that the industry effect was not unsystematic and diversifiable, but systematic. Various indexes would be positively and negatively correlated with each other. In testing his hypothesis, Farrell did not use SIC codes but defined groups that were quite different. To remove interindustry effects, Farrell clustered very similar firms on the basis of economic characteristics that appeared important to him:

1. Dependence on an economic sector (such as dependence on consumer or business spending)
2. Product similarity
3. Stage in the manufacturing cycle

Farrell speculated that these characteristics would lead to earnings similarities and thus contribute to the volatility underlying the firm's covariance with the market. His classification scheme produced four groups of stocks that he labeled cyclical, stable, growth, and oil stocks. Farrell's affinity clusters for stable stocks are shown in Exhibit 3–19. The stable stocks include several subgroups. Note the firms that were classified as stable in his study. These are not firms that might otherwise have been grouped together. Yet they are similar in basic characteristics as Farrell defined them. The average values of the correlation coefficients for each group of stocks with its corresponding index and with the other three indexes show that among the groups there is little relationship, whereas within each group, the relationship is significant. The oil group (not shown here) was the only complete group with no subgrouping within it.

The result of Farrell's efforts was a multi-index model with an efficient frontier that dominated that of the single-index model. The result of using Farrell's model is graphically shown in Exhibit 3–20. We can see that portfolios created using the multi-index framework either reduced risk faster than efficient diversification would suggest or had fewer securities than did portfolios of equivalent risk created on the basis of the single-index model. Put simply, multi-index portfolios outperformed single-index portfolios.

Farrell assumed that his clusters provided information beyond that

Exhibit 3-19

Cluster Diagrams

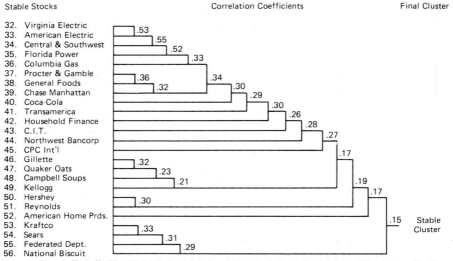

Source: James Farrell, *The Multi-Index Model and Practical Portfolio Analysis* (Charlottesville, Va.: Financial Analysts Research Foundation, 1976), p. 25.

provided by the market alone. What he found was strong covariance, some negative and some positive, between the groups. His approach was quite different from the simple CAPM that used R_m as the only index.

Farrell was not the only practitioner or academic who believed that there was more than one factor that affected expected and realized returns. Using a form of analysis like that used by Farrell, Arnott (1980) studied a larger sample, eliminated unusual data (lying beyond three standard deviations from the mean), and created clusters, but only to the point where Arnott saw unusual groups joining the cluster (Farrell had combined groups until no positive correlations remained). Arnott identified five groups: quality growth, utility, oil, cyclical, and basic stocks. The market (the S&P 500) was also included as a factor. The market explained about 30 percent of the variance in returns for his 600 stocks. The other five indexes improved the R^2 to almost 39 percent, an improvement of about 30 percent. While the market factor was the most important in Arnott's study, he still says that the other factors "can be indispensable in evaluating the risk characteristics of a portfolio."[23] For instance, an investor's portfolio that is concentrated in utility stocks is

[23]Robert D. Arnott, "Cluster Analysis and Stock Price Comovement," *Financial Analysts Journal,* 36 (November–December 1980), 59.

Exhibit 3–20

Ex Ante Efficient Frontier for Single-Index and Multi-Index Models

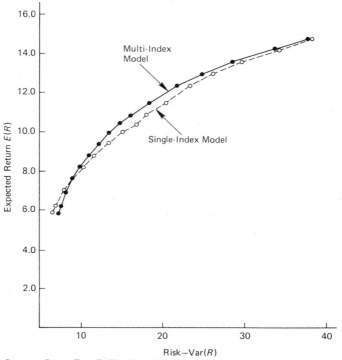

Multi-Index Model

Single-Index Model

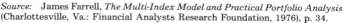

Risk—Var(*R*)

Source: James Farrell, *The Multi-Index Model and Practical Portfolio Analysis* (Charlottesville, Va.: Financial Analysts Research Foundation, 1976), p. 34.

exposed to market risk, but it is also subject to risk from the utility risk factor—a risk that Arnott says the CAPM ignores. By shifting assets into stocks that are insensitive to utility risk, the investor can offset his or her portfolio's unusual exposure to the non-market-related risk that comes from owning utilities. Conversely, the investor wishing to have a portfolio that moves with the utility cluster would choose those stocks with a high coefficient for the utility factor. Exhibit 3–21 provides a sample of the importance of Arnott's various factors for several stocks.

The idea that several factors can and do affect asset prices, is one that many have found intriguing. Sharpe (1982) chose and used factors he believed were important, and for which there were reliable data available for several decades. He did not attempt to identify common factors,

Exhibit 3–21

Sample Factor Betas for Selected Companies

	MAR-KET	GROWTH	UTILITIES	OIL	BASIC	CYCLIC/
IBM	0.93	0.45	−0.24	−0.24	−0.33	−0.26
Digital Equipment	1.28	0.64	−0.80	−0.37	−0.17	0.07
Minnesota Mining	1.16	0.69	−0.43	−0.19	−0.12	−0.30
MGIC	1.70	−0.30	0.06	−0.16	0.33	1.01
AT&T	0.72	−0.31	0.33	−0.15	−0.15	−0.19
Phillips Petroleum	1.14	−0.41	−0.42	0.77	−0.22	−0.20
Sundstrand	1.35	−0.20	0.11	0.05	−0.02	0.84

Source: Robert D. Arnott, "Cluster Analysis and Stock Price Comovement," *Financial Analysts Journal*, 36 (November-December 1980), 61.

and then put names to them as had Farrell and Arnott, but drew on previous research and industry practice. As factors he used the stock's market beta, its alpha (the minimum return the stock had over the prior 60 months), yield, size, and bond beta (the relationship of the stock's returns to those on a long-term government bond index), as well as factors representing eight market sectors, such as transportation, utilities, finance, and energy. In testing these factors Sharpe found that they were frequently significant during the period 1931–79, and, as shown in Exhibit 3–22, he attributed about 40 percent of the variance over time to the 13 factors.

It is important to note that when the only factor was a beta of 1.0, the average R^2 was .25. This is the most naive kind of assumption about the nature and importance of a factor, and one that takes no skill to determine or forecast.

Exhibit 3–22

**Average Time-Series Fit of Models
(Based on 2197 Stocks, 1931–79)**

MODEL	AVERAGE R^2	DIFFERENCE
All beta = 1	.250	
		.089
Beta	.339	
		.043
Common factors	.382	
		.021
Common and sector factors	.403	

Source: William F. Sharpe, "Factors in New York Stock Exchange Security Returns, 1931-1979," *Journal of Portfolio Management*, Summer 1982, p. 9.

Sharpe also calculated the value of each of the factors, and the excess returns (ER) from the S&P 500 and the long-term government bonds over the Treasury bill rate. The results are found in column 1 of Exhibit 3-23. These are simple average annual rates of return. Thus, on average over the period, stocks with high betas outperformed those with low betas, and energy stocks certainly were superior to utilities. Column 3 shows the impact of each factor on the returns of the stocks over this period, and column 4 shows what the model would have forecast. On the basis of the t values (a significant t value would be at least 2.0), Sharpe suggests that it is naive to assume that returns are related only to betas, and to betas created from history alone.

While many would nod knowledgeably at these results, some of these factors seem to be mere proxies for other, more fundamental factors—factors that are at the root of differences in variations of asset return behavior: if utility and finance stocks vary, perhaps it has something to do with interest rates; if cyclical and growth stocks seem to be definite groups, perhaps it has something to do with the level of industrial production. Among others, Chen, Roll, and Ross (1983) have looked at more fundamental macroeconomic variables—variables that may be at the root of the variation in returns. Using a technique somewhat like that used by Farrell and Arnott, they analyzed data from 1947 to 1973. They found five principal factors existed.[24] Using correlation and regression analysis they analyzed the relationship of the five unknown but principal factors, to fundamental macroeconomic variables:

1. A change in expected inflation and unexpected inflation
2. An unexpected change in the term structure of interest rates
3. The growth rate of, and anticipated and unanticipated changes in industrial production
4. Unanticipated change in the risk premium
5. Changes in a stock market index

The market index was included to capture the effect of any variables that had not been explicitly included.

Chen, Roll, and Ross found that "several of the macroeconomic variables were significant in explaining the returns on the factors, most notably, industrial production, changes in the risk premium, excess returns on long bonds, and somewhat more weakly, measures of unanticipated inflation."[25]

[24]Nai-fu Chen, Richard Roll, Stephen A. Ross, "Economic Forces and the Stock Market: Testing APT and Alternative Asset Pricing Theories" (Working paper No. B-73, University of Chicago, December 1983), p. 38.
[25]Ibid., p. 38.

Exhibit 3-23

Returns from Various Factors, 1931–79

FACTOR	AVERAGE VALUE 1926-79 [1]	STANDARD DEVIATION [2]	FACTOR COEFFICIENT [3]	PREDICTED VALUE [4]	t DIFF. [5]
S&P 500 ER	8.295	20.969	NA	NA	(NA)
Long-term government ER	0.518	5.760	NA	NA	(NA)
Z (intercept)	NA	NA	.303	2.51	(−1.32)
Beta (historic)	5.355	18.376	.745	6.18	(−0.31)
Yield	0.237	1.043	−.014	−0.11	(2.37)
Size	−5.563	7.804	−.062	−0.51	(−4.53)
Bond beta	−0.118	2.719	−.009	−0.08	(−0.11)
Alpha	−2.001	4.639	−.086	−0.71	(−1.94)
Basic industries	1.653	7.974	.074	0.61	(0.91)
Capital goods	0.155	5.720	−.014	−0.12	(0.33)
Construction	−1.589	8.862	.103	0.85	(−1.93)
Consumer goods	−0.180	5.173	−.028	−0.23	(0.07)
Energy	6.282	11.042	−.057	−0.47	(4.28)
Finance	−1.478	5.247	−.023	−0.19	(−1.72)
Transportation	−0.570	9.492	−.065	−0.54	(−0.82)
Utilities	−2.622	9.425	−.047	−0.39	(−1.66)

*t value on the difference between the average and predicted values.

Source: Adapted from William F. Sharpe, "Factors in New York Stock Exchange Security Returns, 1931–1979," Journal of Portfolio Management, Summer 1982, pp. 10, 16, and 17.

As you can see, many researchers have identified a factor or factors that appear to be missing from the simple one-factor CAPM. These factor models[26] attempt to capture what is behind the behavior of security returns during a period. Obviously, what we would like is to be able to predict from this analysis of history what is likely to happen. And these researchers seem to indicate that a simple CAPM would give us inadequate and potentially inaccurate forecasts. Unfortunately, factors and the size of their impact can change, and quickly. In addition, factor models are descriptions of what is, and may or may not be normative (what should be) models of behavior.

III. FUTURE DIRECTIONS

Are practitioners and academics, therefore, moving away from the CAPM? Since Roll (1977) questioned the value of empirical testing of the CAPM, many academics have directed themselves away from the CAPM. Whether that is appropriate or not remains to be seen.

As a part of the research into the multifactor models, Ross (1976) proposed a more general model than the CAPM. Called the multifactor model or arbitrage pricing theory (APT), this model breathed fresh air into research at a time when academics were tiring of seemingly untestable asset pricing models and when many of the tests of the CAPM, and allied factor analysis, had seemed to show that it was inadequate or misspecified. The Ross model suggested that several factors contributed to returns. While Ross did not identify what the factors might be, this multifactor model could be tested and was intuitively appealing to both academics and practitioners, who, in the main, were certain that a single factor alone, the market, was not all that determined the expected or realized returns of assets.

This model is an interesting alternative to the CAPM and MPT. Since its introduction by Ross, it has been discussed, evaluated, and tested. Its intuitive appeal alone makes it worth greater discussion. In addition, it is not an extension of the CAPM; rather, some suggest, it is a more general form of the CAPM. Thus, in Chapter 7 you will find a discussion of APT, the theory, the tests of the model, and the current state of thinking about this most recent asset pricing model.

Another variety of model that academics have been discussing is

[26]For a readable article about factor analysis as it relates to asset pricing models, see H. Russell Fogler, "Common Sense on CAPM, APT, and Correlated Residuals," *Journal of Portfolio Management*, Summer 1982, pp. 20–28.

called the *state-preference model.*[27] This type of model is based upon an investor-forecasted "state of nature" (states of nature include such things as changes in market or economic conditions). The preferences of the individual investor or groups of investors will depend upon the forecasted "state" and the investors' preference given that world. This class of model would obviously be much richer, more descriptive, more specific, and much more difficult to manage than a CAPM. Yet the world of investors and investment assets *is* richer, less general, and perhaps much more difficult to understand.

There has also been some discussion that leads us back to or near to the original Markowitz portfolio model. Major problems existed with using that model when it was first proposed. Mechanically estimating pairwise correlations for numerous assets was laborious at best, but processing the necessary correlations was virtually impossible. The increased availability and lower per-unit cost of computer time, and the increased technical competence among analysts, have made the more complex but more descriptive Markowitz method more attractive than it seemed in the past.[28]

Arbitrage pricing theory and Black and Scholes's (1973) option pricing theory[29] are two of the more recent possibilities suggested for use in describing investor behavior.

Although a number of intriguing questions remain to be answered, the simple CAPM has provided a better description of the complex security-pricing process than we have had before. Does it abstract from reality? Yes. But even using ex post data, we find that an average of 33 percent of the changes in returns for a single security are related to changes in the market returns (average R^2 about .33). This is a better average than we were able to sustain with the pre-CAPM multivariate pricing models. For portfolios, the results are even better.

Still, there are important questions to consider before we accept the CAPM as an equity pricing model—such questions as

1. Can we assume a single pricing mechanism in a liquidity sector market? Should liquidity, market-value size, inflation, or basic macroeconomic variables be built into the CAPM?

---

[27]For a discussion of state-preference models, see, for example, Thomas E. Copeland and J. F. Weston, *Financial Theory and Corporate Policy,* 2nd ed. (Reading, Mass.: Addison-Wesley, 1983).

[28]For a discussion of this technique, see, for example, Edwin J. Elton, M. J. Gruber, and M. W. Padburg, "Simple Criteria for Optimal Portfolio Selection," *Journal of Finance,* 31 (December 1976), 1341–57.

[29]For a brief description of the Black-Scholes model and its use, see W. F. Sharpe, *Investments* 2nd ed. (Englewood Cliffs, N.J.: Prentice-Hall, 1981); and Copeland and Weston, *Financial Theory and Corporate Policy.*

2. Can we assume that taxes have no importance in a world where municipal and corporate bonds of like risk and maturity sell at different yields?
3. Can we use a single-period model in a multiperiod world?
4. Can we assume a common undefined horizon when investors have different, nonhomogeneous horizons?

As long as those questions remain unresolved, we cannot mindlessly rely on the CAPM. However, we have not proved that the model is useless. It is difficult—if not impossible—to test an expectational model, and it is also difficult to test a model with inadequate data. Most of the tests to date have not been reliable tests of this expectational model. Thus, our tests do not give us adequate cause to throw out the model. Rather, we must adapt what is valuable within this construct if we are to develop a more apt description of the complex security-pricing process. The obvious frailties of the CAPM are equally obvious opportunities for creative persons to devise more adequate models.

REFERENCES

Arditti, Fred D., "Risk and the Required Return on Equity," *Journal of Finance*, 22 (March 1967), 19-36.

Arnott, Robert D., "Cluster Analysis and Stock Price Comovement," *Financial Analysts Journal*, 36 (November-December 1980), 56-62.

——, "What Hath MPT Wrought: Which Risks Reap Rewards," *Journal of Portfolio Management*, Fall 1983, pp. 5-11.

Banz, Rolf W., "The Relationship between Return and Market Value of Common Stocks," *Journal of Financial Economics*, 9 (1981), 3-18.

Bar Yosef, S., and R. Kolodny, "Dividend Policy and Capital Market Theory," *Review of Economics and Statistics*, 58 (May 1976), 181-90.

Basu, S., "Investment Performance of Common Stocks in Relation to their Price-Earnings Ratios: A Test of the Efficient Market Hypothesis," *Journal of Finance*, 32 (June 1977), 663-82.

Black, Fisher, M. Jensen, and M. Scholes, "The Capital Asset Pricing Model: Some Empirical Tests," in *Studies in the Theory of Capital Markets*, ed. M. Jensen, pp. 79-121. New York: Praeger, 1972.

Black, Fisher, and M. Scholes, "The Pricing of Options and Corporate Liabilities," *Journal of Political Economy*, 81 (May-June 1974), 637-54.

——, "The Effects of Divided Yield and Dividend Policy on Common Stock Prices and Returns," *Journal of Financial Economics*, (May 1974), 1-22.

Blume, Marshall, and I. Friend, "A New Look at the CAPM," *Journal of Finance,* 27 (March 1973), 19-34.

———, "The Asset Structure of Individual Portfolios and Some Implications for Utility Functions," *Journal of Finance,* 30 (May 1975), 585-603.

Chen, Nai-fu, R. Roll, and S. A. Ross, "Economic Forces and the Stock Market: Testing APT and Alternative Asset Pricing Theories," Working Paper No. B-73, University of Chicago, December 1983.

Cohen, K. J., and J. Pogue, "An Empirical Evaluation of Alternative Portfolio Selection Models," *Journal of Business,* April 1967, pp. 166-93.

Cooley, Philip, R. Roenfeldt, and N. K. Modani, "Interdependence of Market Risk Measures," *Journal of Business,* 50 (July 1977), 356-63.

Copeland, Thomas E., and J. F. Weston, *Financial Theory and Corporate Policy,* 2nd ed. Reading, Mass.: Addison-Wesley, 1983.

Douglas, George, "Risk in the Equity Markets: An Empirical Appraisal of Market Efficiency," *Yale Economic Essays,* 9 (Spring 1969), 3-45.

Elton, Edwin J., M. J. Gruber, and M. W. Padburg, "Simple Criteria for Optimal Portfolio Selection," *Journal of Finance,* 31 (December 1976), 1341-57.

Fama, Eugene F., *Foundations of Finance.* New York: Basic Books, 1976.

Fama, Eugene F., and J. D. MacBeth, "Risk, Return and Equilibrium: Empirical Tests," *Journal of Political Economy,* 81 (May–June 1973), 607-36.

———, "Tests of the Multiperiod Two Parameter Model," *Journal of Financial Economics,* 1 (May 1974), 43-66.

Farrell, J. L., Jr., "Analyzing Covariation of Returns to Determine Homogeneous Stock Groupings," *Journal of Business,* 47 (April 1974), 186-207.

———, "Homogeneous Stock Groupings," *Financial Analysts Journal,* 31 (May–June 1975), 50-62.

———, *The Multi-Index Model and Practical Portfolio Analysis,* Charlottesville, Va.: Financial Analysts Research Foundation, 1976.

Fogler, H. Russell, "Common Sense on CAPM, APT, and Correlated Residuals," *Journal of Portfolio Management,* Summer 1982, pp. 20-28.

Fouse, William L., "Risk & Liquidity: The Keys to Stock Price Behavior," *Financial Analysts Journal,* 32 (May–June 1976), 35-45.

———, "Risk & Liquidity Revisited," *Financial Analysts Journal,* 33 (January–February 1977), 40-45.

Francis, Jack C., and S. H. Archer, *Portfolio Analysis,* 2nd ed. Englewood Cliffs, N.J.: Prentice-Hall, 1979.

Friend, Irwin, and Marshall Blume, "Measurement of Portfolio Performance under Uncertainty," *American Economic Review,* 60 (September 1970), 561-75.

Friend, Irwin, R. Westerfield, and M. Granito, "New Evidence on the Capital Asset Pricing Model," *Journal of Finance,* 33 (June 1978), 906-16.

Jensen, Michael C., *Tests of Capital Market Theory and Implications of the Evidence,* Charlottesville, Va.: Financial Analysts Research Foundation, 1975.

King, Benjamin, "Market and Industry Factors in Stock Price Behavior," *Journal of Business,* 39 (January 1966), 139-90.

Kraus, A., and H. Litzenberger, "Skewness Preference and the Valuation of Risk Assets," *Journal of Finance,* 1 (September 1976), 1085-1100.

Lakonishok, Josef, and A. C. Shapiro, "Stock Returns, Beta, Variance and Size: An Empirical Analysis," *Financial Analysts Journal,* 40 (July-August 1984), 36-41.

Lewellen, William, R. Lease, and G. Schlarbaum, "Patterns of Investment Strategy and Behavior among Individual Investors," *Journal of Business,* July 1977, pp. 296-333.

Litzenberger, Robert H., and K. Ramaswamy, "The Effect of Personal Taxes and Dividends Capital Asset Prices," *Journal of Financial Economics,* 7 (1979), 1653-95.

————, "Dividends, Short Selling Restrictions, Tax-Induced Investor Clienteles and Market Equilibrium," *Journal of Finance,* 35 (May 1980), 469-82.

McDonald, Bill, "Functional Forms and the Capital Asset Pricing Model," *Journal of Financial and Quantitative Analysis,* 18 (September 1983), 319-29.

Miller, Merton, and M. Scholes, "Rate of Return in Relation to Risk: A Reexamination of Some Recent Findings," in *Studies in the Theory of Capital Markets,* ed. M. Jensen, pp. 47-78. New York: Praeger, 1972.

————, "Dividends and Taxes: Some Empirical Evidence," *Journal of Political Economy,* 90 (June 1982), 1119-41.

Peterson, Pamela P., and D. R. Peterson, "Divergence of Opinion and Return," *Journal of Financial Research,* 5 (Summer 1982), 125-34.

Reinganum, Marc R., "Misspecification of Capital Asset Pricing: Empirical Anomalies Based on Earning Yields and Market Values," *Journal of Financial Economics,* 9 (March 1981a), 19-46.

————, "Abnormal Returns in Small Firm Portfolios," *Financial Analysts Journal,* 37 (March-April 1981b), 52-56.

————, "A New Empirical Perspective on the CAPM," *Journal of Financial and Quantitative Analysis,* 16 (November 1981c), 439-62.

Roll, Richard, "A Critique of the Asset Pricing Theory's Tests, Part 1: On Past and Potential Testability of the Theory," *Journal of Financial Economics,* 4 (March 1977), 129-76.

Ross, Stephen A., "The Arbitrage Theory of Capital Asset Pricing," *Journal of Economic Theory,* 13 (December 1976), 341-60.

———, "The Current Status of the Capital Asset Pricing Model," *Journal of Finance,* 33 (June 1978), 885-901.

Sharpe, William F., *Investments,* 2nd ed. Englewood Cliffs, N.J.: Prentice-Hall, 1981.

———, "Factors in New York Stock Exchange Security Returns, 1931-1979," *Journal of Portfolio Management,* Summer 1982, p. 9.

Simkowitz, M. A., and W. L. Beedles, "Diversification in a Three-Moment World," *Journal of Financial and Quantitative Analysis,* 13 (December 1978), 903-25.

Swindler, Steve, and P. Vanderheiden, "Another Opinion Regarding Divergence of Opinion and Return," *Journal of Financial Research,* 6 (Spring 1983), 47-50.

Vandell, R. F., and J. Stevens, "Personal Taxes and Equity Security Pricing," *Financial Management,* 11 (Spring 1982), 31-40.

Wallace, Anise, "Is Beta Dead?" *Institutional Investor,* July 1980, pp. 23-30.

chapter
4

Estimating Beta

In Chapter 1 we defined *beta* as a measure of the relative volatility of returns: as the average rate of return from the market moves up and down, what happens to the returns for a given asset? If the asset's returns tend to move up and down more dramatically than do the market returns, the asset is considered relatively more volatile—more risky— and it will have a higher beta. In the capital asset pricing model, beta is the sole asset-specific or portfolio-specific factor. At any given time the forecasts for the risk-free rate and the market premium are the same for every asset or portfolio. Beta alone links the investor's expectations of returns from the asset or portfolio with his or her expectations of returns from the market. Because beta is such a crucial element in the CAPM, its estimation must be accurate.

In this chapter we will look at what we know about estimating beta. To develop a beta forecast, practitioners and academics often extrapolate from history often using some form of regression analysis. Using historical data and regression analysis presents two main problems. The first problem is determining the best way to capture the important information contained in history. In this chapter we will examine the various methods used to calculate beta from historical data. Specifically, we will look at the effect that using different time periods, indexes, risk-free rates, estimation techniques, and holding periods has on beta estimates.

The second problem is the uncertainty over whether a historical beta is useful in forecasting risk. This problem is usually labeled *beta stability*. We will look at whether changes in beta (its instability) are the result of statistical problems or whether changes in beta represent true changes in the underlying risk of the asset. Thus, we will attempt to answer the question, Is a historically based beta stable enough to use as a proxy for expectations? We will conclude the chapter by considering some of the innovative ways developed by academics and practitioners to get better approximations of investors' expectations of an asset's (usually a stock's) systematic risk. In particular, we will look at some attempts that have been made to discover the underlying determinants of beta and to use those factors to predict beta.

Once again, the discussion will neither describe every piece of research nor summarize every article. Rather, this chapter will provide examples of what seem to be some of the most interesting and relevant work that has been done in the area.

To have some idea of the difficulties in making beta estimates, we need only look at the differences among betas estimated by popular beta services. *Beta services* are commercially available lists of betas produced by investment advisory services. Most of the betas shown in Exhibit 4–1 are from beta services and were calculated using historical returns. The exceptions are those provided by Wilshire and Barr Rosenberg Associates. These services use other firm-related historical data to calculate betas. The stocks whose betas are shown were arbitrarily chosen from the available data. Southern California Edison is interesting in that, in 1974, it was estimated to have above-average risk by Merrill Lynch and average risk by Value Line, Rosenberg, and Wilshire. The exhibit vividly demonstrates just how different beta estimates can be from different services, for different stocks, and at different points in time.

We might question the usefulness of beta when such different estimates can be made at the same point in time. Peterson (1972) did so and compared the betas published by four commercial producers—Levy, Value Line, Merrill Lynch, and Oliphant. He ranked the betas from each source and provided the rank-order correlations shown in Exhibit 4–2. A perfect correlation would be 1.00, and that would imply that each stock is ranked by the first service precisely as it is ranked by the second. Any correlation of less than 1.00 shows less than perfect agreement among the advisory services. Thus, we can see from Exhibit 4–2 that Merrill Lynch and Levy estimate the same ranking (but not the same beta) 56 percent of the time. Thus, not only beta but beta rankings can vary from one service to another.

It is important to note at this point that the behavior of beta is of interest to those who wish to test the ability of beta to explain returns

Exhibit 4-1

Betas Calculated by Investment Services for Selected Stocks

JANUARY 1974

	Merrill-Lynch (Adjusted)		Market Model (Adjusted)		Historical	Barr Rosenberg		Value Line
						Short-Term Fundamental	Long-Term Fundamental	
American Airlines	2.04	(1.69)	2.11	(1.01)	2.12	2.35	2.22	2.26
American Cyanamid	0.99	(1.00)	0.97	(0.98)	0.98	1.01	1.03	1.08
Houston Industries	1.08	(1.05)	1.12	(1.00)	1.21	1.12	1.10	0.77
San Diego Gas and Electric	0.99	(0.99)	0.98	(0.99)	1.03	0.87	0.90	0.73
Southern California Edison	1.33	(1.22)	1.33	(1.02)	1.32	0.99	0.99	0.98
					DECEMBER 1972			
American Airlines	1.53	(1.35)	1.15	(0.77)	1.41	1.67	1.60	1.45
American Cyanamid	1.04	(0.84)	0.84	(0.76)	0.95	0.95	0.98	1.05
Houston Industries	1.00	(1.00)	0.69	(0.73)	1.05	1.08	0.98	0.90
San Diego Gas and Electric	0.61	(0.74)	0.48	(0.66)	0.65	0.82	0.88	0.70
Southern California Edison	0.72	(0.81)	0.52	(0.67)	0.72	0.82	0.84	0.80

Source: Diana P. Harrington, "Whose Beta Is Best?" *Financial Analysts Journal*, 39 (July–August 1983), 3.

Exhibit 4–2

Beta Rank-Order Correlations

	LEVY	VALUE LINE	MERRILL LYNCH	OLIPHANT
Levy	1.00	.61	.56	.48
Value Line		1.00	.77	.74
Merrill Lynch			1.00	.85
Oliphant				1.00

Source: D. Peterson, "Suggests Caution in the Use of Betas," *Financial Analysts Journal,* 28 (May–June 1972), 104.

(particularly realized returns), to forecast rates of return, or to evaluate investment portfolios. A review of the assumptions described in Chapter 2 shows that beta is present in the CAPM, but only as a measure of systematic risk—we do not have to restrict the behavior of beta to derive the CAPM.

I. BETA BASICS

Returns for any security are not "caused" by the market. Rather, returns are driven by macroeconomic events. The effect that these economic events have on investors' expectations will depend on three main factors:

1. The responsiveness of the asset's or portfolio's returns to economic events. This responsiveness is measured as the covariance of the asset's rate of return with that of the market [covariance (R_j, R_m)].
2. The relationship of the firm's basic characteristics (such as its debt level) with the average characteristics of firms in the market [covariance (R_j, R_m)].
3. The general uncertainty attached by investors to macroeconomic events (such as changes in the level of oil prices), described as the variance of the market (R_m).

The expected beta for a firm will change if any of the underlying relationships change. For example, if the firm increases its leverage relative to that of the market or undertakes unusually risky ventures, the change would be a real change in the systematic risk of the firm and should be reflected in beta.

Mathematically, beta is

$$\beta_j = \frac{\text{covariance } (R_j, R_m)}{\text{variance } (R_m)}$$

where

$\text{variance } (R_m)$ = the uncertainty attached to economic events

$\text{covariance } (R_j, R_m)$ = the responsiveness of an asset's rate of return (R_j) to those things that also change the market's rate of return (R_m)

j = an asset, stock, or portfolio

m = the market

Covariance itself is defined as $\rho_{jm}, \sigma_j, \sigma_m$

where

ρ_{jm} = the correlation coefficient, a measure of the correlation of the returns of j with the returns of m

σ = the standard deviation of the returns

The mathematical relationship is fairly simple, but each variable is expectational. Much of the difficulty we have had in estimating beta has come as a result of compromise—of our using inadequate proxies for expectational factors. Most often the proxy has been the historical relationship of the stock's rate of return to that of a broad-based index of common stock returns.

Using common stock returns represents a major compromise, and using an index that represents only a portion of the stock market is a further compromise. The market portfolio should be a collection of all risky assets, but common stocks represent only one portion of the universe. While Chapter 6 will discuss this problem further, at this point it is useful to note that since data on common stock returns comes in machine-readable form and thus lends itself to use in computerized studies, much of the focus of CAPM empirical research has been directed toward explaining common stock returns.

Basic Regression Technique

The simplest way to examine the historical relationship between the returns from any asset and those from the market is simply to plot the relationship over time. Exhibit 4-3 illustrates this method. At every

Exhibit 4–3

Security Characteristic Line

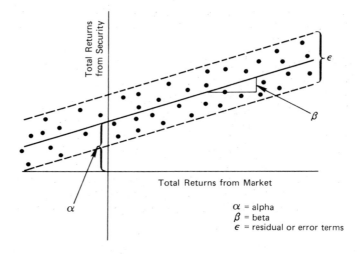

α = alpha
β = beta
ε = residual or error terms

point in time (every interval), the return from the asset and that from the market are represented by a dot on the chart. To convert all the dots to a more manageable descriptive relationship, we could fit a line to the data. This line is called the *security characteristic line*. Now we can describe the relationship by using the formula for a line ($y = a + bx$), the relationship that most of us learned in eighth-grade geometry.

The best-fitting line is one that will minimize the distance that each dot is from the line—the line that minimizes the squared errors. Thus, the method is called a *least-squares regression*. The intercept (a in the formula) is the minimum return from the asset if the return from the market were zero.[1] The slope (b) is the incremental return expected from the asset as the market return becomes higher or lower.

Although this is the basic regression technique, those estimating beta from history use a somewhat more elegant version of the formula for a straight line. This version is called the *market model* and is written as follows:[2]

$$R_{jt} = \alpha_j + \beta_j R_{mt} + \epsilon_j$$

[1]Here we have plotted the total returns from the market and the asset. If we had plotted the excess returns, each asset's and the market's returns less the risk-free rate of return, the line would have gone through the origin and the alpha would have been zero.
[2]This is the total return version of the market model. It can also be written $R_{jt} - R_{ft} = \alpha_j + \beta_j(R_{mt} - R_{ft}) + \epsilon_j$, which is the risk-premium version, where R_f would be the risk-free rate of return.

where

R = total returns[3]

j = a firm or portfolio

t = the time period

m = the market

α = the intercept (or alpha) of the linear regression: the minimum return from the asset when the market return was zero (over all firms and over time the intercept should equal 0)

ϵ = the errors or the residuals (assumed to be normally distributed without any remaining information)

β = the systematic risk (beta), the slope of the line

Because the market model and the CAPM look remarkably alike, many people presume that they are the same. They are not. The market model does not rely on any of the assumptions inherent in the CAPM. It simply states that the returns-generating process is a linear relationship between the returns from the asset and the returns from the market.

In relying on historical data, these regression techniques assume that history is an accurate predictor of the future. The assumption may or may not be true. Just how useful is history? To get some perspective on this question, let us look at two sets of betas calculated using the market model.

Exhibit 4–4 shows the results of plotting the total market returns (using the S&P 500 as a proxy) against the total returns (dividends plus capital gains) from American Telephone and Telegraph (AT&T) from January 1974 to December 1979. Once again, each piece of data is represented by a dot. We could use our own judgment or a computer to fit a line to the dots. Mathematically, the resulting line would be

$$R_{ATT} = 0.432 + 0.575 \, (R_m)$$

Exhibit 4–5 provides the same sort of data for AT&T from 1980 to 1984. This plot does not follow the distinct pattern that the earlier AT&T plot followed. It would be much more difficult to fit a line confidently. However, using the linear-regression package available on all but the simplest calculators, we can calculate a beta. The question is, How useful

[3]Least-squares analysis works best when the independent and dependent variables are normally distributed. Unfortunately, both the risk-free rates of return and the market returns tend to be nonnormal.

Exhibit 4-4

Returns of AT&T vs. Returns of S&P 500, 1974-79

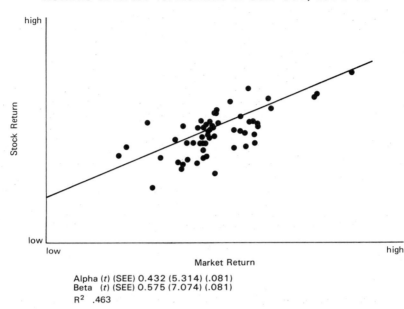

Alpha (*t*) (SEE) 0.432 (5.314) (.081)
Beta (*t*) (SEE) 0.575 (7.074) (.081)
R^2 .463

are these AT&T data in making a forecast for the future? And how useful were the earlier AT&T data? Clearly, changes in the AT&T returns had a closer relationship to changes in the market returns from 1974 to 1979 than they did from 1980 to 1984.

We need not look solely at the plotted data to determine the quality of the results. Using some simple tests, we can tell a great deal about the quality of the regression results. For instance, we can estimate the standard error of the estimated (SEE) beta or alpha. The standard error is like a standard deviation and gives us some idea of how much in error our estimate may be. For instance, if we had a beta of 0.80 and a standard error of 0.3, we could be more than 99 percent confident that the true beta lay in the range of 1.70 to −0.10.[4]

Furthermore, we can also determine the degree of confidence we have in the alpha, the beta, and the entire regression (the *t* and *F* tests) and can determine whether important factors have been omitted (the

[4]This is ±3 standard deviations from the mean. Basic statistics and finance texts provide explanations of the normal distribution and the use of standard deviation.

Exhibit 4–5

Returns of AT&T vs. Returns of S&P 500, 1980–84

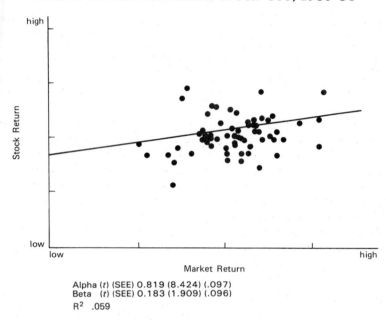

Alpha (*t*) (SEE) 0.819 (8.424) (.097)
Beta   (*t*) (SEE) 0.183 (1.909) (.096)
R^2 .059

Durbin-Watson test).[5] We can also describe how much of the activity of the dependent variable (here, our stock returns) was explained by the independent variable (the market returns)—that is, how well the line fits the data. The measure that describes this association is called the *coefficient of determination,* or R^2. If all the stock-return variation were coincident with market-return changes, the R^2 would be 1.00. Smaller explanatory power would result in a lower R^2. As you can see in Exhibits 4-4 and 4-5, the more dispersed the dots, the lower the R^2.

    The earlier AT&T data have a very good fit; the points are close to the line. AT&T's R^2 of 0.46 is unusually high for a single stock. The AT&T data for the early 1980s, however, are widely spread and the R^2 of 0.06 is very low. This figure means that almost none of the movements of AT&T's returns during this period were related to market changes. This

    [5]For a simple description of these test procedures, see basic statistics textbooks, for example, S. E. Wheelwright and S. Makridakis, *Forecasting Methods for Management,* 2d ed. (New York: John Wiley Interscience, 1980).

makes sense. During the early 1980s, AT&T underwent major changes. Its regulated businesses—with the exception of its long-distance business—were divested, its other markets were opened to significant competition, and the investing public became uncertain about what effect these changes would have on the company. While the divestment did not occur until January 1984, the fact that such a divestiture would occur was known much earlier. Thus, over this period, virtually all the returns were determined by nonsystematic factors and events. History provided some information about AT&T prior to 1980 but few clues about AT&T's future systematic risk in 1984.

The AT&T example is one that is especially interesting. Prior to the order to restructure itself, AT&T's stock had one of the most stable betas of all companies. It was a textbook example. If, however, in the early 1980s, you had used history to predict the future, without knowledge of the changed circumstances of the company, you could have made a major error.

The beta calculated for an average stock has an R^2 of about 0.30. Perhaps we should be pleased that the market "explains" as much as 30 percent of the variance of a typical stock. By itself, this finding is significant but not surprising. Nevertheless, at least 70 percent remains to be explained. The question is, What else drives the price of individual securities? This question will be addressed later in this chapter, for we have not completed our examination of the problems in estimating beta from the history of returns.

Practical Problems in Regression Methodology

As we have seen, one of the conceptual problems in using regression analysis is the assumption that historical data can help us predict the future. But the technique also has some practical problems: the results can vary widely, depending on our choice of input data.

In early work, Jacob (1971) found that betas generated using the market model depended on three factors: the historical period over which the beta was estimated, the average market return during the period studied, and whether the investor actually used the market model as a method for estimating betas. Since Jacob's work, several other factors have been identified: the market proxy chosen, the measurement intervals used within the holding period, and the form of the market model used. To calculate a historical beta, we must make choices for each of these factors. Let us look at the differences that can result when different choices are made for each factor.

Measurement period

The length of time over which we calculate beta is important. The measurement or holding period must be long enough to allow a statistically significant sample, but it must not be so long as to include information that does not reflect the relationships likely to persist into the future.

What is the effect of different holding-period choices? Breen and Lerner (1972) looked specifically at this question. They calculated betas for a number of stocks by using the market model (simple linear regression), with monthly intervals. Exhibit 4-6 shows their results for IBM using the New York Stock Exchange Index for "the market." The betas change significantly as the holding period lengthens. They found similar results for other firms.

One further demonstration of the problem is of interest. Using data from the C. I. Mortgage Group, a firm that eventually declared bankruptcy, Peseau (1977) calculated betas for overlapping periods. We would expect the beta for 1971-74 and that for 1971-75 to be very similar because the latter period includes only one more year of data. Exhibit 4-7, however, demonstrates that the beta for 1971-74 differs dramatically from that for 1971-75. Of course, the low R^2 associated with the 1971-74 beta makes us suspicious of the 1971-74 results. The beta shift among periods with higher R^2s is, nonetheless, dramatic.

Exhibit 4-6

Empirical Beta Estimates for IBM

HOLDING PERIOD IN MONTHS	ALPHA	BETA
6	0.0079	2.2001
12	0.0251	1.1911
18	0.0394	0.9093
24	0.0398	1.0746
30	0.0847	0.7515
36	0.1241	0.5575
42	0.1453	0.4886
48	0.1293	0.3798
54	0.1384	0.4603
60	0.1889	0.4745
66	0.1418	0.8779
72	0.1295	0.7903
78	0.1508	0.4942
84	0.1209	0.6196

Source: W. J. Breen and E. H. Lerner, "On the Use of Beta in Regulatory Proceedings," *Bell Journal of Economics and Management Science,* Autumn 1972, p. 620.

Exhibit 4-7

Betas for C. I. Mortgage Group

TIME PERIOD	INTER-CEPT TERM	(t-VALUE)	BETA	(t-VALUE)	R^2
1971-73	−.013	(− .38)	0.6	(1.96)*	.17
1971-74	−.045	(−1.96)	0.6	(1.29)	.04
1971-75	.010	(− .43)	2.6	(4.28)*	.32
1972-75	−.008	(− .29)	3.0	(4.69)*	.35
1972-76	−.016	(− .63)	3.0	(4.89)*	.33

*Indicates significance.

Source: D. Peseau, "Direct Testimony before the Public Utility Commissioner, State of Oregon in the Matter of Portland General Electric Co." (Oregon Docket No. UF-3339, September 1977).

The length of the holding period does affect the beta. Again, the bad news is that the CAPM does not help us in choosing the appropriate holding period. History, as always, is a difficult proxy for the future. Alexander and Chervany (1980), studying beta stability, estimated the optimal interval over which to calculate a beta. Using data from 1950–67, they found smaller absolute errors were associated with a six-year horizon, although they were insignificantly different from four years, as shown in Exhibit 4-8. While these results are, of course, subject to verification for different time periods and samples,[6] many had previously believed, from a statistical point of view, that the longer the period the better the beta.

Interval choice

The length of the intervals within the chosen holding period can affect the beta estimate. For instance, we might use weekly, monthly, quarterly, or annual intervals within the chosen period. Many experts contend that the interval is irrelevant; however, Levhari and Levy (1977) demonstrated that the betas estimated using different intervals are different. Using data from 1948–68, they calculated betas for a number of stocks using intervals of from 1 to 30 months. Their results are shown in Exhibit 4-9. The betas for most of the stocks change considerably as the interval lengthens. Others, for instance Phillips and Segal (1975), found similar results.

[6]For different results see, for instance, Nicholas Gonedes, "Evidence on the Information Content of Accounting Numbers: Accounting-Based and Market-Based Estimates of Systematic Risk," *Journal of Financial and Quantitative Analysis,* 8 (June 1973), 407–43; and Jerome Baesel, "On the Assessment of Risk: Some Further Considerations," *Journal of Finance,* 29 (December 1974), 1491–94.

Exhibit 4–8

Means and Absolute Errors–Beta Forecasts

PENTILE	ESTIMATION INTERVAL				
	1 Year	2 Years	4 Years	6 Years	9 Years
1: Mean	−2.2891	−1.7272	−1.2204	− .4833	− .3740
MAD	2.4978	2.1435	1.7078	.7805	1.1480
2: Mean	− .6746	− .2531	− .2869	− .3599	− .0235
MAD	1.2616	1.0734	1.2523	.7221	1.1764
3: Mean	.0147	− .1088	− .1982	− .0732	.4374
MAD	1.1390	1.1751	1.4893	.6650	1.5144
4: Mean	.6190	.5123	.1920	.2487	.1622
MAD	1.4024	1.4212	1.6673	.8802	1.6028
5: Mean	2.1760	1.0354	.5002	.8189	1.7987
MAD	2.5991	2.0068	1.7991	1.0149	2.3389
Overall:					
Mean	− .0308	− .1083	− .2027	− .0302	.4002
MAD	1.7800	1.5640	1.5831	.8125	1.5561
H Tests:					
Mean	1135.22*	295.21*	63.84*	67.19*	29.86*
MAD	453.35*	108.84*	17.61*	14.20*	24.07*

*Significant at the 5 percent level.

Source: Gordon J. Alexander and N. L. Chervany, "On the Estimation and Stability of Beta," *Journal of Financial and Quantitative Analysis,* 15 (March 1980), 129.

More recently, Hawawini (1983) estimated daily, weekly, biweekly, triweekly, and monthly betas over the period 1970-73. As shown in Exhibit 4-10 he found them to be quite different. Hawawini speculated as to why this occurred. He believed that, in general, companies whose shares had large market values would have betas that would increase as the interval was shortened. Betas of companies with smaller equity market values would decline as the interval shortened. In part, this movement had to do with whether their betas led or lagged the market.

Perhaps even more interesting than the interval problem is another problem that was first discovered in 1972 during a regulatory commission hearing considering the Communications Satellite Corporation (COMSAT). In that case, two expert witnesses calculated betas for COMSAT that would be used to establish comparable risk classes for estimating COMSAT's cost of equity. Each expert witness used the same interval (monthly) and the same total period (five years). Yet their beta estimates were not the same. The cause of the discrepancy, they discovered, was that one had used data from the third week of each month to calculate beta, whereas the other had used data from the fourth week.

A beta can be very sensitive to the interval chosen for the regres-

Exhibit 4-9

The Estimate of the Systematic Risk of Ten Defensive Stocks

HORIZON (IN MONTHS)	IDAHO POWER CORP.	AMERICAN CAN CAN CORP.	NATIONAL DAIRY PRODUCTS	P. LORILLARD CORP.	AMERICAN TOBACCO	BORDEN, INC.	ABBOTT LABORATORY	STANDARD BRANDS	GREYHOUND CORP.
1	0.4282	0.5167	0.5281	0.6166	0.6296	0.6372	0.6576	0.6650	0.6752
2	0.4012	0.4886	0.4655	0.5711	0.4652	0.5912	0.5717	0.6147	0.6651
3	0.3796	0.3755	0.4475	0.3496	0.4993	0.5684	0.5892	0.5578	0.5773
4	0.3329	0.3311	0.3400	0.4881	0.3697	0.6142	0.5284	0.6397	0.5340
5	0.1881	0.2631	0.4428	0.2604	0.3283	0.3449	0.6319	0.4331	0.6709
6	0.3862	0.3402	0.4119	0.4253	0.3706	0.4330	0.3811	0.6112	0.5294
8	0.4322	0.0621	0.5309	0.4815	0.3020	0.4627	0.2398	0.7987	0.4907
10	0.2312	0.1236	0.4777	−0.0656	0.2438	0.4272	0.4729	0.5325	0.4800
12	0.2367	−0.0118	0.3511	−0.4615	0.0364	0.3390	0.4227	0.4289	0.6188
15	0.1556	0.0702	0.4544	−1.0612	−0.0365	−0.0561	0.1243	0.2008	0.1541
16	0.3016	0.2049	0.5016	−1.0387	0.1400	0.2723	0.1463	0.7473	0.1719
20	0.1142	−0.2563	0.3283	−1.1855	−0.1060	0.2336	0.0247	0.4002	0.2378
24	0.1068	−0.2690	0.3996	−2.0036	0.1657	0.0849	0.2474	0.3771	0.7826
30	0.2210	0.0101	0.2781	−2.8251	0.1187	0.1360	−0.3863	−0.0150	−0.5545

Source: D. Levhari and H. Levy, "The Capital Asset Pricing Model and the Investment Horizon," *Review of Economics and Statistics*, 59 (February 1977), 102.

Exhibit 4-10

Betas Estimated on the Basis of Various Return Intervals,* January 1970–December 1973

	MONTHLY BETA	TRI-WEEKLY BETA	BIWEEKLY BETA	WEEKLY BETA	DAILY BETA
Wayne-Gossard	0.976	0.692	0.986	0.654	0.459
Michigan Seamless Tube	0.973	0.883	0.917	0.784	0.433
Publicker Industries	1.521	1.491	1.513	1.277	1.006
Great Western United	2.496	2.311	2.122	1.911	1.442
Family Finance	1.268	1.324	1.212	0.821	0.795
Bobbie Brooks	1.874	1.889	1.818	1.592	1.405
Monogram Industries	2.950	2.887	2.844	2.403	2.144
Faberge	1.882	1.511	1.511	1.416	1.449
Dillingham Corp.	1.004	1.164	0.990	0.750	0.725
Vornado	2.329	1.628	2.170	1.823	1.765
Big Three Industries	1.339	0.970	1.283	0.969	0.712
Cabot Corp.	0.752	0.898	0.844	0.805	0.756
General Development	1.423	1.628	1.657	1.382	1.358
Addresso-Multigraph	2.094	2.341	1.566	1.414	1.733
Great Western Financial	2.246	1.820	2.043	2.158	1.917
Colgate-Palmolive	1.131	1.002	1.011	0.958	0.850
Aluminium Co. of America	1.115	1.221	1.118	1.150	1.118
Shell Oil	0.930	1.093	0.827	0.860	0.742
S.S. Kresge	1.190	1.326	1.299	1.308	1.237
Eastman Kodak	0.932	0.859	0.958	1.166	1.251

*Returns are measured as the logarithm of investment relatives. Market returns are those of the S&P 500. All betas are statistically significant at the 5 percent level.

Source: Gabriel Hawawini, "Why Beta Shifts as the Return Interval Changes," *Financial Analysts Journal,* 39 (May–June 1983), 74.

sion. The real difficulty is that we still must choose an estimation interval. Curiously enough, however, since we assumed all investors' horizons are identical, by choosing a particular interval we define the horizon of the market. In addition, we presume that over the horizon investors are not reallocating their portfolios; that is, they are not buying and/or selling their assets. However, the returns we are measuring are, in fact, driven by transactions that come as investors do reallocate their portfolios. Thus, we have direct evidence that all investors do not have the same horizon. How do we deal with such a conflict?

Since the CAPM gives us no guidelines for the choice of a horizon, those wishing to estimate a beta have looked elsewhere for direction. Sampling theory suggests that an adequate amount of data is needed to ensure a reasonably normal sample distribution. Since most of the hypotheses that are tested rest on the assumption of normalcy, as does the CAPM, sampling concerns (more is better) and computing constraints (less is better) have dictated the sample size. With the availability of monthly data in computer-readable form, and the need for a reasonably sized sample, the 60-observation, or five-year, estimation period became widely used. In fact it was so widely used many believed that it was *the* horizon. However, evidence about the importance of interval in the estimation of beta suggests that this standard may not be the best choice. We only know that we must have an adequate amount of data, without including old data that has little relevance to the current situation,[7] and to minimize the absolute deviations.

The market proxy

In earlier CAPM history, many believed that the index choice was not a particularly important issue.[8] Indexes were highly correlated;[9] hence, they were assumed to be virtually interchangeable.

Since that early lack of concern about choosing an index, our theoretical and statistical knowledge has become more sophisticated. We now know that if the proxy for the market is not fully diversified (is not a good reflection of the market for all risky assets), the market model will not properly distinguish between diversifiable and nondiversifiable risk. The result would be that we could have an informationless or wrong

---

[7]In addition, we must avoid some known problems, such as the Fisher effect: because some stocks are not widely traded, the end-of-week or end-of-the-day price can yield an inadequate estimate of the true price, thus biasing the estimated beta.

[8]See S. C. Myers, "The Application of Finance Theory to Public Utility Rate Cases," *Bell Journal of Economics and Management Science,* 3 (Spring 1972), 58–97.

[9]Remember that correlation is the degree of relationship between indexes. If returns moved together exactly, we would have a perfect correlation of 1.0. If they were perfectly negatively related, the correlation would be −1.0.

beta, or we could believe that nonsystematic risk was larger or smaller than it actually was. Correlation analysis was used in the past to rationalize index choice. But this method is not enough: two indexes could be highly correlated with each other and still not be correlated with the underlying market for all risky assets. Thus, finding a true proxy may be impossible, and tests using an incorrect index would be useless. A more important statement about the dangers of using widely acceptable but still incomplete indexes was made by Roll (1977).

Although these problems are disturbing, they may be more theoretical than practical. First, if all our available indexes yield approximately equivalent beta results or ranks, we can have some confidence in our results. Furthermore, indexes are what investors use as benchmarks, and thus they at least provide some practical information.

Therefore, the real question is whether the choice of index actually affects results. The data in Exhibit 4–11 provide a perspective on the practical side of the index question. Frankfurter (1976) used the Dow Jones Industrial Average (DJIA), the Standard & Poor 425, and a Scholes Value-Weighted Index in calculating betas. For some stocks, the beta estimates were quite similar; but for other stocks, they were not. We can see that the choice of an index is not only a theoretical problem but a practical one as well.

Stocks alone make up the indexes used by Frankfurter. Building a broader index is still in the experimental stage, although Sharpe (1973) gave us some idea of the changes that might occur as our sophistication

Exhibit 4–11

Alphas and Betas of Randomly Selected Securities

	GMI		S&P 425		DJIA		
	α	β	α	β	α	β	Mean Return
Cerro	−0.638	1.308	−0.270	1.612	−0.319	1.547	0.358
Falstaff Brewing	−1.426	1.028	−1.083	1.228	−1.132	1.116	−0.644
Graniteville	−0.425	1.051	−0.031	1.133	−0.136	1.169	0.375
Scott Foresman	−0.099	1.130	0.288	1.321	0.269	1.125	0.761
Hall WF	−0.202	0.695	0.002	0.909	−0.075	0.920	0.327
Gulf Oil	−0.236	0.528	−0.163	0.920	−0.201	0.840	0.167
Fedders	2.035	1.302	2.359	1.861	2.284	1.697	3.026
AMP	1.196	0.784	1.403	1.000	1.367	0.975	1.793
Chrysler	−0.747	1.107	−0.513	1.701	−0.628	1.657	0.096
Zayre	2.369	1.471	2.867	1.738	2.768	1.649	3.489

Source: G. M. Frankfurter, "The Effect of Market Indexes on the Ex-Post Performance of the Sharpe Portfolio Selection Model," *Journal of Finance,* 31 (June 1976), 953.

in creating indexes increases. Exhibit 4–12 shows the hypothetical differences suggested by Sharpe. The *PST* line is the hypothetical capital market line using stocks alone. The *PBC* line could be the line using bonds, and the *PMR* line could be the quite different result of using a combined stock-bond index. Sharpe suggests the combined indexes would result in a higher line.

While we have reasonable proxies for the stock market, we do not have the same for bonds (or for other assets), although money management organizations are developing more extensive indexes.[10] What is obvious is that there are clear differences among the markets, and, as the 1970s and 1980s have shown, each market changes over time.[11] Still data from the stock market, although limited in the assets they contain, are an available and widely used accommodation.

Exhibit 4–12

Opportunity Sets Using Different Indexes

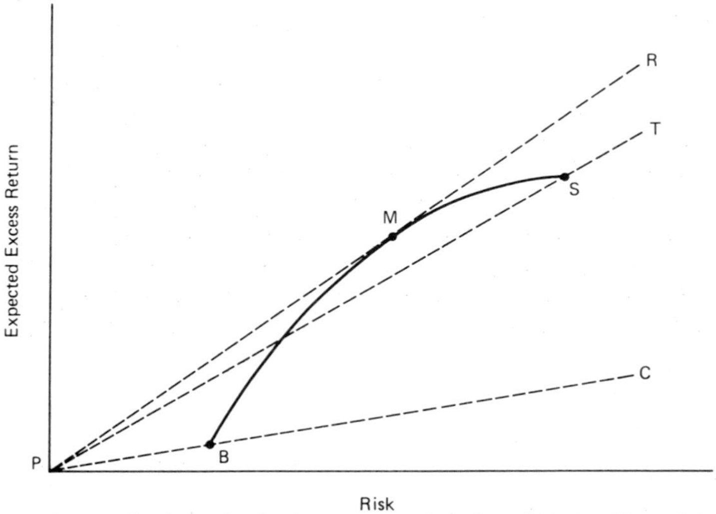

Risk

Source: W. F. Sharpe, "Bonds vs. Stocks: Some Lessons from Capital Market Theory," *Financial Analysts Journal,* 29 (November–December 1973), 75.

[10]See, for instance, First Chicago Bank's First Chicago Investment Advisors' Multiple Markets Index, which includes large and small capitalization, and international equities, venture capital, domestic and international dollar and nondollar bonds, real estate, and cash equivalents.

[11]The relative volatility of the bond markets since the mid-1970s has been markedly higher than the volatility previously experienced.

The market model form

There is little in the academic literature about the impact that different forms of the market model have on beta. If the form of the market model changes, all else staying the same, will the beta change? It should not.

There are a variety of versions of the market model. We have a simple market model:

$$R_j = \alpha_j + \beta_j R_m + \epsilon_j$$

We have the risk-premium version, where we could use anything from T-bills to AA utility bonds for R_f.

$$R_j - R_f = \alpha_j + \beta_j(R_m - R_f) + \epsilon_j$$

There is a less compact form of the risk-premium version:

$$R_j = \alpha_j + \beta_{j1}(R_f) + \beta_{j2}R_m + \epsilon_j$$

If all of these market model forms are equivalent, the betas should be the same and the intercept terms should be equal. This means that the α_j of the simple model would be equal to the term α_j, $+ R_f$ of the risk-premium model and equal to the term $\alpha_j + \beta_{j1}(R_f)$ of the less compact risk-premium model.[12]

Exhibit 4–13 shows the results of using the different models in cal-

Exhibit 4–13

The Results of Three Versions of the Market Model for a Public Utility (Monthly Data)

	α	β_1*	β_2†	R^2
Simple model	−0.0027		0.544	.467
Risk-premium model‡	−0.0041		0.615	.378
Multifactor‡	−0.0043	0.17	0.612	.497

*Coefficient for R_f in the multifactor model.
†Coefficient for market volatililty factor.
‡R_f proxy is the return on Treasury bills.

Source: D. Harrington, "The Capital Asset Pricing Model and Regulated Utility Cost of Equity" (Ph.D. dissertation, 1978), 164.

[12]These models exist in both compound (geometric) form and arithmetic form. Because market returns are normally reported as compound rates of return, many prefer the geometric form.

culating betas for one utility. And neither the betas nor the intercepts are equal from model to model. These forms are all variations of the basic CAPM. None have been modified to deal directly with the problems of misspecification.

We have considered the results of changing some of the simple parameters that are necessary for estimating a beta using historical data. The choice of each input changes the output, and the size of the difference is enough to cause concern. How should betas be measured, using history? The disconcerting answer is that we do not know. Finding the best way to measure beta is not merely a theoretical problem; it is a practical one. The search still requires trial-and-error experimentation.

II. TESTING THE STABILITY OF HISTORICAL BETAS

Now that we have outlined some of the problems involved in measuring historical betas, let us return to the more fundamental issue of the usefulness of history in predicting the future. If historical betas are reasonable predictors of future betas, then we should definitely spend the time required to refine our statistical tools. If historical betas are not reasonable predictors, then we must look for a better way to make beta forecasts. Because the use of historical data to predict the future assumes that betas are stable over time, most tests of the usefulness of historical betas have focused on the issue of the stability of historical betas. If historical betas remain relatively unchanged over time, then historical betas may be useful surrogates for forecasted (ex ante) betas. If, however, historical betas vary over time, then they will have little predictive ability.

What are the results of tests of the stability of historical betas?

1. ANALYSIS OF INDIVIDUAL SECURITIES' BETAS

Bey (1983) used a sophisticated statistical approach to look at the stability of the betas of public utility and industrial stocks. Exhibit 4–14 shows some of his results for individual (not portfolios) utility stocks. For different industries, Exhibit 4–15 shows mean betas and the proportion that were stationary. Note that the ordinary-least-squares (OLS) betas change quite dramatically from period to period—they were not stable.

The average beta is an imprecise estimate. Blume (1971) reported that although the market's average beta was 1.0 (as we would expect), the average standard error (0.30) resulted in a 95 percent confidence in-

Exhibit 4–14

Beta and Market Model Stationarity

UTILITY NAME	ESTIMATED OLS BETAS			
	1/60–12/64	1/65–12/69	1/70–12/74	1/75–12/79
Consolidated Edison Co. N.Y. Inc.	0.59*	0.46*	0.55*	1.12*
Consolidated Natural Gas. Co.	0.59	0.61	0.39*	0.89
Consumers Power Co.	0.69	0.67	0.59*	1.04*
Dayton Power & Light Co.	0.76	0.99	0.39	0.78*
Delmarva Power & Light Co.	0.85	0.82	0.72*	0.75*
Detroit Edison Co.	0.64	0.50	0.55*	0.98*
Duquesne Light Co.	0.52	0.27	0.46	0.84*
El Paso Co.	0.69	0.54*	0.84*	1.00
Empire District Electric Co.	0.67	0.58	0.25*	0.57
Enserch Corp.	0.47	0.94*	1.02*	0.62

*Nonstationary beta for $\alpha = 0.05$.

Source: Roger P. Bey, "Market Model Stationarity of Individual Public Utilities," *Journal of Finance and Quantitative Analysis,* 18 (March 1983), 74.

terval from 0.4 to 1.6. (That is, one can be 95 percent sure that the average historical beta was between 0.4 and 1.6.) This could not be called a beta estimate made with confidence. Blume must also be credited for his finding that, over time, betas tend to drift toward the market average of 1.0. We are not now sure whether this movement is caused by true changes in the riskiness of the securities or by statistical problems, but the phenomenon is clear. Exhibit 4–16 shows the problem that Blume documented. From the first to the second period, each beta—with only one exception—becomes closer to 1.0.

As a result of this finding, called beta drift, several commercial beta producers began to adjust their forecasted betas toward 1.0 in an effort to improve their forecasts. However, Elgers, Haltiner, and Hawthorne (1979) believed that this beta drift was a statistical aberration and demonstrated that betas drift similarly toward 1.0, regardless of whether they are calculated moving forward or backward through time. Exhibit 4–17 shows their results. From periods 1 to 2 and from periods 2 to 1 their OLS and their Bayesian-adjusted betas drift toward 1.0. Thus, the drift appears to be a statistical aberration. It cannot be relied upon to help analysts to determine the stability of calculated historical betas or to adjust forecasts.

Exhibit 4-15
Mean β and Percentage of Securities with Market Model Nonstationarity

SIC CODE	NO. OF SECURITIES	MEAN BETA ESTIMATE				PERCENTAGE OF SECURITIES NONSTATIONARY*			
		1/60–12/64	1/65–12/69	1/70–12/74	1/75–12/79	1/60–12/64	1/65–12/69	1/70–12/74	1/75–12/79
10	11	0.57	0.78	0.86	0.97	18	18	36	36
20	32	0.94	1.04	0.93	1.00	34	13	28	47
22	10	0.96	1.41	1.06	1.37	50	0	20	70
26	14	1.10	1.15	1.03	1.19	29	21	36	57
28	42	1.22	1.17	1.07	1.06	29	19	36	38
29	18	0.82	0.89	0.99	0.80	44	44	22	39
30	12	1.16	1.26	1.08	1.20	50	33	58	58
32	16	1.08	1.47	1.07	1.34	38	44	25	56
33	27	1.17	1.27	1.05	1.21	30	22	19	44
34	14	1.03	1.24	0.97	1.29	36	43	14	43
35	41	1.17	1.28	1.16	1.32	24	22	41	34
36	29	1.36	1.30	1.24	1.35	38	10	48	48
37	34	1.04	1.45	1.11	1.52	24	24	38	41
38	10	1.34	1.38	1.33	1.42	40	20	10	50
40	10	1.16	1.07	1.09	1.03	40	20	30	30
45	10	1.61	1.72	1.80	1.62	40	30	10	50
49	89	0.71	0.63	0.65	0.78	21	17	41	62
53	13	0.86	1.09	1.14	1.21	23	8	31	69
67	21	0.93	1.18	0.99	1.09	24	33	38	57
Total	453					30	22	34	49

* α = 0.05.

Source: Roger P. Bey, "Market Model Stationarity of Individual Public Utilities," *Journal of Finance and Quantitative Analysis*, 18 (March 1983), 76.

Exhibit 4-16

Estimated Beta Coefficients for Portfolios of 100 Securities in Two Successive Periods

PORT-FOLIO	7/26– 6/33	7/33– 6/40	7/33– 6/40	7/40– 6/47	7/40– 6/47	7/47– 6/54	7/47– 6/54	7/54– 6/61	7/54– 6/61	7/61– 6/68
1	0.528	0.610	0.394	0.573	0.442	0.593	0.385	0.553	0.393	0.620
2	0.898	1.004	0.708	0.784	0.615	0.776	0.654	0.748	0.612	0.707
3	1.225	1.296	0.925	0.902	0.746	0.887	0.832	0.971	0.810	0.861
4			1.177	1.145	0.876	1.008	0.967	1.010	0.987	0.914
5			1.403	1.354	1.037	1.124	1.093	1.095	1.138	0.995
6					1.282	1.251	1.245	1.243	1.337	1.169

Source: M. Blume, "On the Assessment of Risk," *Journal of Finance*, 26 (March 1971), 7.

Exhibit 4-17

Portfolio Betas in Successive Time Periods

PORT-FOLIO NUMBER	PERIOD 1 (7/54-6/61)		PERIOD 2 (7/61-6/68)	PORT-FOLIO NUMBER	PERIOD 2 (7/61-6/68)		PERIOD 1 (7/54-6/61)
	OLS	Adjusted	OLS		OLS	Adjusted	OLS
1	0.381	0.522	0.592	1	0.393	0.515	0.558
2	0.581	0.676	0.634	2	0.566	0.653	0.709
3	0.774	0.825	0.780	3	0.727	0.782	0.825
4	0.950	0.962	0.872	4	0.855	0.884	0.921
5	1.093	1.072	0.940	5	0.974	0.980	1.149
6	1.252	1.194	1.061	6	1.139	1.111	1.177
7	1.621	1.480	1.286	7	1.510	1.408	1.315

Source: P. T. Elgers, J. R. Haltiner, and W. H. Hawthorne, "Beta Regression Tendencies: Statistical and Real Causes," Journal of Finance, 34 (March 1979), 262.

In another early study of beta stability, Meyers (1973) hypothesized that if the amount of variance explained by the market varied from one period to the next, then betas would not be stationary from one period to another. Exhibit 4–18 shows some of Meyers's results. The portfolio beta, as we would expect, was quite stable. Virtually the same variance occurred in both periods, showing that beta estimation errors canceled each other. For many individual securities, however, the amount of the returns' behavior explained by the market (the R^2) was quite different from period to period. For instance, Coca-Cola showed what Meyers would call instability.

In reviewing such results, one must use logic. To demonstrate Meyers's contention, let us graphically represent the variances for the Shell Oil Company stock, which is one of the stocks listed in Exhibit 4–18. To the left in Exhibit 4–19 are graphed the results for the first period: 34.6 percent of the changes in returns from this stock reflected the changes in market returns. The remainder of the changes in the stock's returns came from unsystematic sources—from factors specifically related to the firm or industry. Perhaps Shell had unexpected good fortune in securing

Exhibit 4–18

Percentage of Variance (R^2) Explained by First Principal Component (Market Factor) from Stock Price Relatives

COMPANY NAME	AUGUST 1952–AUGUST 1960	JANUARY 1961–DECEMBER 1967
Allegheny Power System	46.2	14.1
Allied Chemical	43.8	44.9
American Motors	5.2	15.3
American Tobacco Co.	11.0	40.7
Atchison, Topeka and Santa Fe	60.0	40.4
Chesapeake and Ohio	50.0	53.3
Coca-Cola	11.1	29.2
Consolidated Edison of NY	11.1	8.5
Detroit Edison	14.3	15.4
General Electric	34.3	27.6
IBM	25.8	45.9
ITT	37.8	46.2
Maytag	25.0	26.0
Pacific Gas and Electric	30.0	26.4
Shell Oil	34.6	6.3
Southern California Edison	17.9	22.9
Average of 94 companies	33.4	33.5

Source: Adapted from S. C. Meyers, "The Stationarity Problem in the Use of the Market Model of Security Price Behavior," *Accounting Review*, 48 (April 1973), 320.

Exhibit 4-19

Percentage of Total Risk from Systematic and Unsystematic Sources for Shell Oil Company

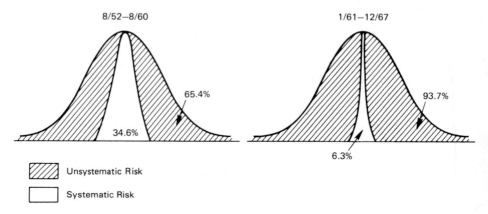

a new source of oil or reducing delivery costs. In the second period (graphed to the right), 6.3 percent of the changes were related to systematic factors. Does this result mean that the beta changed? There is no way to tell from these data. We can say that the returns from one company's stock were more influenced by marketwide forces in one period than in another, but we can say nothing about the beta.

Meyer's results showed that the portfolio beta was relatively stable. Blume (1971, 1975) and Porter and Ezzell (1975) also looked at the stability of portfolios. Using two different methods for forming portfolios, they had what appeared to be conflicting results: increasing the size of the portfolio may or may not increase the stability of beta. After correcting for the different ways in which Blume and Porter and Ezzell created their portfolios, Alexander and Chervany (1980) found that their results were not in conflict—beta was more stable in more diversified portfolios. In addition, they found that most of the improvement in beta stability occurred by the point where there were ten securities in the portfolio. Added securities lent small improvements.

Thus, it appears that portfolio betas are relatively stable, and, by inference, easier to predict than the betas for individual stocks.

2. ANALYZING RISK CLASSES

Another way of assessing beta stability is to look at beta rankings. The hypothesis is that if the firm stays in the same beta class from period to period, betas could be said to be relatively stable and thus reasonable predictors. Blume (1971) used two similar methods of ranking the betas to test for stability. Looking at the last column in Exhibit 4-20, we can see the results of his test for the period 1954-61 versus the period 1961-68. Portfolios with only one security remained in the same risk class 62 percent of the time. This means that 38 percent of the stocks changed risk class. This is a stronger result than those obtained from studies that found betas for individual securities were unstable. Larger portfolios were more apt to remain in the same risk class and portfolios with 50 securities had very accurate risk rankings; only 3 percent of these portfolios changed rank between the two periods. Of further interest is the fact that Blume found virtually no shares that moved in a direction opposite to that of the market (there were almost no negative correlations).

Baesel (1974), using another technique called a *transition matrix*, further tested the stability of risk classes. Baesel classified securities into five risk classes and then tested them in the next period to see whether the securities remained in the same risk class. Exhibit 4-21 shows his transition matrix, indicating the stability of securities' risk classes from one period to the next. Each number in the table represents the frequency with which securities fell into a single risk group in both periods. For instance, 12 percent of the securities in class 1, period *t*, remained in class 1 for the next period (*t* + 1). Conversely, 88 percent of those in class 1 in the first period changed to a different class in the following period. Baesel himself characterized his results as strong enough to say that betas for single securities were not random, but that is all. Admittedly, Baesel's grouping technique does have some problems. Because classes 1 and 5 include all those falling outside the three central classes, the range is broad. The information regarding the three central classes is more reliable. Confirming this suspicion, Alexander and Chervany found, in a closer examination of the behavior of the betas in the extreme groups, that "larger changes in the beta occurred in the extreme pentiles than in the interior pentiles for all but one case."[13]

In both Blume's and Baesel's tests, betas for randomly generated portfolios were more stable than were betas for individual securities. Others have confirmed these results.[14]

[13]Gordon J. Alexander, and N. L. Chervany, "On the Estimation and Stability of Beta," *Journal of Financial and Quantitative Analysis,* 15 (March 1980), 125.

[14]R. C. Klemkosky and J. D. Martin, "The Adjustment of Beta Forecasts," *Journal of Finance,* 30 (September 1975), 1123-28, used standard errors for the betas rather than beta levels in testing various-sized portfolios. They showed that the standard errors decreased as the portfolio size increased. This result indicates that betas for larger portfolios captured or explained more of the historical variation. R. Burr Porter and J. R. Ezzell, in "A Note on the Predictive Ability of Beta Coefficients," *Journal of Business Research,* 3 (October 1975), 365-71, also studied the question.

Exhibit 4-20

Product Moment and Rank-Order Correlation of Betas for Portfolios of N Securities

NUMBER OF SECURITIES PER PORT- FOLIO	7/26–6/33 and 7/33–6/40		7/33–6/40 and 7/40–6/47		7/40–6/47 and 7/47–6/54		7/47–6/54 and 7/54–6/61		7/54–6/61 and 7/61–6/68	
	P.M.	Rank	P.M.	Rank	P.M.	Rank	P.M.	Rank	P.M.	Rank
1	0.63	0.69	0.62	0.73	0.59	0.65	0.65	0.67	0.60	0.62
2	0.71	0.75	0.76	0.83	0.72	0.79	0.76	0.76	0.73	0.74
4	0.80	0.84	0.85	0.90	0.81	0.89	0.84	0.84	0.84	0.85
7	0.86	0.90	0.91	0.93	0.88	0.93	0.87	0.88	0.88	0.89
10	0.89	0.93	0.94	0.95	0.90	0.95	0.92	0.93	0.92	0.93
20	0.93	0.99	0.97	0.98	0.95	0.98	0.95	0.96	0.97	0.98
35	0.96	1.00	0.98	0.99	0.95	0.99	0.97	0.98	0.97	0.97
50	0.98	1.00	0.99	0.98	0.98	0.99	0.98	0.98	0.98	0.97

Source: M. Blume, "On the Assessment of Risk," Journal of Finance, 26 (March 1971), 7.

Exhibit 4-21

Twelve-Month Estimation Interval Transition Matrix

RISK CLASS	RISK CLASS PERIOD t + 1				
PERIOD t	1	2	3	4	5
1	.12	.16	.17	.21	.34
2	.15	.21	.22	.21	.23
3	.18	.18	.23	.21	.13
4	.22	.23	.19	.21	.12
5	.33	.22	.19	.14	.12

Source: J. Baesel, "On the Assessment of Risk: Some Further Considerations," *Journal of Finance,* 29 (December 1974), 1492.

3. ANALYZING STANDARD ERRORS

Klemkosky and Martin (1975) examined what caused the size of errors to decrease as the number of securities in randomly generated portfolios increased. They broke the mean-squared error into three portions: bias, inefficiency, and randomness. *Bias* indicates that a prediction overestimates or underestimates the actual result. *Inefficiency* indicates that a prediction has positive errors for low betas and negative errors for high betas. *Random* errors are the unexplainable errors.

In Exhibit 4-22 we see that the betas of Klemkosky and Martin's random portfolios for July 1962–June 1967 versus July 1967–June 1972 showed little bias but significant inefficiency. Most prediction errors tended to be correlated with the beta: for low-beta stocks, the betas over-forecast the actual result, whereas for high-beta stocks, the betas were underforecasts. Random errors decreased as the portfolio size increased, because random errors could offset one another in larger portfolios.[15]

Klemkosky and Martin tested a variety of adjustment techniques that practitioners were using to reduce the portion of the error ascribable to inefficiency. Exhibit 4-23 shows their results. The Bayesian adjustment, tested by Klemkosky and Martin, combined the beta estimated for the security with the average beta for a group of firms similar to the firm issuing the security in question. For instance, if we were predicting

---

[15]This same mean-squared error technique has been used to measure the effect of the length of the estimation period on the quality of the forecast. Eubank and Zumwalt found that the longer the period and the larger the portfolio, the smaller the mean-squared error. The improvement was largely due to increased efficiency. See Arthur A. Eubank, Jr., and J. K. Zumwalt, "Impact of Alternative Length Estimation and Prediction Periods on the Stability of Security and Portfolio Betas," *Journal of Business Research,* 9 (September 1981), 321–25.

Exhibit 4-22

Source of the Mean-Squared Errors in Beta Predictions, July 1962–June 1967 vs. July 1967–June 1972

	PORTFOLIO SIZE (NUMBER OF SECURITIES)				
	1	3	5	7	10
MSE	.16122	.08363	.06880	.05982	.05465
Portions of MSE due to:					
Bias	.00093	.00100	.00093	.00097	.00119
Inefficiency	.03992	.03947	.03993	.03975	.03800
Random errors	.12036	.04314	.02792	.01908	.01545

Source: Adapted from R. C. Klemkosky and J. D. Martin, "The Adjustment of Beta Forecasts," *Journal of Finance*, 30 (September 1975), 1125.

an electric utility's beta, our choice might be the average beta for all utilities or that for Moody's 24 Electrics. The Blume adjustment combines the current beta estimate with the prior-period betas. The "MLPFS" is the Merrill Lynch technique of weighting the calculated beta with the market beta of one.

As we can see, Blume's technique reduces inefficiency, and the Bayesian adjustment reduces bias. On the whole, however, the total error is largely caused by random errors, and little besides increasing the portfolio size can be done about that. The law of large numbers is of slight comfort to those evaluating individual securities.

An active portfolio manager might like to know how many securities it takes to control ex ante portfolio betas, to, say, ±2 percent of their weighted average. The surprising answer is that it takes more securities to control beta mismeasurement than to control unsystematic risk in terms of their impact on portfolios. The number is about 800—a number large enough to seriously dilute any benefits from active management.

Randomly composed portfolios reduce beta instability. Is this statement also true for structured portfolios? Beta reliability and stability, of course, improve, but not as much as they improve by randomly composed portfolios. The practical problems of beta instability, in short, remain serious for the practicing manager with active management objectives for his or her portfolio.

Beta is unstable, as much of the evidence clearly shows. In fact, a number of researchers, using quite different methods for estimating beta, have found that much of the regression error (the residual risk), and the relationship between the residual risk and beta, may come from misestimating a nonstationary beta.

Exhibit 4-23

Forecast Errors of Adjusted Versus Unadjusted Beta Coefficients

	INDIVIDUAL SECURITIES				PORTFOLIOS (SIZE TEN)			
	Unadjusted	Bayesian	Blume's	MLPFS	Unadjusted	Bayesian	Blume's	MLPFS
Period 2								
Mean Square Error (MSE)	.18387	.13111	.11123	.11015	.08544	.03460	.01259	.01153
Portion of MSE due to:								
Bias	.00084	.00004	.00183	.00075	.00095	.00006	.00178	.00072
Inefficiency	.07367	.02372	.00004	.00004	.07370	.02355	.00002	.00002
Random error	.10935	.10735	.10936	.10936	.01078	.01100	.01078	.01078
Period 3								
Mean Square Error (MSE)	.12385	.11609	.12207	.12293	.02332	.01356	.02155	.02238
Portion of MSE due to:								
Bias	.00018	.00011	.00000	.00087	.00018	.00011	.00000	.00083
Inefficiency	.00730	.00043	.00571	.00571	.00725	.00047	.00567	.00567
Random error	.11636	.11555	.11636	.11636	.01587	.01298	.01587	.01587
Period 4								
Mean Square Error (MSE)	.16122	.13082	.14660	.14934	.05465	.02018	.04215	.04485
Portion of MSE due to:								
Bias	.00093	.00000	.00263	.00537	.00119	.00000	.00252	.00522
Inefficiency	.03992	.00981	.02361	.02361	.03800	.00980	.02418	.02418
Random error	.12036	.12101	.12036	.12036	.01545	.01037	.01545	.01546

Source: R. C. Klemkosky and J. D. Martin, "The Adjustment of Beta Forecasts," *Journal of Finance*, 30 (September 1975), 1127.

Typically we have estimated beta from history, using a fixed-coefficient model like ordinary-least-squares regression. These models estimate one beta over time. Using a time-varying model, one where the beta is allowed to vary over time, Chen (1981) found that "the use of the OLS method (or fixed-coefficient model) will overestimate the portfolio residual risk if individual security beta coefficients are changing over time."[16] Once Chen removed the beta variability from the residual risk, the residual risks were stationary and the relationship between residual risk and beta was eliminated.[17]

The time-varying models do appear to eliminate some of the problems that unstable betas create. As for creating a beta coefficient that can be used to estimate future returns, however, these models have their limitations.

Kryzanowski and To (1984) believe that much of the cause of beta instability is not real instability at all. They suggest that estimates of betas using time-series analysis of historic data rely on the past returns, whereas beta is a function of the expected return. Thus, they say that "betas estimated using ex-post return data can be expected to exhibit intertemporal non-stationarity, even when the underlying ex-ante security returns are serially independent and obey a stationary distribution over time."[18]

4. STABILITY OF CORRELATION COEFFICIENTS

A correlation coefficient (R) is an ingredient needed to estimate a beta. If the correlation coefficient is unpredictable, then researchers believe that it would be difficult to say that the beta is stable or predictable. Elton, Gruber, and Urich (1978) looked at six methods of estimating the correlation coefficients. They did not break their results down into error components, as Klemkosky and Martin did, but they did test some interesting methods of predicting correlations. The methods tested, which were different from those in the Klemkosky-Martin study, were the following:

1. The overall mean, a simple average correlation coefficient for the stocks included in the test

[16]Son-Nan Chen, "Beta Nonstationarity, Portfolio Residual Risk and Diversification," *Journal of Financial and Quantitative Analysis,* 16 (March 1981), 95–112.
[17]For a study using another technique to adjust betas and reduce residual error, see Lawrence Fisher and Jules Kamin, "Forecasting Systematic Risk: Estimates of 'Raw' Beta That Take Account of the Tendency of Beta to Change and the Heteroskedasticity of Residual Returns," *Journal of Financial and Quantitative Analysis,* 20 (June 1985), 127–50.
[18]Lawrence Kryzanowski and Minh Chau To, "The Telescopic Effect of Past Return Realizations on Ex-Post Beta Estimates," *Financial Review,* 19 (March 1984), 1.

2. A perfect correlation of 1.0
3. The Vasicek method, similar to the Bayesian method described previously
4. The full historical method, which uses the average coefficient of five years of data for the particular stock or portfolio

Their results, shown in Exhibit 4–24, indicate that in both time periods studied, the overall mean was the superior method of predicting correlations—better than the more sophisticated methods. The *overall mean* is a very cynical method of forecasting. It is tantamount to saying that the best forecast is just an average for the whole sample. Any added efforts to refine the estimate for a single security are fruitless.

In a more recent study of a variety of commercially available beta services, Harrington (1981) found that some services did demonstrate a measure of forecast skill. Although none of the forecasts were accurate, some did perform better than others and did so consistently. The study results for a sample of utility stocks are shown in Exhibit 4–25. These results are those for a forecast horizon of three years. Although a number of periods and samples were tested in the study, the magnitude of the errors is similar. The study also looked at the use of these betas in the CAPM framework to forecast returns and found those were even more difficult to forecast.

Thus, we find that betas for individual securities are not particularly stable, nor do most securities remain in the same risk class from one period to another. Analysis of mean-squared errors shows that although some components of error can be reduced, the major portion of standard error can be lessened only by adding more securities to the portfolio. Finally, we find that the best way to estimate a correlation coef-

Exhibit 4–24

Average Absolute Error* for Correlation Coefficient Forecasts

FIRST FIVE YEARS		SECOND FIVE YEARS		COMBINED	
1. Overall Mean	.1169	1. Overall Mean	.1415	1. Overall Mean	.1292
2. Blume Beta	.1270	2. Blume Beta	.1499	2. Blume Beta	.1385
3. Vasicek Beta	.1289	3. Unadjusted Beta	.1539	3. Vasicek Beta	.1419
4. Unadjusted Beta	.1348	4. Full Historical	.1545	4. Unadjusted Beta	.1444
5. Beta = 1	.1378	5. Vasicek	.1548	5. Full Historical	.1491
6. Full Historical	.1436	6. Beta = 1	.1776	6. Beta =1	.1577

*All differences are statistically significant unless grouped by a bracket.

Source: E. J. Elton, M. J. Gruber, and T. J. Urich, "Are Betas Best?" *Journal of Finance,* 33 (December 1978), 1378.

Exhibit 4-25

Forecast Errors from Commercially Available Beta Sources
(Based on Three-Year Horizon for 52 Utilities)

	MEAN SQUARED ERROR	BIAS	INEFFI-CIENCY	RAN-DOM ERROR	MEAN FORE-CAST
Beta = sample mean	.086635	.047169	.006294	.033171	.6348
Beta = 1	.227116	.189320	.000773	.037023	1.0000
Market Model	.093383	.021973	.049222	.022188	.4709
Market Model (adjusted)	.091748	.028899	.031198	.031649	.5933
Merrill Lynch	.122362	.053966	.046581	.021815	.6348
Merrill Lynch (adjusted)	.135069	.079422	.033839	.021806	.7031
Barr Rosenberg (historical)	.114077	.054682	.036136	.023257	.7554
Barr Rosenberg (short-term fundamental)	.099353	.058151	.009978	.031223	.7860
Barr Rosenberg (long-term fundamental)	.116526	.076802	.008655	.031066	.8312
Value Line	.079898	.038051	.010821	.031025	.7241

Source: D. R. Harrington, "Predicting Returns Using Commercially Available Beta Forecasts " (Paper presented at the Southern Finance Association Meeting, November 1981), p. 11.

ficient is to use the average coefficient for an entire universe of stocks. If historical betas are not particularly stable and we cannot refine them significantly, they cannot be very useful in estimating future betas. After reviewing these data, one of my colleagues commented: "Stock betas are very nearly random variables with almost no economic content." Is that so?

5. IMPACT OF MACROECONOMIC CHANGE ON BETA:
   THE IMPACT OF INTEREST RATES

If beta changes over time, perhaps it is due to fundamental shifts in the structure of the economy—major political, social, or economic events, not just randomness. McDonald (1985) suggested that "if an extended inflationary period caused a structural shift in the market components, the significance of an inflation factor appended to the single-factor CAPM would simply reflect the rigidity of a static model."[19] Using a method that could identify any cross-sectional shifts concentrated in a single pe-

[19]Bill McDonald, "Making Sense Out of Unstable Alphas and Betas," *Journal of Portfolio Management*, Winter 1985, p. 20.

riod, he found, as shown in Exhibit 4-26, that significant shifts occurred in 1933, 1939-41, and 1974-75. These shifts coincided with major economic upheavals. On the basis of these results, McDonald suggested that analysts or researchers using historical data must exercise caution in the choice of a time period over which to estimate a beta, in order to avoid major periods of nonstationarity.

The major structural changes that McDonald identified were accompanied by major changes in interest rates. Notice that the beta accounts for uncertainty about the economic scenario, not for changes in the levels of interest rates. Exhibit 4-27 shows that because the market line is uncertain, the analyst is uncertain whether scenario A, B, or C will occur, and that the returns for higher beta assets are more uncertain. Distributions X, Y, and Z represent the systematic risk associated with assets with betas of 0.5, 1.0 and 1.5, respectively. Note, the distributions are shown sideways, to demonstrate the systematic risk. What is not accounted for in this risk is the potential for shifts in the overall level of interest rates, that is, changes in the intercept.

Some researchers have looked explicitly at the effect of interest rate changes on the systematic risk of assets. Borrowing a measure of risk widely used in analyzing bonds, duration,[20] a measure of the impact of yield-curve shifts on the price of a bond, they have attempted to meld

Exhibit 4-26

Percent of Securities with Significant Shift 1931-75 (monthly)

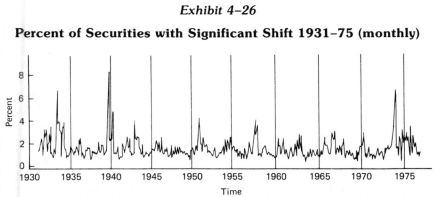

Source: Adapted from Bill McDonald, "Making Sense Out of Unstable Alphas and Betas," *Journal of Portfolio Management*, Winter 1985, p. 21.

[20]Duration is a measure of the years until half the investment will be received in present value terms. For a general description of bond duration and its uses, see Frank K. Reilly and Rupinder S. Sidhu, "The Many Uses of Bond Duration," *Financial Analysts Journal*, 36 (July-August 1980), 58-72. See Ronald Lanstein and W. F. Sharpe, "Duration and Security Risk," *Journal of Financial and Quantitative Analysis*, November 1978, pp. 653-68, for a description of duration as it applies to equities.

Exhibit 4-27

Multiscenario Risk and the CAPM

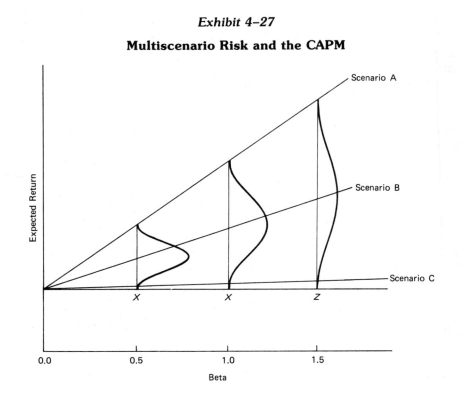

interest rate risk with the kind of risk inherent in the CAPM. Boquist, Racette, and Schlarbaum (1975) show that a security's beta can be described as a function of duration. There has been considerable discussion[21] about the relevance of this measure, whether it captures systematic, or unsystematic risk, and how it might be used. While this certainly is an innovative attempt to join two sorts of risk, we are not certain of its usefulness. Nevertheless, at least one money management organization has created duration betas.[22] These duration betas can be quite different from the betas for the securities. Exhibit 4-28 provides a list of the expected rates of return, durations, betas, and duration betas (the duration of the stock divided by the duration of the market). The

---

[21]See, for instance, R. Lanstein and W. F. Sharpe, "Duration and Security Risk," *Journal of Finance and Quantitative Analysis,* 13 (November 1978), 653–68; M. Livingston, "Duration and Risk Assessment for Bonds and Common Stocks: A Note," *Journal of Finance,* 33 (March 1978), 293–95; and John S. Bildersee and G. S. Roberts, "Beta Instability When Interest Rate Levels Change," *Journal of Financial and Quantitative Analysis,* 16 (September 1981), 379–80.

[22]Drexel, Burnham, Lambert, Inc., has published duration betas.

Exhibit 4-28

Analysts' Estimates of Risk and Return

	EXPECTED RETURN	BETA	DURATION	DURATION BETA
McDonald's	12.7%	1.53	35.7	1.31
Times Mirror	12.9	1.33	24.3	0.86
Digital	11.6	1.27	42.3	1.51
Baxter Travernol	11.7	1.19	41.3	1.51
Northwest Bankcorp	13.4	1.17	23.9	0.88
Western Bankcorp	15.8	1.09	16.4	0.60
Burroughs	10.9	1.09	43.8	1.61
Manufacturers Hanover Bank	14.6	1.07	17.4	0.64
Pfizer	11.7	1.07	30.4	1.12
Jefferson Pilot	11.7	1.03	31.4	1.15
Middle South Utilities	15.3	1.03	14.0	0.51
Kimberly Clark	14.2	0.98	19.0	0.69
Eastman Kodak	11.4	0.98	33.6	1.23
Gulf Oil	16.1	0.97	14.4	0.53
Revlon	11.1	0.97	36.4	1.35
Mobil	15.2	0.96	16.3	0.60
American Home Prods.	11.3	0.96	33.2	1.22
International Harvester	17.7	0.96	13.5	0.50
IBM	11.9	0.95	28.7	1.06

Source: Adapted in part from Tony Estep, N. Hanson, and C. Johnson, "Sources of Value and Risk in Common Stocks," *Journal of Portfolio Management,* Summer 1983, p. 8.

expected rates of return are estimates made by the analysts at one money management organization; the durations were also developed by the analysts. The information in the exhibit is meant only to provide an example of how beta, the risk of systematic change, and duration, the impact of changes in interest rates, can lead to quite different ideas about the risk an investor may be taking with any security.

Still, beta (or relative volatility) does represent a very important kind of risk that should be important to investors: over time, returns do and will vary from our forecasts. Some firms and the returns from their securities are profoundly influenced by socioeconomic and political events. Other firms' returns have been (and perhaps will continue to be) dominated by microeconomic, firm-specific factors: superior management, market power, patent protection, or process innovation. Nonetheless, no firm and thus no security can escape the direct or indirect effects of events in the larger world. It is the desire to find a way to measure this macroeconomic sensitivity that spurs the search for a better beta. Despite the instability of historical betas, the concept of beta is not easily dismissed.

III. FUNDAMENTAL AND CREATIVE BETA PREDICTION

Many analysts believe that we are simply putting too much emphasis on history. Beta is likely to appear nonstationary because a firm's risk conditions change. The problem with instability is that we do not know whether risk is changing or whether our statistical techniques are at fault. History, as usual, presents problems and the future remains unknown.

Other methods of estimating beta have been devised. Beaver, Kettler, and Scholes (1970) attempted to understand the underlying determinants of beta. If we knew what determined beta, we could then use the same factors to estimate it. Beaver, Kettler, and Scholes used ratios from the firms' financial statements and then regressed these ratios against betas derived using the market model. This method, called *multivariate analysis*, is similar to the market model, but the regression includes a larger number of variables in the formula.

Exhibit 4-29 shows the coefficients of the regressions that Beaver, Kettler, and Scholes formed. Their regressions were more stable than those derived using simple historical returns and showed promise for better beta estimates. Remember, however, that these data were still cal-

Exhibit 4-29

Contemporaneous Association of Beta with Accounting Measures of Risk (Correlation Coefficients)

	INDIVIDUAL STOCKS		PORTFOLIOS (5 STOCKS)	
	1947–56	1957–66	1947–56	1957–66
Payout	−.49	−.29	−.79	−.50
Growth	.27	.01	.56	.02
Leverage	.23	.22	.41	.48
Liquidity ratio	−.13	.05	−.35	.04
Size of firm	−.06	−.16	−.09	−.30
EPS variability	.66	.45	.90	.82
Total returns	.44	.23	.68	.46

Source: W. Beaver, D. Kettler, and M. Scholes, "The Association between Market Determined and Accounting Determined Risk Measures," *Accounting Review*, 45 (October 1970), 669.

culated from historical data—but historical financial ratios were used in addition to historical returns.

Other researchers have developed fundamental betas.[23] This type of beta is called *fundamental* because it is based on many of the firm-specific variables that we believe—intuitively or theoretically—can affect a security's risk. Rosenberg and Marathe (1975), in a major study which ultimately produced Rosenberg's fundamental beta, used 54 factors in six categories to develop beta estimates. Eleven of the 14 factors in the market variability category, factors derived from a market model regression (such things as historical beta, beta squared, and beta multiplied by the residual errors) were ranked as the 11 most important factors in this study. Such factors as price-earnings ratio and return on equity were ranked in importance as number 40 and number 36, respectively. Although called fundamental, the factors of primary importance were those derived from the market model using historical returns.

By the way, Rosenberg and Marathe also attempted to predict unsystematic (microeconomic) risk. As we have seen, this risk can be a source of a substantial portion of the total risk for individual assets. Furthermore, the error from the regressions is usually so large that we might suspect that unsystematic risk could instead be systematic or predictable.

Corporate financial experts have long believed that financial leverage (the amount of debt financing a company's assets) and operating leverage (the relationship of fixed and variable costs) are fundamental factors that affect the risk of a company. Thus, they conclude that they should also be determinants of the risk of a stock.

Hamada (1972) described the impact that changes in leverage should have on the beta of a stock; the results of tests by Rosenberg and McKibben (1973), Logue and Merville (1972), Beaver, Kettler, and Scholes (1970), Breen and Lerner (1973), Melicher and Rush (1974), Hill and Stone (1980), and Fuller and Kerr (1981) provide conflicting answers regarding the impact of the effect of leverage on beta.[24]

---

[23]See, for example, D. J. Thompson, "Sources of Systematic Risk in Common Stock," *Journal of Business,* 46 (1973), 173–87, who used covariant forms of dividends, earnings, earnings multiples, and asset growth. Among others, the following have also looked at the fundamental determinants of beta: N. Gonedes, "Evidence on the Information Content of Accounting Numbers"; William Beaver and J. Manegold, "The Association between Market-Determined and Accounting-Determined Measures of Systematic Risk: Some Further Evidence," *Journal of Financial and Quantitative Analysis,* 10 (June 1975), 231–84; and Barr Rosenberg and W. McKibben, "The Prediction of Systematic and Specific Risk in Common Stock," *Journal of Financial and Quantitative Analysis,* 8 (March 1973), 317–34.

[24]Ned C. Hill and B. K. Stone, in "Accounting Betas, Systematic Operating Risk, and Financial Leverage: A Risk-Composition Approach to the Determinants of Systematic Risk," *Journal of Financial and Quantitative Analysis,* 15 (September 1980), 595–637, summarize the research in the area of determining the fundamental, corporate factors behind beta, in addition to examining the impact of operating and financial leverage.

Creative practitioners are developing new approaches to estimating beta. For instance, researchers at Drexel, Burnham, Lambert (and earlier at Bache and Co. with American General Life Insurance Co.) have developed what they call a *market-cycle beta*. They contend that historical betas are better measured if strong trends in the stock market are taken into account. These betas are calculated by using history and are plotted over time. Exhibit 4-30 shows two of their beta series over time. The bar indicates the standard error of the beta; the dot in the middle is the estimated beta. The market cycles are indicated by the dates opposite each beta estimate. The usefulness of these betas remains to be seen.

1. CAN ANALYSTS ADD VALUE?

Fundamental betas are still being derived from *historical* measures of return and/or firms' risk characteristics and return changes relative to the market. In analyzing historical returns or considering the firm's future risk characteristics, can the analyst add value to the beta estimate by forecasting some of the conditions that will affect future fundamental beta measurement? We don't know for sure. Let us examine the question further by looking at the results of a study that uses analysts' estimates to mechanically adjust betas.

Using data from Lynch, Jones and Ryan, a firm that tracks analyst forecasts, Carvell and Strebel (1984) developed a beta adjusted by the uncertainty of analysts' forecasts. Since analysts' forecasts of beta are not available, Carvell and Strebel developed a beta from earnings forecasts. They contend that if the standard error of the beta from a historical regression analysis and/or the analysts' forecast variance is small, estimation risk is not important. This, they say, is the case with the stocks of large, well-researched firms. In fact, they suggest that estimation error is inversely related to market value size—and the number of analysts following the firm. Carvell and Strebel placed each stock into a portfolio according to the number of analysts that followed it. They believed that if they could eliminate unlikely results, such as a size effect, that their adjusted beta would be superior. As shown in Exhibit 4-31, they found that their adjusted betas outperformed the simple, historical beta, at least for the period they tested, 1976 to 1981. The excess return for lightly followed stocks of 0.0023 that was derived when the historical beta was used dropped to 0.0004 using their analyst-adjusted beta—the abnormal returns virtually disappeared. This study is one of the few that has used analyst forecasts to adapt historical beta.

In addition to this mechanical adaptation of beta for analysts' forecasts, practitioners have been using beta and adapting it for some time. Fouse (1976), a practitioner interested in adapting the elegant but cantankerous CAPM for use as a portfolio management tool, attempted to

Exhibit 4–30

Market-Cycle Betas

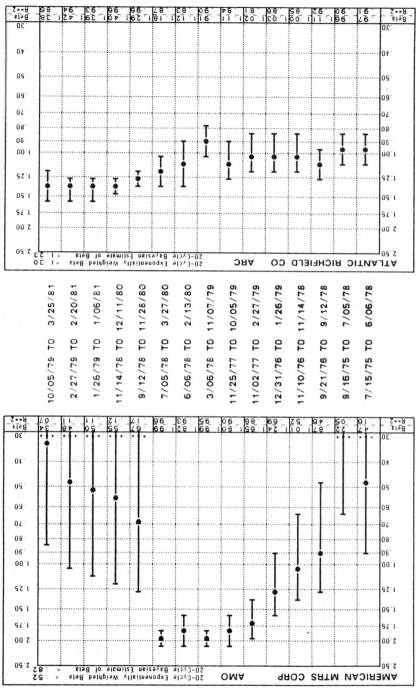

Source: Drexel, Burnham, Lambert, Inc., *Market-Cycle Moving Betas* (New York: August 1981).

Exhibit 4-31

Portfolio Risks and Excess Returns Betas Adjusted for Analyst Forecasts

PORT-FOLIO	AVERAGE NO. OF ANALYSTS	COEFFI-CIENT OF VARIATION	HISTORICAL BETA	NEW BETA	RETURN	EXCESS RETURNS—HISTORICAL BETA	EXCESS RETURNS—NEW BETA
1	22	.050*	1.038*	1.278*	.009*	−.0032*	−.0039*
2	11	.086*	1.135*	1.685*	.013*	.0005	−.0019
3	4	.101*	1.209*	1.822*	.017*	.0023*	.0004

*Significant at 95% percent level or above.

Source: S. Carvell and P. Strebel, "A New Beta Incorporating Analysts' Forecasts," *The Journal of Portfolio Management,* Fall 1984, pp. 83–84.

join modern capital market theory with old, fundamental, classical value theory. He felt that academics, in their attempts to implement the CAPM, ignored price formation in order to concentrate on the behavior and construction of portfolios. Thus, academics could test their models only with ex post data, data that could never convince professional investors or even other academics. Fouse argued that because beta is an expectational estimate based on (1) the financial risk and business risk of a firm and (2) the degree to which a firm's business covaries with the total economy, beta should be predictable. Fouse expected that because analysts had traditionally been concerned with these problems, their estimates should add value.

Analyst-estimated or analyst-adjusted betas are increasingly being used by practitioners and will undoubtedly be tested just as rigorously as other beta-prediction techniques when institutions have been predicting long enough to yield adequate data for a test.

2. CAN BETAS BE USED FOR PRACTICAL PURPOSES?

Because we have discussed major problems in estimating beta, we must certainly ask whether we can still use beta in practice. Perhaps the best way to answer this question is to describe the use that one firm has made of betas. In our example firm, analysts make projections for

1. Five years of expected dividends
2. Five years of expected earnings
3. Five years of expected growth
4. A payout ratio
5. A return on equity
6. A projection of growth after the initial five years
7. Beta, usually using a market model estimate adjusted by the analyst

The first six factors are turned into a forecast of the expected rate of return for the stock in question. Using a variation of the *dividend-discount model*,[25] they find the expected return. For example, in Exhibit

[25]The dividend-discount model is

$$P_O = \sum_{n=1}^{\infty} \frac{D_n}{(1 + R)^n}$$

where

P = market price at time 0
D = dividends
n = the year from year 1 to infinity (∞)
R = the expected rate of return
Σ = the sum

Exhibit 4-32

Analysts' Forecasts Used to Estimate Returns

Values at Maturity: Growth Rate: 10.3% Payout Ratio: 45.0% Implicit ROE: 18.7%

	STOCK RATING	PRICE	DBL BETA		EPS	CHG. IN %	DIV.	CHG. IN %	PAYT. RATIO	GROWTH RATE	ILMPL. ROE	ADD. YRS.	TRANS. YRS.	EXP. RTN. BETA	EXP. RE-TURN	PER-IOD CON-TRIB.
American Motors Corp. (AMO)	S2	3.50	0.82	1980	−6.00	—	0.00	—	20.0%	5.0%	6.3%	4	5	1.17	17.0%	18.5%
				1981	−3.00	—	0.00	—								14.8%
				1982	−1.00	—	0.00	—								66.7%
				1983	0.75	—	0.15	—								
				1984	1.50	100.0	0.30	100.0								
				1985	1.57	5.0	0.31	5.0								
				Eps Growth 1980 to 1985		98.1%								ROR1 = 3.5%		
				Div Growth 1980 to 1985		31.0%										
Ford Motor Co. Del (F)	N2	19.88	0.40	1980	−12.83	—	1.20	—	27.9%	5.0%	6.9%	3	5	0.67	20.3%	38.4%
				1981	−7.00	—	1.20	0.0								18.2%
				1982	1.60	—	1.20	0.0								43.4%
				1983	13.00	712.5	2.00	66.7								
				1984	13.00	0.0	3.00	50.0								
				1985	10.76	−17.2	3.00	0.0								
				Eps Growth 1980 to 1985		214.4%								ROR1 = 29.8%		
				Div Growth 1980 to 1985		25.1%										
General Motors Corp. (GM)	B1	45.75	0.41	1980	−2.65	—	2.95	3.4	48.6%	5.0%	9.7%	3	5	0.59	19.4%	49.4%
				1981	4.75	—	3.05	80.3								17.8%
				1982	11.25	136.8	5.50	36.4								32.8%
				1983	16.00	42.2	7.50	0.0								
				1984	14.70	−8.1	7.50	0.0								
				1985	15.43	5.0	7.50	0.0								
				Eps Growth 1980 to 1985		128.6%								ROR1 = 22.5%		
				Div Growth 1980 to 1985		24.5%										

Source: Drexel, Burnham, Lambert, Inc., *Analysts' Long Term Earnings and Dividend Forecasts* (New York: September 1981).

4–32 the Drexel, Burnham, Lambert, Inc., analysts' estimated return for American Motors is 17 percent. Some money investment management organizations then take this return forecast and an estimate of beta for each stock and portray them as shown in Exhibit 4–33. To this sea of dots, one for each stock, a line of best fit (a least-squares estimate) is plotted. This line, like the dashed line in Exhibit 4–33, is the consensus or the expected marketwide risk-return trade-off forecast by these analysts. Theoretically, all stocks should plot on the line if the market were perfectly efficient. Obviously, here they do not.

The distance that any dot lies from the trade-off (or market-price-of-risk) line is called its *superior, risk-adjusted return,* or *alpha.* The investment firms using this approach believe that the alpha indicates the stock's relative attractiveness.[26] Those stocks with positive alphas (plotting above the line) are expected to outperform the market—that is, to provide a superior return for their risk. The stocks plotting below the line are stocks with less attractive prospects than average. These stocks should be reconsidered if they are already held, but they should certainly not be purchased.

Exhibit 4–33

Expected Return and Risk for a Universe of Stocks

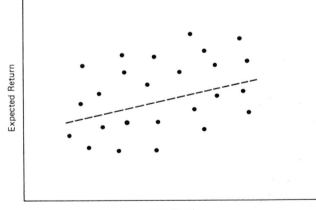

Risk (Beta)

[26]Recall that there have been a number of studies that have found that the alpha, the excess return, could have come from the misestimation of beta. Time-varying models and betas adapted for analysts' estimates seem to have significantly reduced the size of the excess returns. Care must be taken to separate real excess returns from estimation errors. The analyst faced with an excess return should determine whether it is a real potential for profit—that is, whether the return is more than enough to offset the risk.

These alphas and betas depend on the analyst's skill at predicting the future. The question of whether alphas provide better information than total returns for selecting stocks can be answered, We don't know. This technique remains to be tested, but many practicing investment managers believe that alphas derived in this fashion are useful.

This example of one use of beta is one of the curious uses of efficient-market theory. A theoretical concept based on market efficiency is used to identify market inefficiencies—undervalued and overvalued securities. Despite the paradox, the process may be fruitful.

IV. CONCLUSION

We know

> That simple changes in the parameters of a time-series beta can result in a significant change in the resulting beta. (We do not know which are the best ways to make estimates. Consistency is a stopgap policy.)
>
> That time-series betas are not good predictors of single-asset future betas.
>
> That beta is a summary measure and may prove to be too austere. Much that underlies the movements of returns in the marketplace may be better described by a richer model than the CAPM. Unsystematic risk may not be irrelevant—even in the portfolio context.

Despite these disheartening results, it is still too soon to reject beta. Academics and practitioners are using beta and are developing better tests of the predictive value of beta. More important, they are working to unravel the problems of estimating beta and are using beta to make better stock selections, examine performance, and create portfolios. We have learned that we cannot simply extrapolate the future from the past. But analysts exercising careful judgment can interpret historical data and add judgment and insight in an effort to predict the future.

REFERENCES

Alexander, Gordon J., and N. L. Chervany, "On the Estimation and Stability of Beta," *Journal of Financial and Quantitative Analysis*, 15 (March 1980), 123-38.

Baesel, Jerome, "On the Assessment of Risk: Some Further Considerations," *Journal of Finance*, 29 (December 1974), 1491-94.

Beaver, W., P. Kettler, and M. Scholes, "The Association between Market Determined and Accounting Determined Risk Measures," *Accounting Review,* 45 (October 1970), 654-82.

Beaver, William, and J. Manegold, "The Association between Market-Determined and Accounting-Determined Measures of Systematic Risk: Some Further Evidence," *Journal of Financial and Quantitative Analysis,* 10 (June 1975), 231-84.

Bey, Roger P., "Market Model Stationarity of Individual Public Utilities," *Journal of Finance and Quantitative Analysis,* 18 (March 1983), 67-85.

Bildersee, John S., and G. S. Roberts, "Beta Instability When Interest Rate Levels Change," *Journal of Financial and Quantitative Analysis,* 16 (September 1981), 379-80.

Blume, Marshall, "On the Assessment of Risk," *Journal of Finance,* 26 (March 1971), 1-10.

——, "Betas and Their Regression Tendencies," *Journal of Finance,* 30 (June 1975), 785-96.

Boquist, John, George Racette, and Gary Schlarbaum, "Duration and Risk Assessment for Bonds and Common Stocks," *Journal of Finance,* 30 (December 1975), 1360-1365.

Breen, W. J., and E. M. Lerner, "On the Use of Beta in Regulatory Proceedings," *Bell Journal of Economics and Management Science,* Autumn 1972, pp. 612-21.

——, "Corporate Financial Strategies and Market Measures of Risk and Return," *Journal of Finance,* 28 (May 1973), 339-52.

Carvell, Steven, and P. Strebel, "A New Beta Incorporating Analysts' Forecasts," *Journal of Portfolio Management,* Fall 1984, pp. 81-85.

Chen, Son-Nan, "Beta Nonstationarity, Portfolio Residual Risk and Diversification," *Journal of Financial and Quantitative Analysis,* 16 (March 1981), 95-112.

Drexel, Burnham, Lambert, Inc., *Market-Cycle Moving Betas.* New York: August 1981.

——, *Analysts' Long Term Earnings and Dividends Forecasts.* New York: September 1981.

Elgers, Pieter T., J. R. Haltiner, and W. H. Hawthorne, "Beta Regression Tendencies: Statistical and Real Causes," *Journal of Finance,* 34 (March 1979), 261-63.

Elton, Edwin J., M. J. Gruber, and T. J. Urich, "Are Betas Best?" *Journal of Finance,* 33 (December 1978), 1375-84.

Estep, Tony, N. Hanson, and C. Johnson, "Sources of Value and Risk in Common Stocks," *Journal of Portfolio Management,* Summer 1983, pp. 5-13.

Eubank, Arthur A., Jr., and J. K. Zumwalt, "Impact of Alternative Length Estimation and Prediction Periods on the Stability of Security and Portfolio Betas," *Journal of Business Research,* 9 (September 1981), 321-25.

Fisher, Lawrence, and Jules Kamin, "Forecasting Systematic Risk: Estimates of 'Raw' Beta That Take Account of the Tendency of Beta to Change and the Heteroskedasticity of Residual Returns," *Journal of Financial and Quantitative Analysis,* 20 (June 1985), 127-50.

Fouse, W. L., "Risk and Liquidity: The Keys to Stock Price Behavior," *Financial Analysts Journal,* 32 (May-June 1976), 35-45.

Frankfurter, George M., "The Effect of Market Indexes on the Ex-Post Performance of the Sharpe Portfolio Selection Model," *Journal of Finance,* 31 (June 1976), 949-55.

Fuller, Russell J., and H. S. Kerr, "Estimating the Divisional Cost of Capital: An Analysis of the Pure-Play Technique," *Journal of Finance,* 36 (December 1981), 997-1009.

Gonedes, Nicholas, "Evidence on the Information Content of Accounting Numbers: Accounting-Based and Market-Based Estimates of Systematic Risk," *Journal of Financial and Quantitative Analysis,* 8 (June 1973), 407-43.

Hamada, Robert S., "The Effect of the Firm's Capital Structure on the Systematic Risk of Common Stocks," *Journal of Finance,* 18 (May 1972), 435-52.

Harrington, Diana R., "The Capital Asset Pricing Model and Regulated Utility Cost of Equity Determination." Ph.D. dissertation, University of Virginia, 1978.

———, "Predicting Returns Using Commercially Available Beta Forecasts." Paper presented at the Southern Finance Association Meeting, November 1981.

———, "Whose Beta Is Best?" *Financial Analysts Journal,* 39 (July-August 1983), 2-8.

Hawawini, Gabriel, "Why Beta Shifts as the Return Interval Changes," *Financial Analysts Journal,* 39 (May-June 1983), 73-77.

Hill, Ned C., and B. K. Stone, "Accounting Betas, Systematic Operating Risk, and Financial Leverage: A Risk-Composition Approach to the Determinants of Systematic Risk," *Journal of Financial and Quantitative Analysis,* 15 (September 1980), 595-637.

Jacob, Nancy, "The Measurement of Systematic Risk for Securities and Portfolios: Some Empirical Evidence," *Journal of Finance and Quantitative Analysis,* 6 (March 1971), 815-34.

Klemkosky, R. C., and J. D. Martin, "The Adjustment of Beta Forecasts," *Journal of Finance,* 30 (September 1975), 1123-28.

Kryzanowski, Lawrence, and Minh Chau To, "The Telescopic Effect of Past Return Realizations on Ex-Post Beta Estimates," *Financial Review,* 19 (March 1984), 1-25.

Lanstein, Ronald, and W. F. Sharpe, "Duration and Security Risk," *Journal of Financial and Quantitative Analysis,* 13 (November 1978), 653-68.

Levhari, David, and H. Levy, "The Capital Asset Pricing Model and the Investment Horizon," *Review of Economics and Statistics,* 59 (February 1977), 92-104.

Livingston, M., "Duration and Risk Assessment for Bonds and Common Stocks: A Note," *Journal of Finance,* 33 (March 1978), 293-95.

Logue, Dennis E., and L. J. Merville, "Financial Policy and Market Expectations," *Financial Management,* 1 (Summer 1972), 37-44.

McDonald, Bill, "Making Sense Out of Unstable Alphas and Betas," *Journal of Portfolio Management,* Winter 1985, pp. 19-22.

Melicher, Robert W., and D. F. Rush, "Systematic Risk, Financial Data, and Bond Rating Relationships in a Regulated Industry Environment," *Journal of Finance,* 29 (May 1974), 537-44.

Meyers, S., "The Stationarity Problem in the Use of the Market Model of Security Price Behavior," *Accounting Review,* 48 (April 1973), 318-22.

Myers, S. C., "The Application of Finance Theory to Public Utility Rate Cases," *Bell Journal of Economics and Management Science,* 3 (Spring 1972), 58-97.

Peseau, Dennis, "Direct Testimony before the Public Utility Commissioner, State of Oregon in the Matter of Portland General Electric Co." Oregon Docket No. UF-3339, September 1977.

Peterson, D., "Suggests Caution in the Use of Betas," *Financial Analysts Journal,* 28 (May-June 1972), 104.

Phillips, Herbert E., and J. P. Segal, "Data: A Mixed Blessing in Portfolio Selection?" *Financial Management,* 4 (Autumn 1975), 50-53.

Porter, R. Burr, and J. R. Ezzell, "A Note on the Predictive Ability of Beta Coefficients," *Journal of Business Research,* 3 (October 1975), 365-71.

Reilly, Frank K., and Rupinder S. Sidhu, "The Many Uses of Bond Duration," *Financial Analysts Journal,* 36 (July-August 1980), 58-72.

Roll, R., "A Critique of the Capital Asset Pricing Theory's Tests, Part 1: On Past and Potential Testability of the Theory," *Journal of Financial Economics,* 4 (March 1977), 129-76.

Rosenberg, Barr, and W. McKibben, "The Prediction of Systematic and Specific Risk in Common Stock," *Journal of Financial and Quantitative Analysis,* 8 (March 1973), 317-34.

Rosenberg, Barr, and V. Marathe, "Tests of the Capital Asset Pricing Hypothesis." Working Paper No. 32 of the Research Program in Finance.

Berkeley: Graduate School of Business and Public Administration, University of California, May 1975.

Sharpe, W. F., "Bonds vs. Stocks: Lessons from Capital Market Theory," *Financial Analysts Journal,* 29 (November-December 1973), 74-80.

Thompson, D. J., "Sources of Systematic Risk in Common Stock," *Journal of Business,* 46 (1973), 173-87.

Vandell, R. F., "Testimony in the Case of Pacific Power and Light." Oregon Public Utility Commission, 1977.

Wheelwright, S. E., and S. Makridakis, *Forecasting Methods for Management,* 2nd ed. New York: John Wiley Interscience, 1980.

chapter

5

Estimating the
Risk-Free Rate

The risk-free rate (R_f) is the least discussed of the three CAPM factors. Whether in academic research or in practical applications of the CAPM, the 90-day Treasury bill rate has been virtually the only proxy used for the risk-free asset. Remember that this rate is only a proxy for the risk-free rate, which must be estimated, just as beta and the market return must be.

The risk-free rate is usually used twice in the CAPM. It is first used as the minimum rate of return (R_f), and it is used again to create the risk premium $(R_m - R_f)$. Thus, an error in estimating the risk-free rate of return would lead to a misestimate of the expected rate of return for an asset or portfolio. The risk-free rate can also be used in the market model for examining historical results—for estimating the historical betas and alphas. Choosing an incorrect risk-free rate would mean that the analyst would misunderstand the sources of the asset's returns, the quality of its performance, or have poor data on which to make forecasts. As a result, it is important that we examine the risk-free proxy choices and do not accept the customary 90-day Treasury bill rate without due consideration. In this chapter we will discuss the alternatives and the practical and theoretical problems evident in choosing a proxy for the risk-free asset.

I. THEORETICAL PROBLEMS
WITH THE TREASURY BILL AS A PROXY

In CAPM theory, the risk-free asset is one of the two asset choices available to the investor. The investor can reduce the risk of a portfolio by increasing the amount of the risk-free asset in that portfolio, or the investor can increase the risk by reducing the risk-free asset position or by borrowing at the risk-free rate to further invest. In effect, the risk-free rate is the rate that will entice investors to choose between current or future consumption—between savings or investment. The price required to induce an investor to forgo current consumption for a certain future sum, to forgo liquidity, is the price of time, or the riskless or risk-free rate of return.

If the CAPM is to be accurate, the investor's choice of assets must, in essence, depend *solely* on expected returns and on his or her aversion to risk. Based on some work by Tobin (1958), this concept is known as the *Tobin separation theorem*. Essentially, the theorem states that investors make portfolio choices solely on the basis of risk and return, separating that decision from all other characteristics of the securities. If particular assets are chosen on the basis of other factors, then the CAPM is incomplete because it ignores relevant factors.

If the Tobin separation theorem is to work, two things must be true about the risk-free rate of return. The R_f proxy must have no variance and no covariance with the returns from the market. These required characteristics for R_f cause some problems when choosing a proxy.

First, zero variance can exist only for a single period—the single period of this one-period model. In a multiperiod world, there would be variance in proxies for R_f from period to period. For instance, if 90-day Treasury bills were chosen as the proxy for R_f, and the single period were longer than 90 days, the rate on those bills would change from period to period. The change is variance, or risk: the rate of return on the reinvestments would be uncertain.[1]

The second problem is that with variance comes potential covariance. If R_f and R_m covary, the beta for R_f would not equal zero, and the line connecting the R_f and R_m, the capital market line, would not be straight but would be convex (as measured by mean and variance). In either instance, the 90-day Treasury bill would not be risk free. There is some evidence that covariance is present between R_f and R_m, at least

---

[1]In *The Behavior of Interest Rates* (New York: Basic Books, 1970), Richard Roll reports that successive, nonoverlapping, Treasury bill rates are serially correlated—that returns and prices do not follow a random walk. In addition, he found that the serial correlation was not perfectly positive, which confirms the existence of some reinvestment risk.

historically. Ibbotson and Sinquefield (1979) reported significant negative covariance between common stock total rates of return and U.S. Treasury bills over the period 1926–79. The Ibbotson and Sinquefield data also indicate strong serial correlation in the Treasury bill return series. This correlation is no doubt due to inflation. Serial correlation suggests a pattern to the returns over time; they are not a random walk. In addition, Casabona and Vora (1982), even after converting the Treasury bill rate to a perpetuity, show that there is a significant degree of correlation with the market return, both ex ante and ex post. The ex ante and ex post correlations were, however, quite different. Ex ante they found a negative correlation between their Treasury bill perpetuity and market, and ex post the correlation was positive.

Tobin's (1958) work suggested that there is a third problem with using the Treasury bill as a proxy for the risk-free asset. Tobin theorized that an asset's liquidity is critical to investors: highly liquid assets are particularly attractive to investors. Consequently, these assets would be available at a premium price (that is, their returns would somewhat lower than their prices would imply).

Treasury bills are highly liquid. Suppose that investors would be willing to pay a premium for this liquidity. Treasury bills might then be placed at point T in Exhibit 5–1. Here we have a Treasury security T that does covary with the market (thus, it does not lie on the x-axis).

Exhibit 5–1

Treasury Bills and the Capital Market Line

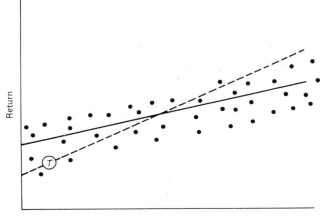

Furthermore, because of its liquidity premium, T plots below the average return for assets of average liquidity. If we use Treasury bills as the R_f proxy we could, in effect, be forcing the market line to be like the dashed line. The intercept would be underestimated and the slope overestimated relative to the real relationship—the solid line. Such a possibility could account for some of the curious results we discussed in Chapter 3.

There is another reason why we might overestimate the return expected from portfolios of above-average risk—if the investor is not able to borrow at the risk-free rate. We can use Exhibit 5-1 to show why this might happen. Presume that the dotted line is the capital market line when lending or borrowing at the risk-free rate. At the far left, the investor's portfolio has a beta of zero, and everything is invested in the risk-free asset (for example, all of the investor's wealth is lent to a riskless borrower). Investors desiring more risk would have less and less of their portfolios lent to the risk-free borrower and more of their wealth in the market portfolio, at least according the CAPM. When the investor lends nothing to the risk-free borrower, the whole portfolio would be invested in the market, and the portfolio's beta would be 1.0—the same as the market portfolio. A risk-taking investor could either borrow at the risk-free rate and invest the proceeds in the market portfolio, or sell short some of the assets held in the portfolio. In either case, the risk-taking investor's return would lie on the right end of the dotted line. If, however, the investor cannot borrow at the risk-free rate, the expected return will lie below the dotted line. Thus, investors, and those evaluating performance, might misestimate the return expected.

In Chapter 3 we described the results of the research done to determine whether history fits what the CAPM would have predicted. In these tests, researchers usually used the 90-day Treasury bill rate as the minimum rate, or the intercept, for the CAPM. Although there is no theory to justify its choice, this rate or a shorter-term Treasury bill rate was often used. We found that in most instances, the Treasury bill rate was lower than the actual minimum return calculated for the period. Some researchers have used these results as evidence to discredit the CAPM. Perhaps they should have, instead, questioned their choice of a proxy for R_f.

The only capital instrument that would seem to fit all the theoretical criteria would be an instantaneous or microsecond Treasury bill. With that kind of security there is no variance and no covariance or default risk. This choice represents an extreme position of pure Tobin liquidity theory, and because the CAPM is a single-period model, the choice implies that investors have virtually instantaneous horizons. If we believe that investors' horizons exceed an instant—as, of course, they realistically do—then an instantaneous bill would have variance due to the constant reinvestment. While minimizing default risk and the impacts of inflation, this security would nonetheless exacerbate reinvestment risk—unless economic conditions were perfectly stable.

It is obvious that the rate on any available asset will violate one or more of these theoretical requirements. But such a problem is frequent in implementing a theory. Often the best solution is to use the least flawed of the choices. Let us look at some of the practical problems that the choices pose.

II. PRACTICAL PROBLEMS WITH USING THE TREASURY BILL RATE

1. FEDERAL RESERVE BOARD INTERVENTION

The first problem in choosing the Treasury bill rate is that it is not a pure market rate. Rather, these rates are influenced, either directly through interest rate control, or indirectly by controlling the money supply, by the Federal Reserve Board in its pursuit of such things as employment, economic growth, and the international stability and value of the dollar. Thus, the rates reflect more than the investors' required compensation for illiquidity and their expectations concerning inflation.

The actions of the Federal Reserve Board certainly affect bond (and stock) prices and thus their yields. However, the effect of rising Treasury rates is to force down stock and bond prices. But are stock and bond prices reduced by the same magnitude? The joint movement of stock and bond prices indicates a covariance between Treasury securities and the stock and bond markets. Because R_f and R_m are theoretically independent, this covariance is not good news for this proxy.

2. SHORT-TERM RATE VOLATILITY

A second practical problem with using a Treasury security is that short-term Treasury securities show significant variability over time. And that variability has increased over time, as Exhibit 5-2 shows. Even when the rates of return are calculated over longer periods of time, the variability between periods is quite dramatic. Carleton and Lakonishok (1985) looked at the volatility from 1926 to 1980 over periods of from 5 to 25 years, and found the average returns and standard deviations shown in Exhibit 5-3. As you see, the means increase as the period becomes more current. Furthermore, for Treasury securities of different maturities the shift can be quite dramatic in a short time, as shown in Exhibit 5-4. This

Exhibit 5-2

Yields on Three-Month Treasury Bills

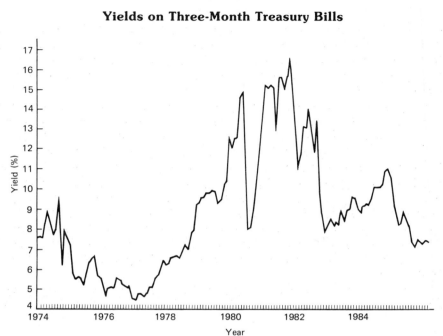

Source: Data from Salomon Brothers, Inc., *An Analytical Record of Yields and Yield Spreads* (New York: 1984).

variability could come from either of the two components of the risk-free rate: the nominal rate of return or the return to compensate for expected inflation.[2]

Expected inflation, one component of the risk-free rate, has changed over time. Fama (1975) found that after reducing the Treasury bill rate by 3 percent, the remaining return proved to be a reasonably accurate forecast of the rate of inflation over the remaining life of the bill. Although inflation, at least as measured by the Consumer Price Index, has been relatively stable over the long term, the middle and late 1970s and early 1980s were certainly not typical. Inflation rates during these years were atypically high and volatile.

The basic component of the risk-free rate is the investor's real return to compensate for illiquidity, although there is some disagreement

[2]Irving Fisher, *The Theory of Interest,* (New York: Macmillan, 1930), was perhaps the first to decompose nominal rates of interest into real rates plus a rate to compensate for expected changes in the level of prices.

Exhibit 5–3

Annualized Historical Returns and Standard Deviations on Long-Term Government Bonds and Treasury Bills

PERIOD	BONDS		BILLS		STANDARD DEVIATION	
	Geom. Mean	Arith. Mean	Geom. Mean	Arith. Mean	Bonds	Bills
1926–80	3.0%	3.2%	2.8%	2.8%	5.7%	2.7%
1931–80	2.8	3.0	2.7	2.8	5.9	2.8
1936–80	2.6	2.7	3.0	3.0	5.6	2.8
1941–80	2.3	2.4	3.4	3.4	5.8	2.8
1946–80	2.0	2.2	3.8	3.9	6.0	2.7
1951–80	2.2	2.3	4.3	4.4	6.4	2.6
1956–80	2.3	2.5	4.9	4.9	6.8	2.5
1961–80	2.6	2.8	5.5	5.6	6.4	2.4
1966–80	2.6	2.9	6.3	6.4	7.3	2.2
1971–80	4.0	4.2	6.8	6.8	6.9	2.5
1976–80	1.9	2.1	7.8	7.8	8.3	2.9

Source: Adapted from Willard T. Carleton and J. Lakonishok, "Risk and Return on Equity: The Use and Misuse of Historical Estimates," *Financial Analysts Journal,* 41 (January–February 1985), 40.

among academics about the factor or factors that determine the real rate of return. Whether it depends on the balance between the forces of supply and demand for capital, perhaps due to the relative savings rate of a society as it matures (more capital is available for savings in societies with more mature populations), or the rate of growth in the economy, the very high interest rates in the 1970s and early 1980s spurred considerable controversy over the true, real rate of return. Studies that did not include this period had found that the real rate of return was between 2 and 3 percent. The question that remained to be answered was, Had the real rate of return during the late 1970s and early 1980s increased, or was the implicit forecast contained in the nominal rate for high inflation?

There have been some questions about the composition of the Treasury bill rate. Even after subtracting the best estimates of expected inflation, many believe that the remaining real rate of return has been above the usual 2.5 to 3.0 percent. Exhibit 5–5 is a graph of the real rates of return on Treasury bills. These are realized returns, not expected returns. Still there is quite a difference in the real rates of return in the early 1980s from averages from prior periods. Was inflation misestimated? Did nonindexed taxes force higher required real returns to provide the investor with equivalent after-tax returns? Or was some new premium for risk being included by investors—a premium to reflect their general inability

Exhibit 5–4

Bond Yields over Time for U.S. Government Securities by Maturity

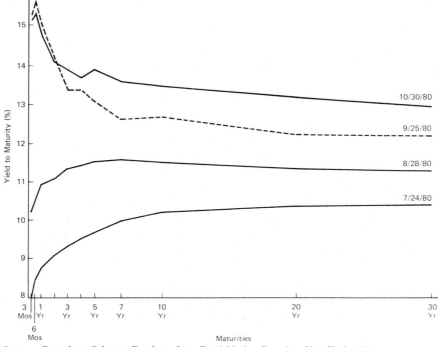

Source: Data from Salomon Brothers, Inc., *Bond Market Roundup* (New York: 1981).

to forecast in the economic environment of the early 1980s? It remains to be seen if these or any other causes lie behind the apparently higher real rate, and whether some of the rate differences may have been reduced during the major bond market rally during the spring of 1986. However, 2.5 to 3.0 percent is still being broadly used as an approximation of the real risk-free return.

Finally, there is another phenomenon that must concern the practitioner. As the horizon lengthens, short-term risks tend to cancel out. Longer cycles, with lower volatility, become important. Risk, therefore, changes over time. Exhibit 5–6 shows the annual average Treasury bill rate. The series is less volatile than the monthly rates shown in Exhibit 5–2. The longer the holding period, the less the volatility and the less the risk.

Exhibit 5–5

Real Interest Rates, 1931–83
(Average 90-Day T-Bill — Change in CPI)

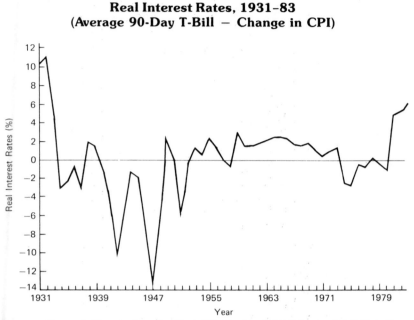

Sources: Economic Report of the President, (Washington, D.C.: February 1984). Data from
Citibank N.A., *Citibase,* (New York: 1978). U.S. Dept. of Commerce, Bureau of the Census,
Historical Statistics of the United States, Colonial Times to 1970. (Washington, D.C.), pp. 1001,
1210–11.

To further illustrate this changing of risk over time, let us look at
a study of portfolio timing. Vandell, Harrington, and Levkoff (1978) considered a variety of combinations of stocks and bonds (asset mixes) over
several lengths of time. As the holding period went from 4 quarters to
17 and to 34 quarters, the variability of the returns dropped. Exhibit 5–7
reproduces results for two asset mixes—one composed of bonds only and
the other composed of 50 percent bonds and 50 percent stocks. The standard deviation over the longer horizon is clearly, and significantly, lower
for either portfolio. From these data we can conclude that the length of
the horizon is quite important in estimating the future.

The volatility of Treasury bill rates underlies a broader problem for
the CAPM practitioner. That problem is that small changes in R_f trans-
late directly into changes in the cost-of-equity estimate. If we use a very
volatile proxy, the estimated cost of equity may vary substantially over
relatively short periods of time. Equity rates are unstable, but are they
that volatile? Are they that closely tied to the Treasury bill rate?

Exhibit 5–6

Annual Treasury Bill Yields

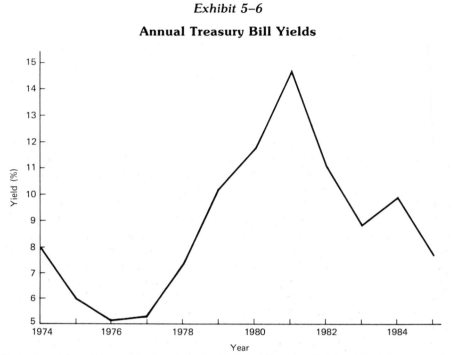

Source: Data from Salomon Brothers, Inc., *An Analytical Record of Yields and Yield Spreads* (New York: 1984).

Exhibit 5–7

Risk and Return for 17- and 34-Quarter
Nonoverlapping Holding Periods, 1926–76

	PORTFOLIO COMPOSITION	
	100% debt	50% debt/50% equity
17-quarter holding period mean	4.08%	7.30%
Standard deviation	.0268	.0405
Mean + 1 standard deviation	6.90%	11.75%
Mean − 1 standard deviation	1.33%	3.05%
Coefficient of dispersion	.670	.574
34-quarter holding period mean	4.08%	7.32%
Standard deviation	.0220	.0154
Mean + 1 standard deviation	6.39%	8.98%
Mean − 1 standard deviation	1.82%	5.68%
Coefficient of dispersion	.549	.217

Source: R. F. Vandell, D. R. Harrington, and S. Levkoff, "Cyclical Timing: More Return for Less Risk," Darden School Working Paper No. 78-12 (Charlottesville, Va.: Darden Graduate School of Business Administration, 1978).

3. THE TREASURY RATE AND THE MINIMUM RATE OF RETURN

Although Treasury bill rates are volatile, they may still provide an adequate proxy for R_f if they are found to be comparable with the minimum rates of return required in the past. Are Treasury rates comparable with ex post minimum rates of return?

Using a technique that calculates the actual minimum required rate of return (plotted as the regression intercept) for a large number of stocks, we can look at the results for several periods, as shown in Exhibit 5-8.[3] The intercepts and the Treasury bill rates are quite different. We have seen this result before in the Black, Jensen, and Scholes study reported in Chapter 3, when the ex post intercept of the market line was higher than the Treasury bill rate for almost every period. Even if we use the Treasury bill rate for the preceding year as the best estimate for the rate in the next period (column 3, Exhibit 5-8), the results are not much better. Thus, the model's theoretical predictions and the actual rates using Treasury bill securities for the same or the following period are quite different.

Many of the tests that we described in Chapter 3 had results that were suspect. The primary reason was that the CAPM is expectational, whereas the data used in the studies describe what actually occurred— these are two quite different worlds. Is the discrepancy between the intercept and the Treasury bill rate yet another case of our using ex post data to test an ex ante concept?

We have increasing evidence that this discrepancy occurs with expectational data as well as with ex post data. Exhibit 5-9 provides forecast data from a study by Vandell and Stevens (1982). Column 2 shows analysts' forecasts for the security market line intercept, and column 1 shows the 90-day Treasury bill yields as of the dates listed. The method used is similar to the one we described at the end of Chapter 4 for evaluating undervalued and overvalued securities. These intercepts in column 2 were not forecasts of the risk-free rate but of the minimum return for the universe being evaluated. As we can see, the projected intercept and the 90-day Treasury bill rate were quite different in all but one period. It is interesting to note how quickly the size of the intercept changed in the one-year period from January 1974 to January 1975 and how stable were the subsequent forecasts.

---

[3]This technique, described in Chapter 3, is the instrumental variable approach like that used by Fisher Black, M. Jensen, and M. Scholes, "The Capital Asset Pricing Model: Some Empirical Tests," in *Studies in the Theory of Capital Markets*, ed. M. Jensen (New York: Praeger, 1972), pp. 79–121; and Eugene F. Fama and J. D. MacBeth, "Risk, Return and Equilibrium: Empirical Tests," *Journal of Political Economy*, 81 (May–June 1973), 607–36.

Exhibit 5-8

Estimated Intercept vs. Treasury Bills

	ESTIMATED INTERCEPT [1]	TREASURY BILL RETURN [2]	UNDERPREDICTION (OVERPREDICTION) [1−2]	TREASURY BILL RATE PRECEDING ONE YEAR [3]	UNDERPREDICTION (OVERPREDICTION) [1−3]
1935–6/68	7.5%	1.7%	5.8%	.2%	7.3%
1935–45	4.7	0.2	4.5	.2	4.5
1946–55	10.9	1.2	9.7	.3	10.6
1956–68	7.4	3.3	4.1	1.6	5.8
1935–40	2.9	0.2	2.7	.2	2.7
1941–45	6.9	0.3	6.6	.0	6.9
1946–50	6.1	0.7	5.4	.3	5.8
1951–55	15.8	1.7	14.1	1.2	14.6
1956–60	19.2	2.8	16.4	1.6	19.6
1961–6/68	1.2	4.6	(3.4)	2.7	(1.5)

Source: This intercept was derived from E. F. Fama, *Foundations of Finance: Portfolio Decisions and Securities Prices* (New York: Basic Books, 1976), p. 362, who used an instrumental variable approach like that of Fisher Black, M. Jensen, and M. Scholes, "The Capital Asset Pricing Model: Some Empirical Tests," in *Studies in the Theory of Capital Markets*, ed. M. Jensen (New York: Praeger, 1972), pp. 79–121.

Exhibit 5–9

Projected Intercept vs. 90-Day Treasury Bill Rate

FORECAST DATE	90-DAY TREASURY BILL [1]	PROJECTED INTERCEPT [2]	DIFFERENCE [3]
1/74	7.76%	7.71%	−.05%
1/75	6.49	12.12	5.63
1/76	4.96	12.94	7.98
1/77	4.60	11.33	6.73
1/78	6.45	12.98	6.53
12/78	9.12	13.67	4.55

Source: Adapted in part from Robert F. Vandell and J. L. Stevens, "Personal Taxes and Equity Security Pricing," *Financial Management,* 11 (Spring 1982), 31–40.

Whether the forecasted intercept is a better proxy for R_f remains to be seen. Because R_f is a forecast, using forecasts rather than historical data for R_f seems more reasonable when implementing the CAPM.

III. PRACTICAL ACCOMMODATIONS

Because of the empirical evidence that the intercept is consistently higher than a Treasury security, and the fact that the Treasury bill rate is heavily influenced by Federal Reserve activity (and is thus not a free market rate), many practitioners suggest the use of a long-term government bond rate or an Aa industrial bond rate as proxy for the risk-free rate, particularly when using the CAPM to look at assets that are clearly long-lived. Grey (1974) of Harris Trust summarized the argument:

> *In theory, the appropriate rate of discount for an investment would include a risk-free rate plus some risk premium. Because U.S. Treasury bills are usually considered to be the closest available approximation to a risk-free investment, the discount rate on Treasury bills is often used as the risk-free rate. This creates some very serious problems, however, because the rate of Treasury bills, like that on most short-term marketable instruments, is quite volatile. . . . One way to approach the problem of dealing with the risk premium factor is to use the long-term interest rate instead of the risk-free rate. The long-term interest rate for investment grade bonds should still be less than the discount rate on common stocks because the latter are riskier. . . .* [4]

[4]W. S. Grey, "Discount Rates and Return Forecasts," *Financial Analysts Journal,* 30 (May–June 1974), 55–56.

We are left with approximations. The longer-term rates (such as the rate for a high-grade intermediate-term corporate bond) fit our tests of history better than Treasury bill rates. Exhibit 5-10 shows the relative levels and movement of several longer-term debt securities. Although these rates are not as volatile as Treasury bills, using such a rate begs the issue: the longer-term rate is still just an approximation and is not based on theory.

There are more questions that the analyst must answer. It is not simply a choice between alternative instruments—Treasury bills versus bonds, some other debt instrument, or a zero-beta portfolio. The analyst must also decide whether to use compound (geometric) or simple (arithmetic) rates of return. Exhibit 5-11 illustrates the difference between the two methods. Here we have an investment with beginning value of $100 growing to $200 at the end of the second year. The arithmetic average shows a mean return of 25 percent; the geometric, 0 percent. If investors evaluate investments as if the proceeds are to be reinvested, then the

Exhibit 5-10

Interest Rates for Debt of Different Qualities

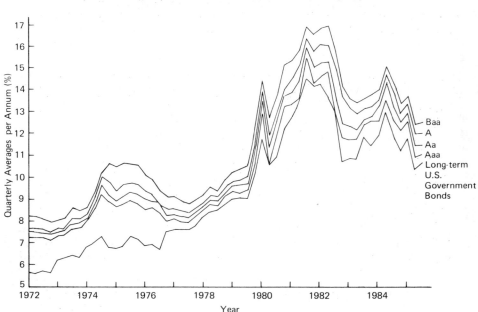

Sources: Data from *Moody's Bond Record* (1985) for corporate yields; *Federal Reserve Bulletin* (1976-85) for U.S. government yields.

Exhibit 5–11

Investment Returns: Arithmetic vs. Geometric Returns

YEAR(t)	RATE OF RETURN (R)
1	+100%
2	−50

$$\text{Arithmetic mean} = \frac{\Sigma R_t}{t}$$

$$= \frac{1.00 + (-.5)}{2}$$

$$= .25 \text{ or } 25\%$$

$$\text{Geometric mean} = \sqrt[t]{(1 + R_t)} - 1$$

$$= \sqrt[2]{(1 + 1.0)(1 - .5)} - 1$$

$$= \sqrt[2]{1} \qquad - 1$$

$$= 0.0 \text{ or } 0\%$$

geometric return is appropriate. However, if returns are viewed as a single holding period's return, then the arithmetic average would be the proper choice.

There are several real and theoretical problems in making the arithmetic-geometric choice. First, many academics believe that because the CAPM is a single-period model, the simple (arithmetic) method is appropriate. We do not, however, have any evidence indicating that investors ignore the compounding effect of a multiperiod world. Furthermore the simple method ignores the capital market custom of quoting bond yields or growth rates as geometric averages, not as simple averages. It is academically interesting, and also practically important, that the geometric average produces a lower estimated market return. Exhibit 5–3 gives both the arithmetic and geometric means and standard deviations. You can see that the differences between the two can be quite dramatic.

Once again, we have no clear answer to give regarding the best way to get an estimate for the risk-free rate. What we do have are some warnings about easy acceptance of conventional wisdom. Anyone using the CAPM must choose the R_f proxy with great care. The most widely used proxies, 30- or 90-day Treasury bill rates, are empirically inadequate and theoretically suspect. A mechanic who simply takes the current 90-day Treasury bill rate as the R_f choice ignores the facts: no single, defensible choice for R_f exists. Moreover, the substitution of the intercept from a historical period is fraught with the problems that history consistently presents: which period is the one that will be most like the future?

Work now being done in testing the forward bill and bond rates holds promise. And creative analysts are refining their ability to estimate this risk-free or minimum required rate. Throughout the chapter we have pointed out the options available. The choice is really up to the practitioner.

In the next chapter we will consider the last of the three forecasts needed to use the CAPM: the market rate of return. In addition, we will look at the risk premium that results from subtracting the risk-free rate from the market premium.

REFERENCES

Board of Governors of the Federal Reserve System, *Federal Reserve Bulletin,* 1976 to 1985.

Black, Fisher, M. Jensen, and M. Scholes, "The Capital Asset Pricing Model: Some Empirical Tests," in *Studies in the Theory of Capital Markets,* ed. M. Jensen, pp. 79-121. New York: Praeger, 1972.

Carleton, Willard T., and J. Lakonishok, "Risk and Return on Equity: The Use and Misuse of Historical Estimates," *Financial Analysts Journal,* 41 (January-February 1985), 38-47.

Casabona, Patrick A., and A. Vora, "The Bias of Conventional Risk Premiums in Empirical Tests of the Capital Asset Pricing Model," *Financial Management,* 11 (Summer 1982), 90-95.

Fama, Eugene F., "Short Term Interest Rates as Predictors of Inflation," *American Economic Review,* 65 (June 1975), 269-82.

———, *Foundations of Finance: Portfolio Decisions and Securities Prices.* New York: Basic Books, Inc., 1976.

Fama, Eugene F., and J. D. MacBeth, "Risk Return and Equilibrium: Empirical Tests," *Journal of Political Economy,* 81 (May-June 1973), 607-36.

Fisher, Irving, *The Theory of Interest.* New York: Macmillan, 1930.

Grey, W. S., "Discount Rates and Return Forecasts," *Financial Analysts Journal,* 30 (May-June 1974), 53-61.

Ibbotson, R. C., and R. Sinquefield, *Stocks, Bonds, Bills and Inflation. 1985 Yearbook: Market Results for 1926-1984* (Chicago: Capital Market Research Center, 1985).

Moody's Investors' Services, Inc., *Moody's Bond Record.* New York: 1985.

Roll, Richard, *The Behavior of Interest Rates.* New York: Basic Books, 1970.

Salomon Brothers, Inc., *An Analytical Record of Yields and Yield Spreads.* New York, 1981, 1984.

——, *Bond Market Roundup.* New York: 1981.

Tobin, James, "Liquidity Preference as Behavior toward Risk," *Review of Economic Studies,* 25 (February 1958), 65–86.

Vandell, Robert F., D. Harrington, and S. Levkoff, "Cyclical Timing: More Return for Less Risk," Darden School Working Paper No. 78-12. Charlottesville, Va.: Darden Graduate School of Business Administration, 1978.

Vandell, Robert F., and J. L. Stevens, "Personal Taxes and Equity Security Pricing," *Financial Management,* 11 (Spring 1982), 31–40.

chapter

6

___

Estimating
the Market Return

___

In Chapter 4 we discussed beta at length. Both academics and practitioners have found that beta is the most intriguing of the three CAPM factors. Beta is the only CAPM factor that represents the specific asset or portfolio. Estimating it captivates those fascinated by statistics.

However interesting beta may be, we cannot use the CAPM without estimates for the risk-free rate and for the expected returns from the market. The risk premium is the excess rate of return, above the riskless rate, that investors require for assets of varying riskiness. By subtracting this risk-free rate from the market's rate of return, we derive an estimate for the risk premium. In terms of the CAPM, the risk premium is the return expected from an asset or a portfolio with a beta equal to 1.0. An asset with more or less risk would have a proportionally higher or lower premium. For instance, a stock or portfolio with a beta of 2.0, representing a higher-than-average level of systematic risk, would be expected to return $R_f + 2.0(R_m - R_f)$.

The market return, and thus the risk premium, can be estimated in a variety of ways. Keep in mind, however, that the CAPM is expectational and that the risk-premium estimate is equally expectational. We are, therefore, looking for a way to estimate what investors expect the risk premium to be, not what it has been. Because risk-premium estimations are often formulated by subtracting the expected return on a risk-free asset from the expected return on the market $(R_m - R_f)$, both estimates—the market rate return and the risk-free rate—are critical to the development of an adequate risk premium. In Chapter 5 we discussed the risk-free rate. In this chapter we will discuss the problems encountered in estimating the market rate of return.

I. HISTORY AS A PREDICTOR
OF THE MARKET RETURN

Many practitioners estimate future market returns in much the same way that they estimate beta. History is assumed to be relatively stable, and the future is not expected to be very different from the past. Consequently, these practitioners assume that the past is an adequate mirror of the investor's expected market premium.

In looking at beta, we examined the inherent problems of using history to calculate beta and to make forecasts. Many of the same problems face us when we use history to estimate the market return. We will discuss four of the questions that analysts must answer in the process of estimating the market's rate of return:

1. How should the return be calculated?
2. If an index is used, should it be value- or equal-weighted?
3. Over what period should the return be calculated?
4. What proxy should be used for the market?

1. CALCULATING THE MARKET RETURN: SIMPLE
OR COMPOUND RETURNS

Two techniques are used for calculating returns: simple (arithmetic) averages or compound (geometric) averages. Simple and compound rates of return are quite different as seen in Exhibit 5–11. Exhibit 6–1 shows the actual rates of return and standard deviations for a number of assets, and you can see that there is a 2.2 percent difference between the two returns for common stocks from 1926 to 1984, 59 years. Carleton and Lakonishok (1985) looked at the equity market returns from different holding periods, periods of from 5 to 25 years, and found that the differences between the two did not remain constant. Their results are shown in Exhibit 6–2.

Obviously there is a difference between simple and compound rates of return. Which should we use in looking at past performance? We do not know, but Carleton and Lakonishok say that

Exhibit 6-1

Basic Series: Total Annual Returns, 1926-84

SERIES	GEOMETRIC MEAN	ARITHMETIC MEAN	STANDARD DEVIATION	DISTRIBUTION
Common Stocks	9.5%	11.7%	21.2%	
Small Stocks	12.4	18.2	36.3	
Long-term Corporate Bonds	4.4	4.6	7.6	
Long-term Corporate Bonds	3.7	3.9	7.5	
U.S. Treasury Bills	3.3	3.4	3.3	
Inflation	3.0	3.2	4.9	

-90x   0x   +90

Source: Ibbotson Associates, *Stocks, Bonds, Bills and Inflation 1985 Yearbook: Market Results for 1926-19* (Chicago: Capital Market Research Center, 1985), p. 23.

> *the truth is, each is appropriate under particular circumstances. The geometric mean measures changes in wealth over more than one period on a buy and hold (with dividends reinvested) strategy. If the average investor rebalanced his portfolio every period, the geometric mean would not be a correct representation of his portfolio's performance over time. The arithmetic mean would provide a better measure of typical performance over a single historical period.*[1]

Their conclusion does not help us in deciding what to use in forecasting the market return.

2. CALCULATING THE MARKET RETURN: VALUE OR EQUALLY WEIGHTED RETURNS

A discussion continues among academics and practitioners over whether to use a value-weighted index, where each return in the index is weighted by the market value of the stock, or an equally weighted index, where

[1]Willard T. Carleton and J. Lakonishok, "Risk and Return on Equity: The Use and Misuse of Historical Estimates," *Financial Analysts Journal,* 41 (January-February 1985), 39.

Exhibit 6-2

Annualized Equity Premium Estimates

PERIOD	ARITHMETIC MEANS				GEOMETRIC MEANS			
	Bonds		Bills		Bonds		Bills	
	Value-Weighted	Equally Weighted	Value-Weighted	Equally Weighted	Value-Weighted	Equally Weighted	Value-Weighted	Equally Weighted
1926–80	8.2%	13.9%	8.6%	14.3%	6.1%	9.3%	6.3%	9.7%
1931–80	8.7	15.7	8.9	15.9	6.7	11.4	6.8	11.7
1936–80	9.1	13.9	8.8	13.6	7.6	10.7	7.2	8.2
1941–80	10.4	15.2	9.4	14.2	9.1	10.4	8.0	8.0
1946–80	9.7	12.5	8.0	10.8	8.6	10.0	6.8	6.8
1951–80	9.9	13.3	7.8	11.2	8.6	10.7	6.5	6.5
1956–80	7.8	12.2	5.4	9.8	6.6	9.4	4.0	4.0
1961–80	7.3	12.3	4.5	9.5	6.1	9.4	3.2	3.2
1966–80	6.0	11.7	2.5	8.2	4.6	7.4	0.9	0.9
1971–80	6.9	12.7	4.3	10.1	5.1	9.1	2.3	2.3
1976–80	14.6	24.9	8.9	19.2	14.0	24.2	8.1	8.1

Source: Willard T. Carleton and J. Lakonishok, "Risk and Return on Equity: The Use and Misuse of Historical Estimates," Financial Analysts Journal, 41 (January–February 1985), 41.

the returns are simply averaged. As shown in Exhibit 6-2, Carleton and Lakonishok (1985) found that the equally weighted index had a higher return over each of their holding periods. The difference in returns, they suggest, is due to the heavier weighting of smaller companies' stocks in the equally weighted index—there is a difference in risk. Carleton and Lakonishok conclude that the value-weighted index is a better reflection of what occurred in the markets and of investors' experience. Equally weighted indexes, they say, "make no more sense than an index constructed of their names."[2] There are those who would disagree with this conclusion.

3. TIME PERIOD

When we decide to use history as a proxy for the future, the next question must be, What period in history? We have already seen how different the returns can be from different historical periods. In implementing the CAPM, many contend that investors view the market return as a long-term concept. This suggests that investors' opinions about individual assets may change, but that the expected market returns show longer-term stability. Those who suggest that investors look back over long periods of history in forming estimates for the future often use 50 years or more of market returns as proxies for expected market returns. Yet it has been well documented that certain periods of history have a greater impact on individuals than do other periods. For example, the Great Depression had a profound and prolonged effect on the behavior of individuals as well as business firms. Indeed, some firms have determined their current financial structure on the basis of what would have been sound practice during the Depression. The Maytag Company, for instance, avoided all long-term debt until 1984, more than 50 years after the depths of the Depression. Individual investors behave no differently.

However, as any teacher knows, the lessons that were so clear to those who lived through World War II and even the Vietnam conflict are now of little significance except to students of history, most of whom only read about these events. Unless history is taught very well, its impact is minimal. Also minimal is the impact of certain major events that have occurred during the past 50 years. The year 1926 was near the height of a bull market, a point that few of us can remember. But 1973 was near the bottom of a bear market, a point that many of us remember only too well. Similarly, inflation has been so important recently that many of us did not recall the fact that deflation is also a possibility.

Other factors have also changed—institutions now dominate what

[2]Ibid., p. 40.

was, in the past, largely an individual investor's market. The period beginning in 1926 includes the Depression, a world war, the imposition of personal taxes, the introduction of the SEC, and a time of regulated bond yields.

Exhibit 6–3 shows the actual market premiums over a number of different periods. Each period represents a different set of historical events, many of which could recur. For instance, the years 1960–70 represent a long bull-market period, whereas the years 1973–78 represent a period that started with a bear market. These are all *actual*, ex post results.

This exhibit demonstrates one other problem that we must keep in

Exhibit 6–3

Historical Market Returns Compound (Geometric) Averages, Various Holding Periods

HOLDING PERIOD	COMPOUND RATE OF RETURN
Variable-length periods:	
1926–60	10.0%
1926–74	8.5
1926–76	9.2
1926–78	8.9
1931–69	9.9
1931–74	8.4
1950–70	13.0
1950–78	10.6
1960–70	7.5
1960–78	6.5
1970–78	4.5
1973–78	0.9
25-year periods:	
1950–74	10.1
1951–75	10.3
1952–76	10.3
1953–77	9.2
1954–78	9.5
1955–79	8.4
1956–80	8.4
1957–81	7.9
1958–82	9.3
1959–83	8.6
1960–84	8.4

Source: Data from Ibbotson Associates, *Stocks, Bonds, Bills and Inflation 1985 Yearbook: Market Results for 1926–1984* (Chicago: Capital Market Research Center, 1985), 90–91.

mind when extrapolating from history: the result depends on the choice of starting and ending points. If we begin the calculation with a bull-market high (such as the year 1926) and end with a bear-market low (such as the year 1974), the results will be very different from those obtained by starting low (1931) and ending high (1969). The choice of beginning and ending points is important. We are attempting to extrapolate a long-term trend from the short-term cycles. Choosing beginning and ending points with similar market yields (and price-earnings ratios) can reduce the magnitude of the problem.

How do we choose a period of history? The period chosen reflects our best judgment of the period of history that will mostly nearly resemble the market that we expect over the investor's horizon. Exhibit 6–4 gives us the results of one study: the monthly rates of return for several periods in history. On an annualized basis, the monthly rate of .0138 for 1926–68 would have been 17.9 percent. In addition to the mean realized returns, the standard deviations of the monthly returns for 1926–68, 1926–45, 1946–68, and eight subperiods are shown. Fama said that these ex post (realized) returns were high compared with what had been antic-

Exhibit 6–4

**Sample Means and Standard Deviations
of Geometric Market Returns,* February 1926–68**

HOLDING PERIOD	MONTHLY SAMPLE MEAN†	MONTHLY STAN- DARD DEVIATION†
Long Periods:		
2/26–6/68	.0138	.0853
2/26–12/45	.0162	.1165
1/46–6/68	.0117	.0413
Subperiods:		
2/26–12/30	.0019	.0686
1/31–12/35	.0313	.1822
1/36–12/40	.0075	.1135
1/41–12/45	.0274	.0577
1/46–12/50	.0077	.0520
1/51–12/55	.0147	.0325
1/56–12/60	.0090	.0037
1/61–6/68	.0141	.0433

*Equally weighted portfolio.
†These are monthly, not annualized, figures.

ipated: the "average monthly return on NYSE stocks for the post-war period is 1.17%, whereas the average return on U.S. Treasury bills with one month to maturity is .18%."[3]

In addition to changes in the average realized return, Exhibit 6–4 demonstrates another important point. The variability (standard deviation) differed from one period to another.

When analysts choose a period, the major consideration may be not only the level of the rates but their variability. Beginning in 1931 the variability of returns declined over each successive five-year period. The most dramatic change occurred during the years before and during World War II. The postwar standard deviation was 35 percent of the prewar variability. Both the return from the market as a whole and the returns from individual securities were affected.[4] World War II, however, did not seem to provide the real line of demarcation between highly volatile and more stable returns. Instead, the economic conditions of the 1930s seem to have caused the change in volatility patterns for the whole period. The data shown in Exhibit 6–5 suggest that long-term monthly returns distributions are rather stable except for a few periods. The 1930s were a period of severe depression and significant financial uncertainty. Omit that period and the data are more stable than we would otherwise have expected. The Arab oil embargo and its effects made 1973–75 the second most unstable period since 1926.

Fama, who writes extensively about the volatility of past market rates, concludes that the choice of time period must satisfy two criteria: First, "the period should include a sufficient number of months to allow the construction of meaningful frequency distributions," and second, "the choice must take into account the earlier finding that the variability of returns was higher in the 1930's than in subsequent periods."[5] These seem to be realistic criteria, and they suggest that the longest historical series we might consider would begin no sooner than the early 1950s. Exhibit 6–3 provides estimates for compound returns over all possible 25-year periods beginning in 1950. The 51-year market return would have been 8.9 percent. If we omit the volatile 1930s and the effects of World War II, the returns are more stable.

Although Fama's figures do not include the more volatile 1970s, any chosen period that includes the 1930s evidently shifts from the nor-

---

[3]Eugene F. Fama, *Foundations of Finance: Portfolio Decisions and Securities Prices* (New York: Basic Books, 1976), p. 14.

[4]See, for example, Benjamin King, "Market and Industry Factors in Stock Price Behavior," *Journal of Business,* 39 (January 1966), 139–90; and Marshall Blume, "On the Assessment of Risk," *Journal of Finance,* 26 (March 1971), 1–10. Both King and Blume noted the decline in variability of individual securities.

[5]Fama, *Foundations of Finance,* p. 27.

Exhibit 6–5

Behavior of the One-Year Standard Deviation of Monthly Returns on the Market Index, 1926–78

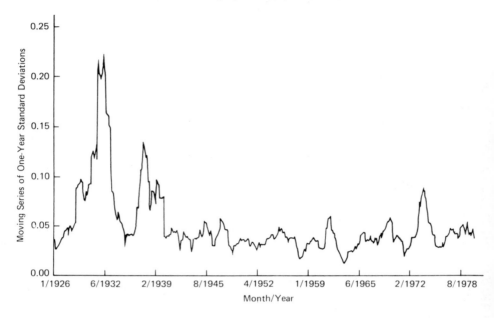

mal return and standard deviation pattern. Also, the market character-istics are more constant than the longer-period averages that include the 1930s, shown in Exhibit 6–4, would suggest.

4. MARKET PROXY

The Ibbotson Associates data used in Exhibits 6–1 and 6–3 rely on the Standard and Poor 500 index as a proxy for the market. This is not the only market proxy that we could use. The S&P 500, the S&P 400, the Dow Jones Industrial Average, and the Wilshire 5000 are among the choices. However, there are problems with each index.[6] The worst prob-lem is one that affects all indexes, as Richard Roll pointed out in 1977. We discussed Roll's argument in Chapter 3: because all indexes are just fragments of the real market for all risky assets, it is difficult, and prob-ably impossible, to know whether an index is an adequate proxy for the

[6]For a brief but thorough description of the various indexes, see W. F. Sharpe, *In-vestments,* 2nd ed. (Englewood Cliffs, N.J.: Prentice-Hall, 1981).

unknown world. Furthermore, since each index is composed of different kinds of stocks, the results can be, and should be, quite different. Exhibit 6-6 shows the returns for six indexes for the year ending June 28, 1985.

In addition to this problem, we must consider whether any single index can represent the circumstances of individual investors. For example, one question is whether the index must reflect the investor's liquidity preference. In Chapter 2 we discussed the effect of liquidity preferences on CAPM theory, and in Chapter 5 we discussed their impact on the risk-free rate of return. We suggested that multiple liquidity market lines result if, for instance, large investors are unable to take positions in less liquid stocks. Would we want to calculate relative performance characteristics or forecast returns using a universe that includes stocks not available to the liquidity-restricted investor? For instance, the Wilshire 5000 Index includes both exchange-listed and over-the-counter stocks. Thus it includes many stocks not available to those managing large portfolios. Does this index represent a relevant universe?

Once we have chosen an index, we are faced with other problems. For instance, if we choose the S&P 500, should it be value- or equal-weighted? The difference between the two is made clear in Exhibit 6-1. That question is always good for a heated discussion, whether it be among academics or practitioners. The index, and the means by which it is calculated, affect the beta and the historical return. Still, to use the CAPM, we must choose a market proxy.

An alternative to using an index emerged from the method that Black, Jensen, and Scholes (1972) used for offsetting beta instability. To use this technique to estimate the risk premium, all securities available (usually those on the CRSP tapes[7]) are broken into 20 beta-grouped port-

Exhibit 6-6

Index Returns for Year Ending June 28, 1985

INDEX	RATE OF RETURN
Standard & Poor 500	18.99%
Standard & Poor 400	15.99
Dow Jones Composite	25.50
Dow Jones Industrials	17.94
Wilshire 5000	−2.25
First Chicago Multiple Markets Index	13.90

[7]The data base available from the Center for Research into Security Prices at the University of Chicago.

folios—the highest betas in portfolio 1 and the lowest betas in portfolio 20. All securities are regrouped each year into beta-ranked (high to low) portfolios. The betas are calculated using the preceding five years' data. The return for each beta-ranked portfolio is then calculated for each time period. The portfolio returns for all portfolios are then regressed against the returns of the market using the market model. From this regression, two pieces of useful information can be obtained: the risk premium (the increment in return for each increment of risk) and the intercept (the return on any asset when the market return is zero). The intercept, or alpha, can also be interpreted as the return on the risk-free (zero-beta) portfolio. The zero-beta return and risk premium are those for the particular universe being evaluated. As shown in Exhibit 6–7, over the period January 1931–December 1975, the arithmetic risk premium calculated with this method was 7.4 percent and the alpha was 7.05 percent, for a total market return of 14.45 percent. Over the same period the Treasury bill rate was 2.2 percent; the high-grade corporate bond yield, 3.6 percent; and the S&P 500 return, 9.01 percent.

Note that when this method is used to calculate a market premium, consistency must be maintained among input variables. Thus, if a firm's cost of capital is calculated using this risk premium, the zero-beta portfolio return (the alpha) should be used for R_f. The use of any other rate for the risk-free return (such as the spot 90-day Treasury bill rate) would be appropriate *only* if the risk-free rate were expected to change to this level with *no* change in the associated risk premium.[8]

Exhibit 6–7

Market Rate of Return, January 1931–December 1975

	ARITHMETIC MEAN	GEOMETRIC MEAN
Annual return on the zero-beta portfolio (alpha)	7.05%	6.84%
Annual risk premium	7.4	7.2
Total market return	14.45%	14.04%

Source: D. Harrington, "The Capital Asset Pricing Model and Public Utility Cost of Equity Capital Determination" (Ph.D. dissertation, University of Virginia, 1978), p. 259.

[8]If another proxy is used for R_f (e.g., the Treasury bill rate) and this rate is not compared with the historical intercept (and any difference found satisfactorily reconciled), the total return estimate would be based on two conceptually different figures—the premium over a historical intercept (R_z) and the premium over a theoretical intercept (e.g., a current Treasury bill rate).

II. THE USUAL RISK-PREMIUM ESTIMATE

To calculate the market premium, the risk-free rate is subtracted from the market's total rate of return. This method is often called *calculating the spread* and was used long before the CAPM was developed. In fact, in many public utility rate cases, experts present testimony regarding the cost of equity based on the spread between the return (realized yield) on the firm's bonds and its stock. To use this approach, we assume that the spread is relatively constant. But is it?

Exhibit 6–8 shows the annual rates of return on corporate bonds and common stocks. The difference between the two lines is the annual spread, which is shown in the bottom graph. The size of the spread is quite erratic. If we had used a Treasury security (which has typically offered more stable returns) instead of corporate bonds, the spread would have been even less stable.

At the least, ex post spreads differ in size and direction over time. The ability to use history to predict the future hinges, as we said earlier, on relative stability. If the spread is erratic, it will not provide a good proxy for expected spread—for the risk premium. As we saw in Chapter 5, the relative stability of the rates and spreads between Treasury and corporate bonds changes over time.

Typically, the CAPM is implemented by using a long period of history (1926–86) to estimate the market return, and a short spot Treasury rate (such as that on 90-day bills) is used as a proxy for R_f. These choices assume the following conditions.

1. *That a long period of history is the best proxy for investors' expectations of future market returns*

The Black, Jensen, and Scholes portfolio reformation method, though technically more complex, makes an equivalent assumption. In addition, we are assuming that current market conditions and trends are not relevant. Although it is true that investors consider present and past market history in determining what the future will hold, how the investor (or analyst) adapts history for current market circumstances and uses it to make future market forecasts is a matter of his or her own judgment. Such judgment is rejected in a pseudomechanical implementation of the model, but judgment exists nonetheless.

2. *That the risk premium required by investors at any point in time depends almost exclusively on changes in R_f*

Exhibit 6–8

Returns on Common Stocks and Bonds

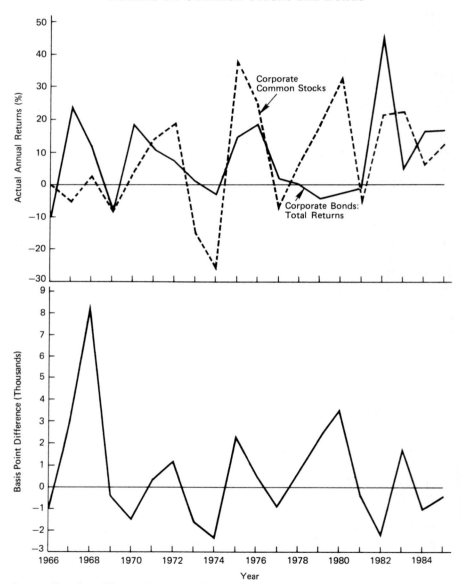

Source: Data from Ibbotson Associates, *Stocks, Bonds, Bills and Inflation 1985 Yearbook: Market Results for 1926–1984,* (Chicago: Capital Market Research Center, 1985).

Because R_m is usually estimated from a large amount of data over a long period of time, changes in the level of this rate occur only slowly—especially when compared with changes in spot Treasury bill rates. The difference between the two, the derived risk premium, thus depends primarily on R_f. In times of very high short-term Treasury rates, the premium for risk would be small, but the cost of equity would be high. For an example of the sort of curious anomaly that can occur, think back to early 1981. At that time, short-term Treasury security rates were at record highs, and in several public utility cases experts were questioned about the existence of a negative risk premium. Because short-term rates exceeded historical average market returns, the traditional, mechanically applied risk-premium models indicated a negative premium on the market.[9] This strange argument rested on the mechanical application of a judgment-based model and on increased concern over the volatility of debt securities.

3. That there is a single risk premium— a single expected capital market line

In almost every application, a single risk premium or narrow risk-premium band is developed, even though we have factors that suggest that multiple capital market lines may exist. Relaxation of certain of the model's assumptions led us in Chapter 2 to consider the possibility of multiple market lines.

III. OTHER MARKET FORECASTS

There is yet another approach to obtaining a market premium. Investment advisory services have begun to publish expected returns for the market. In most cases, the expected market return is derived by plotting the expected risk (beta) and expected return for a broad group of stocks. The expected market return is the forecasted return for a portfolio with a beta of 1.0. One of the benefits of using these analyst-derived estimates is that these estimates tend to provide results that are quite different from those using history alone.

At least one money management organization has added a different dimension—tax sectors—to their forecasts. They believe that investors in very high tax brackets would prefer stocks (or assets) that are differ-

---

[9]For instance, the routine use of Ibbotson Associates' market return for the period 1926–80 and the spot Treasury rate as of January 1981 would yield a premium of $(9.4\%$ $- 15.02\%) = -5.62\%$, a negative risk premium.

Exhibit 6–9

Analysts' Forecasts and Historical Calculation for R_m and R_f

PERIOD	90-DAY TREASURY BILLS	ANALYST FORECAST SECURITY MARKET LINE INTERCEPT	ANALYST FORECAST SECURITY MARKET PLANE INTERCEPT	ANALYST FORECAST SECURITY MARKET LINE RISK PREMIUM	ANALYST FORECAST SECURITY MARKET PLANE RISK PREMIUM
1/74	7.76	7.71	7.89	2.97	3.43
2	7.06	7.36	6.64	3.20	3.44
3	7.99	7.59	6.97	3.07	3.25
4	8.23	7.70	7.09	3.35	3.47
5	8.43	8.17	7.51	3.24	3.42
6	8.15	8.09	7.42	3.30	3.48
7	7.75	8.43	7.82	3.43	3.55
8	8.74	9.29	8.39	4.28	4.55
9	8.36	11.18	10.34	4.41	4.56
10	7.24	11.07	8.75	3.72	5.26
11	7.59	11.26	8.78	3.73	5.40
12	7.18	11.42	8.98	3.78	5.53
1/75	6.49	12.12	9.82	1.73	3.42
2	5.58	12.33	10.09	1.29	3.07

3	5.54	12.33	10.40	.55*	2.68
4	5.69	13.58	10.45	-.89	1.84
5	5.32	13.31	10.97	-.22*	1.85
6	5.19	12.76	10.68	.26	2.06
7	6.16	13.17	11.43	.05*	1.61
8	6.46	13.70	11.48	-.13	1.87
9	6.38	13.82	11.50	.10*	2.12
10	6.08	14.05	11.65	-.36*	1.83
11	5.47	14.24	12.00	-.71*	1.39
12	5.50	13.83	11.52	-.20*	1.88
1/76	4.96	12.94	11.41	-.22*	1.16
2	4.85	12.00	10.38	.65*	1.80
3	5.05	11.59	9.76	.01	2.19
4	4.88	11.59	9.90	1.10	2.17
5	5.19	11.61	9.74	1.28	2.41
6	5.44	11.77	9.76	1.29	2.57

*Insignificant at .05 level.

Source: R. F. Vandell and J. Stevens, "Personal Taxes and Equity Security Pricing," Darden School Working Paper No. 80-05 (Charlottesville, Va.: Darden Graduate School of Business Administration, 1980), p. 30.

ent from those preferred by nontaxable institutions. Instead of a line or a series of lines, these organizations' forecasted security market line would take the form of a three-dimensional plane, with tax rates as the third dimension. The implication for the market premium is quite clear, however. The risk premium expected would vary, if this concept is true, depending on the tax brackets of various investor groups. A single, homogeneous rate may not be particularly useful in estimating the expected return for investors in very different circumstances.

In Exhibit 6-9 Vandell and Stevens (1980) used analyst estimates for beta and return to calculate ex ante security market lines, adding yield forecasts to calculate three-dimensional security market planes. The yield factor was included to reflect the differential effect of taxes. Columns 2, 3, and 4 list the 90-day Treasury bill rate and the intercepts estimated for the ex ante security market line and market plane for 1974–76. In some periods, such as January 1975, the differences between the 90-day bill rate and the security market line and security market plane intercepts were quite significant. In columns 5 and 6, the forecasted risk premiums are also listed. The average premium using the market plane is consistently higher than that forecasted on the basis of risk and return alone, and in no period does it provide a zero or negative forecast. These results are quite different from those that would be obtained if history alone were used.[10]

In another attempt to use forecasts rather than historical data alone, one stock analyst queried portfolio managers about their required returns for public utility common stocks above an average return on an AA-rated long-term utility bond. The portfolio managers responded as shown in Exhibit 6-10.

Brigham and Shome (1981) also forecast a market return. By using the Value Line data for the Dow Jones 29 Electric Utilities, for a 20-year government bond, and for 399 of the S&P 500, they calculated the expected market returns each year from 1964 to 1979. Their results are shown in Exhibit 6-11. Once again these are not forecasts of the market return, but forecasts derived from the Value Line forecasts for the individual securities. To create this market forecast, Brigham and Shome used a method called the *dividend-discount model* to turn the forecasts of individual securities' returns into market forecasts.[11]

---

[10]From some research there is some indication that changes in expectations over time are one of the causes of some of the ex post market lines with negative slopes and intercepts. See, for instance, Diana R. Harrington and R. F. Vandell, "The Effects of Changes in Ex Ante Expectations on Ex Post Results for Equity Securities" (Paper presented at the Midwest Finance Association Meetings, April 1, 1982).

[11]Brigham and Shome used the dividend-discount method (forecasted return equals expected dividend yield $[\frac{D}{P}]$ plus expected growth $[g]$) to make these calculations.

Exhibit 6-10

Required Return for Stock Above the AA Utility Bond, June 3, 1981

Question Asked of Portfolio Managers: Assuming that a double A, long-term utility bond currently yields about 15%, what would be the fair value of a utility common stock for the same company, if the stock's expected total return was:

TOTAL RETURN	INDICATED RISK PREMIUM (basis points)
over 23%	over 800
23	800
22	700
21	600
20	500
19	400
18	300
17	200
16	100
under 16	under 100

Most investors require an 18% to 19% total return or 349 basis points under the bond alternative.

Responses of Portfolio Managers:

Risk Premium	Percent of Respondents	Total Return	Weighted Average Risk Premium
Over 800	1%	Over 23%	8 basis points
800	1%	23	8
700	1%	22	7
600	3%	21	18
500	14%	20	69
400	28%	19	111
300	28%	18	86
200	18%	17	36
100	3%	16	3
under 100	3%	under 16	3
			349 basis points

Source: C. Benore, *A Survey of Investor Attitudes toward the Electric Power Industry* (New York: Paine Webber Mitchell Hutchins, Inc., June 3, 1981), p. 7.

Exhibit 6–11

Expected Constant Growth DFC Return on Equity and 20-Year Government Bond Yield

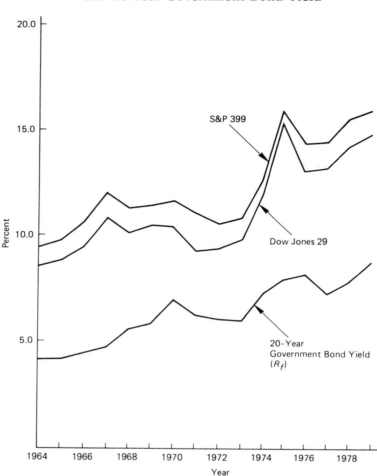

Source: E. F. Brigham and D. K. Shome, "Risk Premium Approach to Estimating the Cost of Common Equity Capital," in *Proceedings of the Iowa State Regulatory Conference* (Ames, Iowa: 1981), p. 258.

In August of 1985 the expected return on the market was 12.3 percent, considerably, and logically, lower that the expected return Brigham and Shome found in 1979 when inflation rates were much higher. In addition, the expected return was higher than the ex post compound return of 9.5 percent Ibbotson Associates found for common stocks from 1926–1985. As you can see in Exhibit 6–12, the expected returns were widely dispersed, and not particularly related to beta. The data shown in the

Exhibit 6–12

Expected Return by Industries

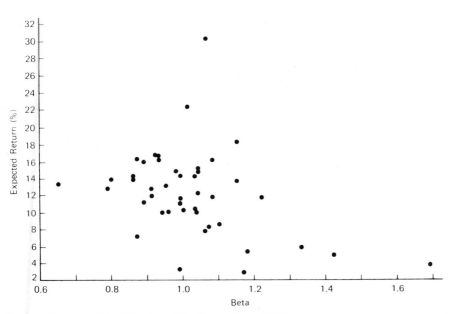

Source: Data from Value Line, Inc., *Value Screen*, August 1985.

exhibit are the averages of the expected returns for 44 industries. Data on the 1000 individual companies that made up the sample showed the same degree of dispersion.

Much more time and effort is now being spent on using available data to forecast the market return (and the market premium). Still, we must be cautious because published, ex ante (expected) returns have been available for a limited time. The forecasts could be biased by the particular group of analysts making the forecasts, or they could be no better than forecasts made using history as a proxy. Better collection and analysis of these forecasts may soon provide better estimates of the expected market return.

IV. CONCLUSION

Much more attention has been focused on estimating beta than on estimating the market premium. In this chapter we have looked at methods of estimating the market return. However, we have again pointed out more problems than practical solutions. Analysts using history to project market returns must choose between arithmetic and geometric methods, must select an appropriate historical period, and must use a suitable index as a proxy for the market portfolio. Analysts must also decide whether single or multiple market lines better reflect a world of diverse investors.

Once again, we find that judgment is required to use the model and that creative new solutions are required to bring greater value in its practical use. As we can see, the forecasted data is different from that derived from history alone. We have no theoretical road maps for making the needed estimates, but new techniques are in the offing. Good analysis seems to yield superior insight over the simple extrapolation from history. The CAPM looks so precise that it has fooled both practitioners and academics—but in use, the CAPM can produce diverse results. Consistency and logic are the best criteria for using the CAPM.

REFERENCES

Benore, Charles, *A Survey of Investor Attitudes toward the Electric Power Industry.* New York: Paine Webber Mitchell Hutchins, Inc., June 3, 1981.

Black, Fisher, M. Jensen, and M. Scholes, "The Capital Asset Pricing Model: Some Empirical Tests," in *Studies in the Theory of Capital Markets,* ed. M. Jensen, pp. 79-121. New York: Praeger, 1972.

Blume, Marshall, "On the Assessment of Risk," *Journal of Finance,* 26 (March 1971), 1-10.

Board of Governors of the Federal Reserve System, *Federal Reserve Bulletin.* Washington, D.C., 1976 to 1980.

Brigham, Eugene F., and D. K. Shome, "Risk Premium Approach to Estimating the Cost of Common Equity Capital," in *Proceedings of the Iowa State University Regulatory Conference,* Ames, Iowa: 1981.

Carleton, Willard T., and J. Lakonishok, "Risk and Return on Equity: The Use and Misuse of Historical Estimates," *Financial Analysts Journal,* 41 (January-February 1985), 38-47.

Fama, Eugene, F., *Foundations of Finance: Portfolio Decisions and Securities Prices.* New York: Basic Books, 1976.

Harrington, Diana R., "The Capital Asset Pricing Model and the Public Utility Cost of Equity Capital Determination." Ph.D. dissertation, University of Virginia, 1978.

Harrington, Diana R., and R. F. Vandell, "The Effects of Changes in Ex Ante

Expectations on Ex Post Results for Equity Securities." Paper presented at the Midwest Finance Association Meetings, April 1, 1982.

Ibbotson Associates, *Stocks, Bonds, Bills and Inflation, 1985 Yearbook: Market Results for 1926-1984.* Chicago: Capital Markets Research Center, 1985.

King, Benjamin, "Market and Industry Factors in Stock Price Behavior," *Journal of Business,* 39 (January 1966), 139-90.

Moody's Investors' Services, Inc., *Moody's Bond Record.* New York: 1980 and 1981.

Roll, R., "A Critique of the Capital Asset Pricing Theory's Tests, Part 1: On Past and Potential Testability of the Theory," *Journal of Financial Economics,* 4 (March 1977), 129-97.

Sharpe, W. F., *Investments,* 2nd ed. Englewood Cliffs, N.J.: Prentice-Hall, 1981.

Vandell, R. F., and J. Stevens, "Personal Taxes and Equity Security Pricing." Darden School Working Paper No. 80-05. Charlottesville, Va.: Darden Graduate School of Business Administration, 1980.

——, "Personal Taxes and Equity Security Pricing," *Financial Management,* Spring 1982, pp. 31-40.

chapter

7

The Arbitrage Pricing Theory

What conclusions can we reach about the capital asset pricing model after academics and practitioners have spent years considering, adapting, and testing it? Not many. Those who have examined the model's assumptions because they believed they were too restrictive and unrealistic did find that making changes in the assumptions would change the model. We are not sure, however, which of the changes are necessary, nor what the overall impact would be if a number of assumptions were relaxed at the same time.

Empirical tests of the CAPM have, in retrospect, produced results that are often at odds with the theory itself. Much of the failure to find empirical support for the CAPM is due to our lack of ex ante, expectational data. This, combined with our inability to observe or properly measure the return on the true, complete, market portfolio, has contributed to the body of conflicting evidence about the validity of the CAPM. It is also possible that the CAPM does not describe investors' behavior in the marketplace.

Theoretically and empirically, one of the most troubling problems for academics and money managers has been that the CAPM's single source of risk is the market. They believe that the market is not the only factor that is important in determining the return an asset is expected to earn. Practitioners have for years organized themselves to study and analyze various other factors such as industries (e.g., autos), or sectors (e.g., interest-rate sensitive stocks). In addition, both academics and practitioners, concerned about the leanness of the CAPM, began adding, or testing the model for the systematic importance of, other factors: price-earnings ratios, stock-issue size, liquidity, taxes, and even the time of the year in which purchases and sales of stocks occurred. With some exceptions, practitioners believed these factors were important, and academic studies appeared to show they were important; added factors seemed to improve the model.

Some of the factors that were added seemed to be of temporary importance; others seemed to be more important at some times than at others. There is no reason why a model containing several factors that explain securities' returns in one period should be significant in another period. Factors change—and their importance changes with time. For example, OPEC, with its influence on oil prices and its consequent impact on the value of all kinds of assets, certainly was an important factor in the mid and late 1970s; increases in oil prices have not had the same degree of importance to asset returns before or since. In 1986 oil price decreases had the reverse impact on the value of assets.

Models that describe the source of returns for assets or a group of assets during any particular period are called multifactor models. These models say nothing about market efficiency or inefficiency, equilibrium or disequilibrium. They only describe the factors that were important for that group of assets at that time. An equilibrium theory, however, makes a statement about the relationship between *expected* returns of securities and the common features of those securities. They describe what will, not what did, influence the prices of assets.

The CAPM is an equilibrium theory of asset pricing, albeit one which says that there is only one thing that is important. Other models take more factors into consideration—for instance, market value, liquidity, or industrial production. Arbitrage pricing theory (APT) is a multifactor equilibrium pricing model.

The arbitrage, or arbitrage pricing, theory relates the expected return of an asset to the return from the risk-free asset and a series of other common factors that systematically enhance or detract from that expected return.

$$E[R_j] = R_f + \beta_{j1} (E [RF_1] - R_f) + \ldots + \beta_{jk} (E [RF_k] - R_f)$$

Where

R_j = the return on an asset

R_f = the risk-free rate of return

β_j = the sensitivity of the asset to a particular factor—that is, the covariance of the asset's returns with the changes in the particular factor

RF_k = the expected return on a portfolio with an average (1.0) sensitivity to a factor, k, that systematically affects returns, a factor common to all asset returns

j = an asset

k = a factor

E = an expected variable

The APT is not only an ex ante, expectational model; just like the CAPM, the model can be written in ex post, realized terms. Realized returns, the returns the investor receives, are the sum of the returns expected as a result of that asset's sensitivity to the common factors, the returns that result from unexpected changes in the common factors, and those that arise from asset-specific, or idiosyncratic, events.

$$\tilde{R}_j = E\,[\tilde{R}_j] + \beta_{j1}\,(\tilde{R}F_1 - E[\tilde{R}F_1]) + \ldots + \beta_{jk}\,(\tilde{R}F_k - E[\tilde{R}F_k] + \epsilon_j$$

Where

ϵ = idiosyncratic risk, assumed to be mutually independent over time and negligible for large numbers of assets

Just as investors are expected to diversify away unsystematic risk in modern portfolio theory (MPT) and the CAPM, they will eliminate idiosyncratic risk if the investor's portfolio is sufficiently large. Thus, when investors look at the market for securities, the prices of assets will reflect the lack of arbitrage profit possibilities.

Arbitrage pricing theory says nothing about either the magnitudes or the signs of the factor coefficients, or what the factors themselves might be; the model does not give us this guidance, nor did Ross (1976, 1977) when he first described the model. Neither does the theory say anything about how the identity and magnitude of the factors should be determined.[1] What it says is that, by active trading of securities with different sensitivities to the important factors, investors trade away opportunities for excessive gains: that since there are only a few systematic

[1]Most researchers have used some variation of a statistical analysis method called *factor analysis* to search for the common, but unspecified, factors in a sample. Factor analysis and the APT are not synonymous. The APT is a theoretical construct that, like the CAPM, says nothing about how the variables are to be identified or measured.

factors affecting returns, many portfolios are close substitutes for each other and thus will have the same value. Excessive gains come only when, by buying some assets and selling others, the investor hedges his or her portfolio and thereby insulates it from risk without eliminating excess return (the return above the risk-free rate). These excessive gains are called *arbitrage profits*. In efficient markets, excess returns are eliminated by trading, and investors cannot, on average or over time, find opportunities to arbitrage for profits.

A simple example might be useful in demonstrating what an arbitrage profit is, and how an investor could take advantage of it, if it were available. For the sake of simplicity, we will describe a market in which there are only three assets, all sensitive to only one factor—for example, inflation. The sensitivities of each of the assets to the common factor, inflation, and the expected returns are shown in Exhibit 7-1. Asset B is expected to have a return of 14.0 percent. Since the return that would usually be expected for an asset with this sensitivity to inflation is 12.5 percent, asset B promises an excess return of 1.5 percent. To take advantage of this excess return, *and to do so with no risk,* an investor can arbitrage among the three assets: the investor with $2000 need only buy $1000 of asset B and short-sell $667of the risk-free security, A, and $333 of asset C. The result of the buying and short-selling activities is shown in Exhibit 7-2.

The investor garners the 1.5 percent excess return, and does so without risk: the factor sensitivity of asset B is offset by the average sensitivity of the short-sold portfolio. An opportunity like this would be similar to finding two bonds, issued by the same company, on the same day, with the same maturities, yields, and other features, offered at two different prices. Obvious inequities offer opportunities to arbitrage. Such opportunities attract investors rapidly, who bid the prices of the assets up or down to eliminate the excess returns. Thus, arbitrage profits are hard to find and capture, and come only when assets are mispriced.[2]

The example we have just used is a simple one. The same situation exists when assets are priced on more than one factor.[3] Arbitrage seems intuitively logical, and seems to describe the behavior of most investors:

---

[2]Mispricing occurs in two ways. First, the owner of an asset misprices for some reason, perhaps because of naiveté. Second, when there are barriers between markets, and when risk-adjusted rates of return in different markets are different (perhaps because a government lends support to a particular kind of asset or industry), the few investors who can move between the markets can take advantage of inequalities. Thus, to earn the arbitrage profits, an investor either must be particularly insightful or be one of a few able to move between segmented markets.

[3]APT allows for as many factors as are important in the pricing of assets. For a multifactor example see Dorothy Bower, R. S. Bower, and D. E. Logue, "A Primer on Arbitrage Pricing Theory," *Midland Corporate Finance Journal,* 2 (Fall 1984), 31–40.

Exhibit 7–1

Factor Sensitivity and Expected Returns for Three Assets

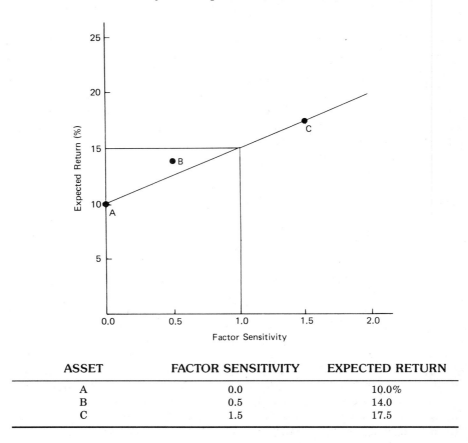

ASSET	FACTOR SENSITIVITY	EXPECTED RETURN
A	0.0	10.0%
B	0.5	14.0
C	1.5	17.5

they are opportunity seekers, believing that opportunities to make profit exist. However intuitive it might be, this model also requires some assumptions.

I. THE APT ASSUMPTIONS

The CAPM makes assumptions about investor preferences (more return is preferred to less, and risk must be rewarded), about investors' behavior (risk is variance of the portfolio, and mean and variance of returns

Exhibit 7–2

Arbitraging Risk and Return

ACTION/AMOUNT	ASSET	EXPECTED RETURN	FACTOR SENSITIVITY
Buy:			
$1000	B	14.0%	0.5
Short-sell:			
$667	A	(6.7*)	0.0
333	C	(5.8†)	(0.5‡)
Total		(12.5%)	(0.5)
Portfolio:			
$2000		1.5%	0.0

*.67 × 10%.
†.33 × 17.5%.
‡.33 × 1.5.

are the normal investor's key considerations), and about the world (investors' forecasts are homogeneous and markets are frictionless). Of the assumptions made by the CAPM, only three appear needed for the APT.

1. Investors seek return tempered by risk: they are risk-averse and seek to maximize their terminal wealth.
2. Investors can borrow and lend at the risk-free rate.
3. There are no market frictions such as transactions costs, taxes, or restrictions on short-selling.

These three assumptions describe investors' behavior in general, but fail to describe the factors on which decisions are made. That is an important difference between the two models. The APT does not make any assumption about the distribution of the returns from assets. It does not require that investors make decisions on the basis of mean and variance, and the troubling CAPM assumption about normalcy of returns is not necessary for the development of the APT. The second assumption, that the risk-free rate is the minimum that an investor would accept for making an investment, is a logical part of any asset pricing model. However, the APT says nothing about the difficult problem of borrowing and lending rates discussed in Chapter 3. Finally, since market frictions impose difficulties in determining pricing, we again assume them away.

While the APT has fewer assumptions than the CAPM, it does have two that are peculiar to it:

4. Investors agree on the number and identity of the factors that are important systematically in pricing assets.
5. There are no riskless arbitrage profit opportunities.

The first of the unique APT assumptions suggests that asset returns are determined by many factors, not just "the market,"[4] and that
investors all believe these are all the factors. The second describes investors' behavior in the marketplace: they seek arbitrage opportunities, and,
through trading strategies designed to capture the riskless profits, eliminate them. As a consequence, "Since any market equilibrium must be
consistent with no arbitrage profits, every equilibrium will be characterized by a linear relationship between each asset's expected return and
its return's response amplitudes on the common factors"[5]—that is, ex
ante and ex post the APT is the same. Whereas Roll and Ross assert
that a reasonable test of the CAPM must be made with the "true market
portfolio," they say that the APT "yields a statement of relative pricing
on subsets of the universe of assets. As a consequence, the APT can be
tested by examining only subsets of the set of all actual returns"[6]—that
is, it can be tested on any set of data, and the research will yield gen-
eralizable conclusions.

While the APT makes relatively few assumptions, it provides little
guidance concerning the identity of the priced factors and the relationships between expected returns and the systematic factors. Herein lie
two of the major empirical challenges that the APT gives researchers—
they must determine the number and identity of the factors.

II.   IS THERE MORE THAN ONE FACTOR
DETERMINING RETURNS?

In Chapter 3 we reviewed some of the studies that have examined various factors affecting returns, in particular the returns on common equities in the United States. There are two ways in which the factors can
be identified. First, the researcher can speculate about the important factors (perhaps on the basis of other theory), and then seek to confirm the
existence of the factors by analyzing the returns from groups of assets.
The other approach is to determine from the returns data whether there
are common factors, and then attempt to identify them. We discussed

---

[4]Since the APT makes no assumptions about the distribution of asset returns or the
nature of the market portfolio, it appears to be free of the problems that Ross (1976) pointed
out in connection with the CAPM. This is because APT does not specify any particular
constructions of the factors, and thus they do not have to be linear combinations of all
market assets.

[5]Richard Roll and S. A. Ross, "An Empirical Investigation of the Arbitrage Pricing
Theory," *Journal of Finance,* 35 (December 1980), 1074.

[6]Ibid., p. 1080.

several studies of both types in Chapter 3. Of the first type, Sharpe (1982), Arnott (1980), and Reinganum (1981), among others, are recent examples. Of the latter type, Farrell (1976), Chen, Roll, and Ross (1983), and Roll and Ross (1980) exemplify the approach. On the basis of their research, and the research of others, we must conclude that we do not know how many factors exist, or what they are.

Much of the research into the determinants of returns, as reported in Chapter 3, included the market as one of the important factors. Researchers repeatedly found that the market factor was the primary and dominant factor related to returns. This and other research has been done in studying market efficiency and the strength of the single-factor CAPM. However, as we have said, the criticisms that have been leveled at CAPM tests may not be applicable to the APT. What have direct tests of APT found?

Roll and Ross (1980) were among the first to look specifically for APT factors. They justified their use of historical data by stating that the same APT equation "not only describes the ex ante individual perceptions of the returns process, but also that the ex post returns are described by the same equation. . . . [Thus, this] permits ex ante theory to be tested by examining ex post data."[7]

Using daily returns for common stocks from 1962–72, and factor analysis,[8] Roll and Ross estimated the number and importance of the common factors for 42 groups of 30 common stocks. They found that when they set the risk-free rate (λ_0) at 6 percent over the test period, 88.1 percent of the groups had at least one significant factor (λ_n), as shown in Exhibit 7–3. Other methods for dealing with the intercept (λ_0) yielded different numbers of significant factors. From their data, Roll and Ross found that there was more than one factor, and "perhaps as many as four,"[9] important in pricing assets.[10]

Fogler (1982) gives us an example of the different sensitivities that different stocks can have to four common, yet undefined, factors. Using principal component analysis, a kind of factor analysis, on the returns of 100 stocks from 1961 to 1969, he found the factor sensitivities (which he called "betas") shown in Exhibit 7–4.

[7]Ibid., p. 1082.

[8]For a straightforward description of factor analysis as it applies to the APT, see H. Russell Fogler, "Common Sense on CAPM, APT, and Correlated Residuals," *Journal of Portfolio Management*, Summer 1982, pp. 20–28.

[9]Roll and Ross, "Empirical Investigation," p. 1093.

[10]See also Marc Reinganum, "The Arbitrage Pricing Theory: Some Empirical Results," *Journal of Finance*, 36 (May 1981), 313–21; and Stephen Brown and M. Weinstein, "A New Approach to Testing Asset Pricing Models," *Journal of Finance*, 38 (September 1983), 711–43, who found comparable numbers of common factors.

Exhibit 7-3

Cross-Sectional Generalized Least-Squares Regressions of Arithmetic Mean Sample Returns on Factor Loadings, (Based on 42 Groups of 30 Individual Securities per Group, 1962-72 Daily Returns, Standard Errors of Risk Premia (λ) Computed from Time Series)

1 FACTOR	2 FACTORS	3 FACTORS	4 FACTORS	5 FACTORS
I.	$\bar{R}_j - 6\% = \hat{\lambda}_1 \hat{b}_{j1} + \ldots + \hat{\lambda}_5 \hat{b}_{j5}$ ($\hat{\lambda}_0$ assumed at 6%)			
Percentage of groups with at least this many factor risk premia significant at the 95% level				
88.1	57.1	33.3	16.7	4.8
Expected percentage of groups with at least this many risk premia significant at the 95% level given no true risk premia ($\lambda = 0$)				
22.6	2.26	.115	.003	.00003
Percentage of groups with factor's risk premium significant at the 95% level in natural order from factor analysis				
76.2	50.0	28.6	23.8	21.4
II.	$\bar{R}_j = \hat{\lambda}_0 + \hat{\lambda}_1 \hat{b}_{j1} + \ldots + \hat{\lambda}_5 \hat{b}_{j5}$ ($\hat{\lambda}_0$ estimated)			
Percentage of groups with at least this many factor risk premia significant at the 95% level				
69.0	47.6	7.1	4.8	0
Percentage of groups with this factor's risk premium significant at the 95% level in natural order from factor analysis				
35.7	31.0	23.8	21.4	16.7

Source: Richard Roll and S. A. Ross, "An Empirical Investigation of the Arbitrage Pricing Theory," *Journal of Finance*, 35 (December 1980), 1092.

In estimating the number of factors, other researchers have had different results. Dhrymes (1984), using a sample similar to that of Roll and Ross, found that

> at the 5% level of significance, with a group of 15 securities, we have at most **two** "common risk" factors; with a group of 30 securities we have at most **three** "common risk" factors; with a group of 45 securities we have at most **four** "common risk" factors; with a group of 60 securities we have at most **six** "common risk" factors; and with a group of 90 securities we have at most **nine** "common risk" factors.[11]

Why does this happen? It occurs because as the number of assets is increased, the number of interrelationships can also increase. For ex-

[11]Pheobus J. Dhrymes, "The Empirical Relevance of Arbitrage Pricing Models," *Journal of Portfolio Management*, Summer 1984, p. 39.

ample, let us assume an initial sample of 30 stocks, 10 stocks each from three industries. It is likely that at least three factors will be needed to explain returns, one for each industry. If the sample were enlarged by 30 stocks, again 10 from each of three different industries, the number of industry factors would, of course, increase. In addition to the industry factors, other common factors could exist. This is a simple example, but one that makes it clear that the number of factors that will be identified can depend upon how many assets are being examined.[12] Dhrymes warns that "if we look at only a small subset of such securities, then we get a distorted view of what such factors may be, and our inferences could be extremely misleading"[13]—that is, the sample we use will have an impact on the results. In another paper, Dhrymes, Friend, and Gultekin (1984) say

> *The fundamental reason for this state of affairs is, essentially, that there is no necessary and simple connection between "factors" found in a 30-security context and "factors" to be determined in the context in which APT models may be held to apply. . . . Rather, the structure simply represents the researchers' rendition of the well-established pattern of covariation among securities returns.*[14]

The authors go on to say that "if, after prolonged empirical investigations, the number of 'factors' found is stabilized and an economic/financial interpretation is attached to them, we may, at that stage, think of such risk factors as reflecting fundamental economic forces at work in the securities markets."[15] Dhrymes, Friend, and Gultekin criticized the Roll and Ross study on a number of statistical and conceptual grounds. Not known for their reticence, Roll and Ross replied.[16] They disagree with the critique. Among other things, they take exception to the conclusion about the number of factors being sample-size dependent. They say that "there are a number of reasons why nonpriced factors will increase with the group size,"[17] but that most of the common factors are diversifiable, and hence will not be priced—that is, are not of concern.

[12]The question of whether the number of factors increases with increases in the sample size is by no means resolved. D. Chinhyung Cho, "On Testing the Arbitrage Pricing Theory: Inter-Battery Factor Analysis," *Journal of Finance*, 39 (December 1984), 1485–1502, using a somewhat different technique, finds that there are five or six factors, but that the number of factors does not depend upon the size of the sample group.

[13]Drhymes, "Empirical Relevance of Arbitrage Pricing Models," p. 38.

[14]Phoebus J. Dhrymes, I. Friend, and N. B. Gultekin, "A Critical Reexamination of the Empirical Evidence on the Arbitrage Pricing Theory," *Journal of Finance*, 39 (June 1984), 331.

[15]Ibid., pp. 331–32.

[16]Richard Roll and S. A. Ross, "A Critical Reexamination of the Empirical Evidence on the Arbitrage Pricing Theory: A Reply," *Journal of Finance*, 39 (June 1984b), 347–350.

[17]Ibid., p. 349.

Exhibit 7-4

Principal Component Betas for Four-Index Model

COMPANY NAME	B_0	B_1	B_2	B_3	COMPANY NAME	B_0	B_1	B_2	B_3
1. Burroughs	.40	-.26	.32	.26	51. International Harvester	.52	-.20	-.29	-.08
2. Eastman Kodak	.60	.06	.34	.01	52. International Paper	.73	.01	-.05	-.10
3. IBM	.65	.01	.50	.07	53. Johns-Manville	.67	-.23	-.21	-.07
4. International Telephone	.70	-.04	.32	.22	54. Joy Manufacturing	.70	-.12	-.04	-.11
5. Merck	.56	.16	.34	.03	55. Kennecott	.56	-.06	-.11	.02
6. Minn. Mining and Manufacturing	.64	.00	.30	.09	56. Mohasco	.62	-.23	-.04	.24
7. Motorola	.56	-.33	.27	.14	57. Monsanto Co.	.55	-.16	-.16	-.17
8. NCR	.53	-.06	.44	.07	58. National Lead	.62	-.12	-.38	.08
9. Pan American	.62	-.32	.04	.17	59. National Steel Corporation	.70	-.25	-.08	-.22
10. Polaroid	.46	-.12	.45	.28	60. Pullman	.63	-.20	-.14	-.08
11. Sears	.53	.06	.28	-.06	61. Square D	.66	.06	-.11	.04
12. Texas Instruments	.51	-.33	.19	.37	62. Sunbeam	.48	-.04	-.05	.22
13. Trane	.49	-.28	.21	.13	63. Timkin	.68	-.18	-.24	-.05
14. UAL Inc.	.62	-.21	.09	.14	64. Gulf Oil	.53	.36	-.13	.32
15. Zenith	.54	-.29	.26	.09	65. Mobil	.46	.40	-.28	.37
16. American Electric Power	.57	.53	-.04	-.18	66. Shell Oil	.56	.24	-.19	.35
17. American Home Products	.60	.13	.23	-.04	67. Standard of California	.54	.42	-.27	.29
18. C.I.T.	.48	.06	.02	-.19	68. Standard Oil (Indiana)	.52	.38	-.24	.32
19. CPC International	.59	.21	.12	-.06	69. Texaco	.68	.41	-.21	.23
20. Central and Southwest	.46	.48	.07	-.27	70. Allegheny Ludlum	.60	-.16	-.14	.03
21. Coca-Cola Company	.60	.15	.37	-.08	71. Armco Steel	.66	-.21	-.06	-.32
22. Columbia Gas	.47	.38	-.09	-.23	72. Bliss and Laughlin Industry	.53	.03	-.02	-.18
23. Federated Department Stores	.56	.09	.28	-.01	73. Brunswick Corporation	.47	-.22	.19	-.21

24. Florida Power Corp.	.49	.39	.26	−.06	74. Chicago Pneumatic	.58	−.13	.12	.27
25. General Foods	.61	.28	.23	−.23	75. Clevite Corporation	.49	.44	−.10	−.20
26. Gillette Company	.54	.08	.31	.15	76. Federal Mogul	.60	−.01	−.14	−.20
27. Hershey	.52	.07	.06	−.10	77. Interlake Steel	.65	−.22	−.23	−.10
28. Household Finance	.57	.20	.14	−.23	78. Mesta Machine	.61	−.37	−.09	.00
29. Kraftco	.60	.23	.06	−.10	79. Midland Ross	.61	−.13	−.24	.17
30. National Biscuit	.41	.24	.13	−.11	80. Quaker State	.36	.04	−.07	.06
31. Procter and Gamble	.57	.21	.24	−.16	81. Republic Steel	.74	−.20	−.14	−.24
32. Quaker Oats	.50	.25	.08	−.07	82. Smith, Kline and French	.61	.11	.26	−.03
33. Reynolds	.60	.01	.10	−.16	83. Abbot Laboratories	.39	.22	.04	.15
34. Transamerica	.73	.29	−.03	−.08	84. Allied Chemical	.67	−.25	−.20	−.21
35. Virginia Electric	.48	.49	.04	−.38	85. American Cyanamid	.69	−.03	−.12	.13
36. American Can	.56	−.01	−.14	.04	86. Celanese Corporation	.69	−.10	−.02	.14
37. American Standard	.52	−.11	−.10	.06	87. Dow Chemical	.63	−.17	.02	.00
38. Bethlehem Steel	.71	−.21	−.24	−.22	88. Dupont	.71	.06	−.10	−.00
39. Borg-Warner	.70	−.14	−.04	−.06	89. FMC Corporation	.76	.03	.05	−.06
40. Burlington Industries	.56	−.25	.00	−.03	90. Hercules	.61	.13	.03	−.06
41. Caterpillar	.59	−.28	−.02	.07	91. Johnson & Johnson	.55	−.13	.23	.02
42. Cinn. Milling	.62	−.15	−.14	.07	92. Libby-Owens Ford Glass	.67	−.04	−.21	−.11
43. Clark Equipment	.60	−.12	−.04	−.01	93. Pfizer	.70	.24	.20	.09
44. Continental Can	.57	−.04	−.24	.11	94. Cities Services	.45	.23	−.44	.15
45. Deere	.47	−.17	−.07	−.17	95. Getty Oil	.57	−.01	.03	.25
46. Eaton, Yale & Towne	.68	−.06	−.15	−.06	96. Kerr McGee Corporation	.60	.21	.12	.26
47. Gardner Denver	.63	−.16	−.19	−.07	97. Lukens Steel	.58	−.27	.01	−.24
48. Georgia Pacific	.68	−.04	.06	−.06	98. Marathon Oil	.41	.21	−.41	.20
49. Goodyear	.65	−.05	−.07	−.30	99. Phillips Petroleum	.64	.23	−.22	.27
50. Ingersoll-Rand Corporation	.77	−.13	−.15	.01	100. ACF Industries	.59	.01	−.15	.11

Source: H. Russell Fogler, "Common Sense on CAPM, APT, and Correlated Residuals," *Journal of Portfolio Management,* Summer 1982, p. 21.

Of the remainder of the Dhrymes (1984) and Dhrymes, Friend, and Gultekin (1984) tests, Ross says that "the remaining tests Dhrymes reports fall into three basic categories. They are either wrong, they are beside the point and misdirected, or they are so mystifying that we cannot determine into which of the first two categories they fall."[18] Typical of new theories receiving their initial tests, the argument between these authors has not ended. Dhrymes et al. (1985) have replied, emphasizing their earlier criticisms.

Shanken (1982) questions the usefulness of factor analysis for identifying priced factors, the very testability of the APT. He says that since "equivalent sets of securities may conform to very different factor structures . . . the usual empirical formulation of the APT, when applied to these structures, may yield different and inconsistent implications concerning expected returns for a given set of securities."[19] He goes on to suggest that, since the APT does not give any direction as to what the correct factors and their magnitudes are, then "the 'equilibrium APT' appears to be subject to substantially the same difficulties encountered in testing the CAPM."[20] Finally, Shanken suggests that the enthusiasm with which the academic community has embraced the APT as a testable alternative to the CAPM may not be appropriate. In a reply to Shanken's comments, Dybvig and Ross (1985) suggest that his analysis has "little relevance for actual empirical tests,"[21] and that the theory is indeed testable. Shanken (1985) in the same issue of the journal, disagrees once again with Dybvig and Ross. He further continues to state that the "equilibrium factors models which they discuss [Dybvig and Ross] have much to offer, but are essentially generalizations of the simple mean-variance CAPM, in a multi-beta form."[22] This controversy is hardly resolved and far from over. What it does is point out the troubling misunderstanding that has followed this model and its testing.

The discussions among Roll and Ross (1980, 1984b), Shanken (1982, 1985), Dybvig and Ross (1985), Ross (1984), Dhrymes (1984), Dhrymes, Friend, and Gultekin (1984), and Dhrymes et al. (1985) are typical of a field of research that is in its infancy—the state of APT research.

---

[18]Stephen A. Ross, "Reply to Dhrymes: APT Is Empirically Relevant," *Journal of Portfolio Management,* Fall 1984, p. 55.

[19]Jay Shanken, "The Arbitrage Pricing Theory: Is It Testable?" *Journal of Finance,* 37 (December 1982), 1134.

[20]Ibid., p. 1136.

[21]Philip Dybvig and Stephen Ross, "Yes, The APT Is Testable," *Journal of Finance,* 40 (September 1985), 1184.

[22]Jay Shanken, "Multi-Beta CAPM or Equilibrium-APT?: A Reply," *Journal of Finance,* 40 (September 1985), 1195.

III.   ARE THE APT FACTORS
ALL THAT ARE PRICED?

While Roll and Ross (1980) found that there were as many as four factors that are systematically priced, they believed their analysis may not have captured all the factors that underlie returns: to have compelling test results, researchers must find that the factors they identify are not correlated to each other,[23] and that no other important factors exist. To test for added factors, Roll and Ross regressed the expected returns derived using five factors they estimated in their factor analysis, against what they call "own variance,"[24] the standard deviation of the individual returns. If they captured all of the factors that are important in pricing the assets, at least for these stocks during this period, then the "own variance" should not affect the returns.[25] Unfortunately, 42.5 percent of the groups showed significant effects from the "own variance." This could suggest that the APT is not a good description of the mechanism for pricing assets: since arbitrageurs should be able to diversify away the noncommon part of variance, it should not be priced. Even though their results showed that "own variance" was priced, Roll and Ross conclude that the negative result might be the fault of having skewed data, and not of a faulty model. Thus, they say the results of their test is inconclusive.

In another test of "own variance," Chen (1983) found that "we cannot reject the null hypothesis that the APT is correct, and the own variance has no explanatory power net of the FL [factors]."[26] The test that Chen used was different from that of Roll and Ross and designed to eliminate some estimation errors. Still the results were not entirely conclusive. However, he believes the evidence points to the APT as a useful model for estimating returns.

Dhrymes et al. (1985) reach the opposite conclusion, saying that "unique risks . . . seem at least as important as common risks measured by factor risk premia. However, neither measure of risk contributes ap-

[23]Not all researchers have found that their factors are uncorrelated. In testing a three-factor model during the period 1975–80, Robert A. Pari and Son-Nan Chen, "An Empirical Test of the Arbitrage Pricing Theory," *Journal of Financial Research,* 7 (Summer 1984), 121–30, found that residual risk was not priced.

[24]Roll and Ross, "Empirical Investigation," p. 1093.

[25]In Chapter 3 we discussed research that had shown that variance, or standard deviation, was related to risk (beta) adjusted returns. If the risk measure or, in the case of the APT, the common factors are properly identified, they will capture all that is systematic in the returns. Thus, variance could not be related to returns.

[26]Nai-fu Chen, "Some Empirical Tests of the Theory of Arbitrage Pricing," *Journal of Finance,* 38 (December 1983), 1406.

preciably in explaining return on individual securities."[27] They go further and suggest that Roll and Ross have substantially modified what they originally meant by the APT.

In addition to looking at "own variance," Chen examined the effect of the size of the market value on the pricing of assets.[28] Recall that size was one of the factors that systematically affected risk-adjusted returns from the CAPM. Chen found that "firm size does not have additional explanatory power after risk is adjusted by the FL [factors]."[29] This indicates that size is either one of the factors not captured by the market factor in the CAPM, or is acting as a proxy for a such a factor.

Chen's study is interesting for a number of reasons. Prime among them is that Chen points out that the methods of estimating the factors and testing for their significance are not entirely resolved. What methods to use, and how to interpret the results, are both problems that are yet to be solved in the exploration of the APT. Until this is done, it remains to be seen whether the APT is superior to the one-factor CAPM.

IV. WHAT ARE THE APT FACTORS?

Chen, Ross, and Roll (1983), in a study the results of which were reported in Chapter 3, derived the common factors from a set of data and then tested them for their relationship to fundamental macroeconomic variables, such as inflation, oil prices, and industrial production. Ross and Roll (1983) reported the four macroeconomic variables important in determining returns:

1. Unanticipated changes in inflation
2. Changes in expected industrial production (which are, by definition, unanticipated)
3. Unanticipated changes in risk premia (as measured by the spread between low-grade and high-grade bonds)
4. Unanticipated changes in the slope of the term structure of interest rates[30]

---

[27]Phoebus J. Dhrymes et al., "New Tests of the APT and Their Implications," *Journal of Finance*, 40 (July 1985), 663.

[28]In part Chen's test was in response to a size effect found by Reinganum, "The Arbitrage Pricing Theory: Some Empirical Results," *Journal of Finance*, 36 (May 1981), 313–321.

[29]Chen, "Some Empirical Tests," p. 1409.

[30]Richard Roll and S. A. Ross, "The Merits of the Arbitrage Pricing Theory for Portfolio Management" (Paper presented at the Institute for Quantitative Research in Finance, Fall 1983b), pp. 14–15.

They were comforted by the economic rationale that lies behind the factors, since "they appear in the traditional discounted cash flow (DCF) valuation formula."[31] Industrial production, they suggest, is a "proxy for real cash flows" and "inflation enters because assets are not neutral— their nominal cash flow growth rates do not match expected inflation rates."[32] The other two variables affect the magnitude of the DCF discount rate.

One word of caution: we are not talking about historical rates of industrial production, inflation, risk premia, or yield curve shifts. It is sensitivity to the *unexpected* changes in those factors that are important, and that determine the returns the investor will get.[33]

Using variables like those described by Roll and Ross (1983), Bower, Bower, and Logue (1984) demonstrate the difference that using the APT and the CAPM can have on the expected rates of return estimated for a

Exhibit 7–5
CAPM and APT Estimates of Expected Return

COMPANY	CAPM	APT
American Broadcasting Company	21.5%	14.3%
American Hospital Supply	22.9	12.8
Baxter Travenol Laboratories	21.0	11.6
CBA	18.2	13.9
Chris Craft Industries	22.2	17.1
Cook International	16.7	20.2
Ipco Corporation	29.3	2.7
Matrix Corporation	24.7	25.3
Metromedia	22.9	19.2
Napco Industries	22.6	16.4
Parker Pen	21.7	22.6
Rollins	24.3	16.2
SBS Technologies	21.7	22.3
Storer Broadcasting	20.4	15.4
Taft Broadcasting	25.2	21.1
Teleprompter	36.0	28.4
Western Union	19.1	10.8
Average	23.0	18.8
Standard Deviation	4.4	6.0

Source: Dorothy Bower, R. S. Bower and D. E. Logue, "A Primer on Arbitrage Pricing Theory," *Midland Corporate Finance Journal,* 2 (Fall 1984), 38.

[31]Ibid., p. 15.
[32]Ibid.
[33]The reader is referred to Nai-fu Chen, R. Roll, and S. A. Ross, "Economic Forces and the Stock Market" (Working Paper Ser. B-73, University of California at Los Angeles, December 1983), for a discussion of how they measured these variables.

number of stocks. As shown in Exhibit 7-5, the difference can be as large as 10 percent.

Estep, Hanson, and Johnson (1983), using a somewhat different time-series approach, show what building sensitivities into portfolios can do to their performance. Among the factors they studied were three that were similar to those found by Chen, Roll, and Ross: GNP growth, interest rate changes, and inflation. The performance of their portfolios is shown in Exhibit 7-6.

Unfortunately, along with the four intuitively pleasing variables, Chen, Roll, and Ross (1983) found, and Ross and Roll reported (1983), that the market—the return on the New York Stock Exchange—is also an important factor. The market index is included as a proxy for factors that may be omitted. If the market index is important in pricing, even after the other common factors have been accounted for, either the factors have been mismeasured, or one or more factors are missing. Born says that "the market portfolio cannot be one of the . . . common factors in the APT's return generating model. . . . Finding a statistically significant 'market' factor suggests that additional return generating factors remain to be identified."[34]

There are other questions that must be raised about the factors that have been identified—for instance, the interest rate factor. Interest rates, or yields to maturity, are defined by the prices of risky bonds. Thus, these rates should be a function of the underlying return-generating process. While their inclusion in an empirical model may prove valuable in explaining returns from common stocks, it probably confounds attempts to identify the "true" factors.

The identification of the factors that are relevant in pricing assets is still at its inception. Considerable work is needed before we begin to know the APT, its foibles, and its strengths.

V.   IS THE APT USABLE?

The real question at this point is not whether the APT is usable, but whether it is being used. Long before academics tired of testing and examining the CAPM, practitioners were using it to select stocks, estimate expected returns, form portfolios, and evaluate performance. The APT

---

[34]Jeffery A. Born, "The Arbitrage Pricing Theory, the Market Portfolio and Ambiguity When Performance is Measured by the Security Market Line" (Working Paper No. FIN-2-84, University of Kentucky (1984), pp. 10–11.

Exhibit 7–6

Relative Performance of Economic Factor Portfolios

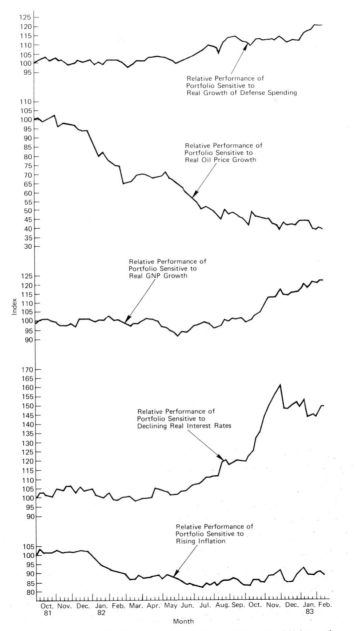

Relative Performance of
Portfolio Sensitive to
Real Growth of Defense Spending

Relative Performance of
Portfolio Sensitive to
Real Oil Price Growth

Relative Performance of
Portfolio Sensitive to
Real GNP Growth

Relative Performance of
Portfolio Sensitive to
Declining Real Interest Rates

Relative Performance of
Portfolio Sensitive to
Rising Inflation

Source: Tony Estep, N. Hanson, and C. Johnson, "Sources of Value and Risk in Common Stocks," *Journal of Portfolio Management,* Summer 1983, p. 11.

has been recommended for each of these activities, and is being used, at least conceptually.[35]

As it was with the CAPM, so it is with APT. Even before the APT was introduced by Ross (1976, 1977), practitioners had organized to take advantage of differences they believed were important in determining prices. Macroeconomic factors have long been of interest to, if not the focus of, stock and bond analysts and portfolio managers. Thus, the APT has an immediate interest for investment practitioners.[36] Whether that interest continues to develop will depend upon the further testing of the model, the ability to identify factors that are stable over time, and the success of its use.

REFERENCES

Arnott, Robert D., "Cluster Analysis and Stock Price Comovement," *Financial Analysts Journal,* 36 (November-December 1980), 56-62.

Born, Jeffery A., "The Arbitrage Pricing Theory, the Market Portfolio and Ambiguity When Performance is Measured by the Security Market Line." Working Paper No. FIN-2-84, University of Kentucky, 1984.

Bower, Dorothy, R. S. Bower, and D. E. Logue, "A Primer on Arbitrage Pricing Theory," *Midland Corporate Finance Journal,* 2 (Fall 1984), 31-40.

Brown, Stephen, and M. Weinstein, "A New Approach to Testing Asset Pricing Models," *Journal of Finance,* 38 (September 1983), 711-43.

Chen, Nai-fu, "Some Empirical Tests of the Theory of Arbitrage Pricing," *Journal of Finance,* 38 (December 1983), 1393-1414.

Chen, Nai-fu, R. Roll, and S. A. Ross, "Economic Forces and the Stock Market." Working Paper Ser. B-73, University of California at Los Angeles, December 1983.

———,"Economic Forces and the Stock Market: Testing APT and Alternative Asset Pricing Theories," Working Paper No. B-73, University of Chicago, (December 1983).

Cho, D. Chinhyung, "On Testing the Arbitrage Pricing Theory: Inter-Battery Factor Analysis," *Journal of Finance,* 39 (December 1984), 1485-1502.

[35]See, for instance, Richard Roll and S. A. Ross, "Regulation, the Capital Asset Pricing Model, and the Arbitrage Pricing Theory," *Public Utilities Fortnightly,* May 26, 1983a, pp. 22-28.

[36]See, for instance, Salomon Brothers' STOCKFACTS system which includes a mechanism for estimating the historic factor sensitivity of a large universe of common stocks to factors similar to those described by Chen, Roll, and Ross, "Economic Forces and the Stock Market."

Dhrymes, Pheobus J., "The Empirical Relevance of Arbitrage Pricing Models," *Journal of Portfolio Management,* Summer 1984.

Dhrymes, Pheobus J., I. Friend, and N. B. Gultekin, "A Critical Reexamination of the Empirical Evidence on the Arbitrage Pricing Theory," *Journal of Finance,* 39 (Summer 1984), 35-44.

Dhrymes, Pheobus J., I. Friend, M. N. Gultekin, and N. B. Gultekin, "New Tests of the APT and Their Implications," *Journal of Finance,* 40 (July 1985), 659-673.

Dybvig, Philip, and Stephen Ross, "Yes, The APT Is Testable," *Journal of Finance,* 40 (September 1985), 1173-88.

Estep, Tony, N. Hanson, and Cal Johnson, "Sources of Value and Risk in Common Stocks," *Journal of Portfolio Management,* Summer 1983, pp. 5-13.

Farrell, J. L., Jr., "Analyzing Covariation of Returns to Determine Homogeneous Stock Groupings," *Journal of Business,* 47 (April 1974), 186-207.

Fogler, H. Russell, "Common Sense on CAPM, APT, and Correlated Residuals," *Journal of Portfolio Management,* Summer 1982, pp. 20-28.

Fogler, H. Russell, K. John, and J. Tipton, "Three Factors, Interest Rates Differentials and Stock Groups," *Journal of Finance,* 36 (May 1981), 323-35.

Kryzanowski, Lawrence, and Minh Chan To, "General Factor Models and the Structure of Security Returns," *Journal of Financial and Quantitative Analysis,* 18 (March 1983), 31-52.

Oldfield, George, and R. J. Rogalski, "Treasury Bill Factors and Common Stock Returns," *Journal of Finance,* 37 (May 1981), 337-50.

Pari, Robert A., and Son-Nan Chen, "An Empirical Test of the Arbitrage Pricing Theory," *Journal of Financial Research,* 7 (Summer 1984), 121-30.

Reinganum, Marc, "The Arbitrage Pricing Theory: Some Empirical Results," *Journal of Finance,* 36 (June 1981), 313-21.

Roll, Richard, and S. A. Ross, "An Empirical Investigation of the Arbitrage Pricing Theory," *Journal of Finance,* 35 (December 1980), 1073-1104.

———, "Regulation, the Capital Asset Pricing Model, and the Arbitrage Pricing Theory," *Public Utilities Fortnightly,* May 26, 1983a, pp. 22-28.

———, "The Merits of the Arbitrage Pricing Theory for Portfolio Management." Paper presented at the Institute for Quantitative Research in Finance, Fall 1983b.

———, "The Arbitrage Pricing Theory Approach to Strategic Portfolio Planning," *Financial Analysts Journal,* 40 (May-June 1984a), 14-26.

——, "A Critical Reexamination of the Empirical Evidence on the Arbitrage Pricing Theory: A Reply," *Journal of Finance,* 39 (June 1984b), 347-50.

Ross, Stephen A., "The Arbitrage Pricing Theory of Capital Asset Pricing," *Journal of Economic Theory,* 13 (December 1976), 341-60.

——, "Risk, Return and Arbitrage." In *Risk and Return in Finance,* ed. James Bicksler and Irwin Friend, pp. 128-189. Cambridge, Mass.: Ballinger Publishers, 1977.

——, "Reply to Dhrymes: APT Is Empirically Relevant," *Journal of Portfolio Management,* Fall 1984, p. 55.

Shanken, Jay, "The Arbitrage Pricing Theory: Is It Testable?" *Journal of Finance,* 37 (December 1982), 1129-40.

——, "Multi-Beta CAPM or Equilibrium-APT?: A Reply," *Journal of Finance,* 40 (September 1985), 1189-96.

Sharpe, William F., "Factor Models, CAPMs, and the APT," *Journal of Portfolio Management,* Fall 1984, 21-25.

chapter

8

Practical Applications
of CAPM and APT Concepts

My role throughout this book has been to act as a sort of Federal Trade Commission of finance theory. I have examined two products—the capital asset pricing model (CAPM), and arbitrage pricing theory (APT)—and provided the appropriate warning labels. At the same time, I have shown that detractors' claims—that the products are definitely worthless—are just as naive as proponents' unquestioning faith in them.

I. THE CAPITAL ASSET PRICING MODEL

Most of this book has been concerned with the CAPM because it has been tested, analyzed, and used longer. Detractors have three main criticisms of this model:

1. The assumptions are too unrealistic; thus, the simple CAPM is probably seriously flawed.
2. Tests of the CAPM prove that it does not describe what has occurred; thus, it is probably wrong.
3. It is virtually impossible to get reasonable people to agree on the best forecasts for beta and for the risk-free and market rates of return; thus, the CAPM is practically useless.

Creative analysts, examining these same criticisms, reach opposite conclusions. They assert that research and experimentation are needed to refine what is valid in the model, to improve the accuracy of forecasts, and to extend the model's uses. We have already described efforts to perfect the model and the input data.

The information and evidence presented in this book are a cross section of what is available to academics and practitioners. While these models must be considered and used with great care, nothing reported in this book is sufficient to cause the thoughtful user to completely discard the model. Indeed, a number of creative uses have been and are being made of the CAPM. Corporate managers, investment practitioners, and public utility rate-of-return analysts have all been engaged in developing the CAPM. Let us look briefly at some of the current uses.

1. CORPORATE MANAGEMENT

Corporate managers have used the CAPM in three related ways: (1) to determine hurdle rates for corporate investments, (2) to estimate the required returns for divisions, strategic business units, or lines of business, and (3) to evaluate the performance of these divisions, units, or lines of business.

Managers often use the corporate cost of capital (usually a weighted average of the marginal costs of debt and equity) as the required rate of return for new corporate capital investments. To develop this overall cost of capital, the manager must have an estimate of the cost of equity capital. To calculate a cost of equity, some managers estimate the firm's beta (often from historical data)[1] and use the CAPM to determine the firm's required return on equity.

Using the CAPM to estimate the cost of equity for the firm is relatively common. Because other equity cost methods require the use of a market-determined stock price and estimates of future growth rates and dividends for the firm, the CAPM is of special interest to managers whose firms are closely held, pay no dividends, or have uncertain future rates of growth.

Some managers are not satisfied with a single corporate hurdle rate

---

[1]For a description of one method of forecasting the firm's beta, see J. F. Weston, "Investment Decisions Using the Capital Asset Pricing Model," *Financial Management*, Spring 1973, pp. 25–33. For a critique of CAPM usefulness in capital budgeting, see S. C. Myers and S. M. Turnbull, "Capital Budgeting and the Capital Asset Pricing Model: Good News and Bad News," *Journal of Finance*, 32 (May 1977), 321–32. For a description of estimating divisional betas, see Russell J. Fuller and H. S. Kerr, "Estimation of Divisional Cost of Capital: An Analysis of the Pure Play Technique," *Journal of Finance*, 36 (December 1981), 997–1009.

as the required rate of return. For firms that have diverse businesses with different risks, a single rate is believed inadequate to represent a fair return for each business segment. As a result, some managers have developed multiple hurdle rates—one for each business unit or line of business. In the past these rates have typically been subjective revisions of the corporate hurdle rate. The CAPM has been adapted to determine directly these multiple rates.

To do this, some managers first choose a group of similar but publicly traded firms as proxies for the untraded business unit or division. The average of the betas for these proxy firms is used as the divisional beta. The divisional required rate of return is then determined in the same manner as the corporate equity cost. Other managers simulate the returns for the division, using several macroeconomic scenarios. The beta is a measure of the sensitivity of the returns to changes in the macroeconomic factors.

In addition to calculating hurdle rates for use in evaluating capital investments, including acquisitions, the corporate strategic planner has become aware of the benefits that can be derived by introducing a more consistent and systematic method of risk analysis into the strategic planning process.[2] At least conceptually, the distinction between systematic and unsystematic, macroeconomic and microeconomic, risk is very useful as a basis for developing this systematic approach to risk analysis in corporate strategic planning.

The same sort of analysis can be used to evaluate past performance and to determine whether the business unit earned its cost of capital: created value, or not.[3] Exhibit 8-1 shows an example of such a historic analysis. The company, AKI, a multidivisional firm, evaluated its divisions, two of which are shown here. The divisions are quite different, and their performances were substantially different as well. The Alaska Gas division earned more than its cost of capital and thus created value. It lies above the diagonal line, the market price of risk, the security market line. The Lockwood division did not fare so well: its returns were less than its cost of capital. However, when AKI evaluated the divisions relative to others in each industry, they found that Alaska Gas had, at best, a lackluster performance, while Lockwood outperformed its competition. Alaska Gas, because it is in a cyclical business, could have been expected to have some years in which performance lagged. The questions that AKI's management faced were, What would happen to the natural gas

---

[2] For a description of the process and how it is implemented in one such firm, see Diana Harrington, "Stock Prices, Beta, and Strategic Planning," *Harvard Business Review,* May–June 1983, pp. 157–64.

[3] Ibid.

Exhibit 8-1

**Performance of AKI and Subsidiaries,
June 1975-December 1977**

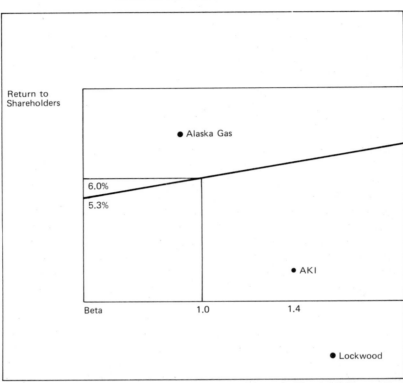

Source: Diana R. Harrington, "Stock Prices, Beta, and Strategic Planning," *Harvard Business Review,* May-June 1983, p. 160.

industry in the future? What about Alaska Gas was causing its relatively poor performance?

Such an analysis of the future is shown in Exhibit 8-2, which shows the expected performance for 52 industries, and in Exhibit 8-3, which shows the expected performance for one of those industries in late April 1984. Interestingly enough, at that point in time taking risk was not being well rewarded—high beta stocks were expected to earn little more than those of lower risk. This was a fairly unusual result. However, as you can see, some industries were expected to do much better than others, but all were expected to do relatively well. This data can be, and has been, used by managers to put expected returns into perspective, and to take corrective action before the results are realized.

Exhibit 8-2

Risk and Return by Industry

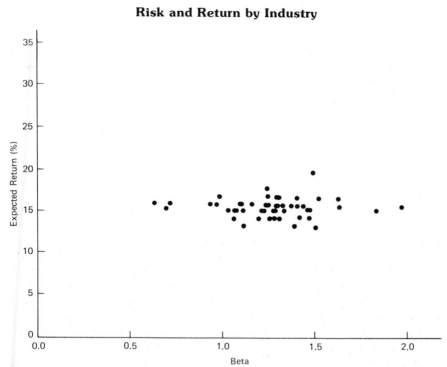

Source: Data from Wells Fargo Investment Advisors, Wells Fargo Bank, *Security Market Plane,* May 1, 1984.

2. REGULATION OF PUBLIC UTILITIES' RATES OF RETURN

The CAPM has been and continues to be used by the managers and regulators of public utilities.[4] Utility rates are set so that all costs, including costs of debt and equity capital, are covered by rates charged to consumers. In determining the cost of equity for the public utility, the CAPM has been used to estimate directly the cost of equity for the utility in question. The procedure is like that followed for any other firm: the beta and risk-free and market rates of return are estimated, and the CAPM is used to determine a cost of equity.

[4] For a list of several public utility proceedings in which the CAPM was used, see Diana Harrington, "Trends in Capital Asset Pricing Model Use," *Public Utilities Fortnightly* 4, August 13, 1981, and Diana R. Harrington, "The Changing Use of the Capital Asset Pricing Model in Utility Regulation," *Public Utilities Fortnightly* 28, February 14, 1980.

Exhibit 8–3

Risk and Return for the Automobile Industry

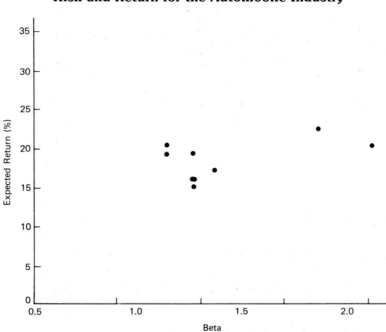

Source: Data from Wells Fargo Investment Advisors, Wells Fargo Bank, *Security Market Plane*, May 1, 1984.

Beta, independent of the CAPM, has also been used in utility regulation as a measure of risk. The beta for a given utility is used to choose a group of comparable firms (firms with similar betas). These proxy firms are usually in nonregulated businesses. The historical return on equity for this group of firms is then used as a forecast of the required equity return for the given utility.

Controversy erupts each time the CAPM or beta is used in the process of setting utility rates.[5] The arguments are the same three listed at the beginning of this chapter.

3. PORTFOLIO MANAGEMENT AND STOCK SELECTION

Investment practitioners have been most enthusiastic and creative in adapting the CAPM for their uses. The CAPM has been used to select stocks, construct portfolios, and evaluate portfolio or stock performance.

[5]For a description of several rate-of-return proceedings in which the CAPM and beta were used, see Diana R. Harrington, "Capital Asset Pricing Model and Public Utility Costs of Equity Capital Determination" (Ph.D. dissertation, University of Virginia, 1978).

Stock selection

Stocks for which supernormal returns are forecast are considered undervalued, that is, attractive candidates for purchase. Overvalued stocks are those with below-normal anticipated returns and are thus candidates for sale. The degree of overvaluation or undervaluation is determined by the stock's alpha, or the distance that the risk-return plot for the stock lies from the market line. This alpha can be calculated in two ways.

The earliest approach was to calculate a beta for a given security using the market model. This was the process we described in Chapter 4 for AT&T, using an ordinary-least-squares, or market-model regression. The alpha was the historical excess return (or loss)—the intercept from the market model regression. The analyst then assumed that the historical alpha would continue into the future. Thus, stocks with positive alphas were attractive while negative alpha stocks were considered overvalued.

Because history is unlikely to repeat itself, many practitioners were not satisfied with this use of history to predict future performance. They sought instead to forecast the alpha or risk-adjusted attractiveness of each stock. To do this, some money management organizations first make independent forecasts of return and beta for each stock. The forecasted beta and return for each stock are then arrayed on the risk-return graph, as shown in Exhibit 8–4. Once the forecasts for all the stocks have been

Exhibit 8–4

Expected Return and Risk for a Universe of Stocks

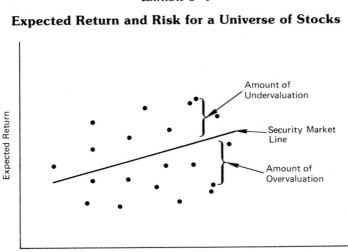

graphically represented, a line of best fit (using a method similar to the market model regression) is drawn. This line, shown in Exhibit 8-4, is a forecast for the security market line. Attractive (undervalued) securities are those whose risk-return characteristics are plotted above the line. Fair-priced securities lie directly on the line, whereas overvalued securities are plotted below the line. The degree of undervaluation or overvaluation (the alpha) is simply the distance from the stock's plot to the line. Alpha represents the analysts' forecast of the stock's relative attractiveness.

In Exhibit 8-2 we showed a graph of the expected risks and returns for 52 industries, made in late April 1984 by the analysts in the investment advisory department of a bank.[6] Atypically, the dots, or the cloud of dots, are rather flat, not widely dispersed, and seem to indicate that the analysts were not anticipating that risk would be well rewarded. On the basis of this graph, some managers would decide that risk taking was not warranted, and choose less risky stocks. As shown in Exhibit 8-5, at other times risk takers expected to be rewarded, or conversely, the prices of risky stocks were so low that the expected return was much higher—investors had to be lured into making such aggressive purchases. Such was the case in December 1974 and again in July 1982.[7] This use of CAPM concepts is not without controversy.

This forecast of stock attractiveness is one of those inefficient uses of an efficient-market concept. In prospect, all forecasts should fall on the market line because beta and expected return are directly and linearly related (theoretically). In practice forecasts do not fall on the market line, and practitioners believe that this process can be used effectively to select securities.

Portfolio optimization

In addition to selecting securities, beta has been used to control the risk level of a portfolio. Although the desired level of risk will depend upon each investor's preference, many portfolio optimization models use

---

[6]The analysts use a variation of the dividend discount model to forecast the returns from each stock. To simplify the graph, Exhibit 8-2 provides their average forecasts for industries, not the individual stocks.

[7]These forecasts are the best long-term forecasts these analysts can make at the time. Investors can, and do, make decisions on the basis of these long-term forecasts. There are managers that use such analysis to play a short-term game. To do so they must forecast the next forecast. For instance, in July 1982 if you were forecasting that the expectations in April 1984 would be as shown in Exhibit 8-5, you would buy the most risky assets in order to make a profit—the expected return on those assets dropped over the two-year period, thus suggesting that the price rose (all else being equal). Lower-risk assets would actually have declined in price in order to offer the higher return required by April 1984. The trick is, of course, to forecast the next forecast.

Exhibit 8–5

Security Risk Line (at Market Yield)

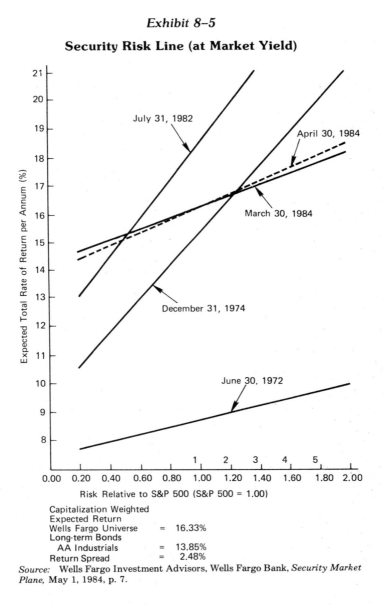

July 31, 1982

April 30, 1984

March 30, 1984

December 31, 1974

June 30, 1972

Expected Total Rate of Return per Annum (%)

Risk Relative to S&P 500 (S&P 500 = 1.00)

Capitalization Weighted
Expected Return
Wells Fargo Universe   =   16.33%
Long-term Bonds
  AA Industrials   =   13.85%
  Return Spread   =   2.48%

Source: Wells Fargo Investment Advisors, Wells Fargo Bank, *Security Market Plane,* May 1, 1984, p. 7.

a linear-programming approach with a particular beta as the risk-level constraint. In using a linear-programming technique, some variable (returns, for instance) is maximized while another factor or factors (risk, for instance) is controlled. Although this is a simplistic description of the more complex portfolio optimization methods, it does convey the essence of how beta is used in managing the level of portfolio risk.

Portfolio performance

Using historical returns and beta, we can evaluate the performance of the portfolio or asset. Portfolios with negative risk-adjusted returns (negative alphas) are said to have underperformed, and those with positive risk-adjusted returns (positive alphas) are said to have shown superior performance. Before using risk-adjusted returns to evaluate performance, the magnitude of returns was most important. We now know that all assets with equivalent returns are equal only if they are equally risky. The beauty of using risk-adjusted performance is that more reasonable information is available.

More sophisticated performance analysis systems take into account restrictions that are placed on portfolios. For instance, if a portfolio manager is restricted to investing in growth stocks, the portfolio's results are compared to the results from other growth stock portfolios. To do otherwise would be to give an unfair advantage or penalty to those who are kept from investing in the broadest possible universe.[8]

II. ARBITRAGE PRICING THEORY

One of the new improved pricing model versions is the arbitrage pricing theory. When it was first introduced, many believed that it would solve the theoretical, empirical, and practical problems that the CAPM had encountered. It has, however, run into many of the same problems that were discovered during the testing and implementing of the CAPM. Still, APT is an alluring new concept, based on intuitively sensible ideas, and some practitioners have begun introducing APT-type analysis into their stock selection and portfolio design and analysis. Perhaps the more im-

---

[8]The use of the security market line (SML) to evaluate performance has been severely criticized and roundly defended. The argument revolves around the theoretical correctness versus the practical usefulness of the CAPM. For discussions of the problems that can occur when the SML is used to evaluate performance see Richard Roll, "Ambiguity When Performance Is Measured by the Securities Market Line," *Journal of Finance,* 33 (December 1978), 1051–69; David Mayers and E. Rice, "Measuring Portfolio Performance and the Empirical Content of Asset Pricing Models," *Journal of Financial Economics,* 7 (March 1979), 3–28; Philip H. Dybvig and S. Ross, "The Analytics of Performance Measurement Using a Security Market Line" and "Differential Information and Performance Measurement Using a Security Market Line," *Journal of Finance,* 40 (June 1985), 401–16 and 383–99 respectively. For a discussion of the practical usefulness of the model, see Barr Rosenberg, "The Capital Asset Pricing Model and the Market Model," *Journal of Portfolio Management,* Winter 1981, pp. 5–16.

portant development in the potential use of APT is the degree to which practitioners are being exhorted by academics to use the APT in estimating cost of capital for public utilities,[9] and for analyzing stocks and planning their equity portfolios.[10]

As intuitively logical as it is to determine the pattern of sensitivities to the primary factors determining returns of a company, division, stock, or portfolio, we have yet to determine, with confidence, what the factors are, and whether the factors that are important in one period maintain their importance over time and for different samples. Even if the preliminary studies that have found effects of unanticipated changes in inflation, industrial production, risk premia, and the term structure of interest rates are correct, we have much work to do to measure these factors with confidence, and to predict them with any degree of accuracy.

Nevertheless, many money managers have long followed basic changes in the structure of the economy, and have used some straightforward ways of incorporating sensitivities to those factors into their stock selection and portfolio management practices. For instance, managers have, through experience or research, identified the stocks that are sensitive to changes in interest rates or inflation, and bought or sold those stocks on the basis of their forecasts for those two factors.

Recently, these models of economic sensitivity have been made more formal. Computer models that will estimate the sensitivity of stocks, or portfolios, to certain economic factors, or that will select stocks and form portfolios to meet factor-sensitivity criteria, have been and are being developed at money management organizations.[11] How successful these models, and APT as a usable concept, will be, remains to be seen.

III. CONCLUSION

These are very brief descriptions of far more complex processes. Whether historically calculated or analyst-forecasted betas and alphas are used for stock selection, portfolio optimization, or performance evaluation, considerable judgment is required and considerable controversy results.

[9]See Richard Roll, "Regulation, the Capital Asset Pricing Model, and the Arbitrage Pricing Theory," *Public Utilities Fortnightly,* May 26, 1983, pp. 22–28; and Dorothy Bower, R. S. Bower, and Dennis Logue, "Arbitrage Pricing Theory and Utility Stock Behavior," *Journal of Finance,* 39 (September 1984), 1041–54.

[10]See, for instance, Richard Roll, "The Arbitrage Pricing Theory Approach to Strategic Portfolio Planning," *Financial Analysts Journal,* 40 (May–June 1984), 14–29.

[11]Salomon Brothers has a computer system called STOCKFACTS that will test the sensitivity of stocks to basic economic changes, and will allow the user to build portfolios that satisfy the user's criteria for factors sensitivities.

The arguments are the same three that we have described repeatedly. Nonetheless, investment practitioners believe that they are making better decisions by using more systematic approaches to investment management.

The picture that has been painted appears negative, but it is not. It is realistic. There are problems with a simple-minded use of a simple concept. To use it, without knowing it, is like using a drug and never reading the label. There are always dangers, lessened if they are known. I have given you the label warnings and I hope that you have found, as I have, a concept worth the risks. It is not a cure for every ill, but a poultice useful as new improved versions are being developed.

REFERENCES

Bower, Dorothy, R. S. Bower, and D. Logue, "Arbitrage Pricing Theory and Utility Stock Behavior," *Journal of Finance,* 39 (September 1984), 1041-54.

Dybvig, Philip H., and S. Ross, "The Analytics of Performance Measurement Using a Security Market Line," *Journal of Finance,* 40 (June 1985), 401-16.

——, "Differential Information and Performance Measurement Using a Security Market Line," *Journal of Finance,* 40 (June 1985), 383-99.

Fuller, Russell J., and H. S. Kerr, "Estimation of Divisional Cost of Capital: An Analysis of the Pure Play Technique," *Journal of Finance,* 36 (December 1981), 997-1009.

Harrington, Diana R., "The Capital Asset Pricing Model and Public Utility Costs of Equity Capital Determination." Ph.D. dissertation, University of Virginia, 1978.

——, "The Changing Use of the Capital Asset Pricing Model in Utility Regulation," *105 Public Utilities Fortnightly,* 28 (February 14, 1980), 28-30.

——, "Trends in Capital Asset Pricing Model Use," *108 Public Utilities Fortnightly* 4 (August 13, 1981).

——, "Stock Prices, Beta, and Strategic Planning," *Harvard Business Review,* May-June 1983, pp. 157-64.

Harrington, D. R., and R. F. Vandell, "The Effects of Changes in Ex Ante Expectations on Ex Post Results for Equity Securities." Paper presented to the Midwest Finance Association, March 1983.

Mayers, David, and E. Rice, "Measuring Portfolio Performance and the Empirical Content of Asset Pricing Models," *Journal of Financial Economics,* 7 (March 1979), 3-28.

Myers, S. C., and S. M. Turnbull, "Capital Budgeting and the Capital Asset Pricing Model: Good News and Bad News," *Journal of Finance,* 32 (May 1977), 321-32.

Roll, Richard, "A Critique of the Asset Pricing Theory's Test," *Journal of Financial Economics,* 4 (1977), 129-76.

———, "Ambiguity When Performance Is Measured by the Securities Market Line," *Journal of Finance,* 33 (December 1978), 1051-69.

———, "Regulation, the Capital Asset Pricing Model, and the Arbitrage Pricing Theory," *Public Utilities Fortnightly,* May 26, 1983, pp. 22-28.

———, "The Arbitrage Pricing Theory Approach to Strategic Portfolio Planning," *Financial Analysts Journal,* 40 (May-June 1984), 14-29.

Rosenberg, Barr, "The Capital Asset Pricing Model and the Market Model," *Journal of Portfolio Management,* Winter 1981, pp. 5-16.

Rudd, Andrew, and B. Rosenberg, "The Market Model in Investment Management," *Journal of Finance,* 35 (May 1980), 597-607.

Wells Fargo Investment Advisors, *Security Market Plane* (San Francisco, California, Wells Fargo Bank), 1975-85.

Weston, J. F., "Investment Decisions Using the Capital Asset Pricing Model," *Financial Management,* Spring 1973, pp. 25-33.

Index